Praise for *Global Slump*

"In this book, McNally confirms—once again—his standing as one of the world's leading Marxist scholars of capitalism. For a scholarly, in-depth analysis of our current crisis that never loses sight of its political implications (for them and for us), expressed in a language that leaves no reader behind, there is simply no better place to go."
—Bertell Ollman, professor, Department of Politics, NYU, and author of *Dance of the Dialectic: Steps in Marx's Method*

"David McNally's tremendously timely book is packed with significant theoretical and practical insights, and offers actually existing examples of what is to be done. *Global Slump* urgently details how changes in the capitalist space-economy over the past 25 years, especially in the forms that money takes, have expanded wide-scale vulnerabilities for all kinds of people, and how people fight back. In a word, the problem isn't neoliberalism—it's capitalism."
—Ruth Wilson Gilmore, University of Southern California, and author, *Golden Gulag: Prisons, Surplus, Crisis, and Opposition in Globalizing California*

"Standard accounts of the present crisis blame the excesses of the financial sector, promising that all will be well when the proper financial regulations are in place. McNally's path-breaking account goes far deeper. He documents in great detail how the roots of the crisis are found in the systematic failings of capitalism. At this moment in world history the case for a radical alternative to the capitalist global order needs to be made as forcefully as possible. No one has done this better than McNally."
—Tony Smith, professor of Philosophy, Iowa State University, and author of *Globalisation: A Systematic Marxian Account*

D1463649

▮SPECTRE▶

Editor: Sasha Lilley

Spectre is a series of penetrating and indispensable works of, and about, radical political economy. Spectre lays bare the dark underbelly of politics and economics, publishing outstanding and contrarian perspectives on the maelstrom of capital—and emancipatory alternatives—in crisis. The companion Spectre Classics imprint unearths essential works of radical history, political economy, theory and practice, to illuminate the present with brilliant, yet unjustly neglected, ideas from the past.

Spectre
Greg Albo, Sam Gindin, and Leo Panitch, *In and Out of Crisis: The Global Financial Meltdown and Left Alternatives*

David McNally, *Global Slump: The Economics and Politics of Crisis and Resistance*

Sasha Lilley, *Capital and Its Discontents: Conversations with Radical Thinkers in a Time of Tumult*

Spectre Classics
E. P. Thompson, *William Morris: Romantic to Revolutionary*

Global Slump:
The Economics and Politics of Crisis and Resistance

David McNally

Global Slump: The Economics and Politics of Crisis and Resistance
David McNally
© PM Press 2011

ISBN: 978-1-60486-332-1
Library of Congress Control Number: 2010927764

Cover by John Yates/Stealworks
Interior design by briandesign

10 9 8 7 6 5 4 3 2

PM Press
PO Box 23912
Oakland, CA 94623
www.pmpress.org

Printed in the USA on recycled paper, by the Employee Owners of Thomson-Shore in Dexter, Michigan. www.thomsonshore.com

Published in Canada by Fernwood Publishing
32 Oceanvista Lane, Black Point, Nova Scotia, BoJ 1Bo
and 748 Broadway Avenue, Winnipeg, MB R3G 0X3
www.fernwoodpublishing.ca

Library and Archives Canada Cataloguing in Publication
McNally, David
Global slump : the economics and politics of crisis and resistance
/ David McNally.
Includes bibliographical references.
ISBN: 978-1-55266-396-7

1. Global Financial Crisis, 2008–2009. 2. International finance.
3. Capitalism.
I. Title.

HG3881.M39 2010   332'.042   C2010-904888-1

Published in the EU by The Merlin Press Ltd.
6 Crane Street Chambers, Crane Street, Pontypool NP4 6ND, Wales
www.merlinpress.co.uk
ISBN: 978-085036-678-5

For the incredible "Fergallys"—
Liam, Sam, Adam, and Sue

Contents

Preface and Acknowledgements

As fate would have it, I was in New York for the annual Left Forum in mid-March 2008 when the Wall Street investment bank Bear Stearns melted down. "This is big," I told my partner, as I pored through the financial newspapers trying to get a handle on the dimensions of what was happening. "This could be the start of a major crisis," I speculated. In fact, while I was miles ahead of mainstream economists in my understanding—no great claim to fame, as we shall see—I still had only the haziest sense of just how profound an event was unfolding.

In many respects, this book represents my effort to clarify the nature of the Great Recession, where it came from, and how it is likely to unfold in the years ahead. It also represents my attempt to think through what all this means for movements of resistance, struggles for global justice, and anticapitalist politics. But this has been no solitary quest. At every step of the way, I have been engaged in action and discussion with radical activists and scholars about the issues that are covered here. Throughout, I have felt the urgency of making sense of events that are rapidly changing the world in which we live, events that are throwing up huge new challenges to social justice movements everywhere. This urgency is driven by the conviction that we need to map the character of the global slump as best we can in order to more adequately fashion our resistance to its devastating effects.

This book is my small contribution to that cause. Whatever its deficiencies, which are surely many, they would be even greater were it not for the feedback, inspiration, and encouragement I received from many quarters.

I would particularly like to acknowledge the great spirit of nonsectarian radical inquiry that ran through the day schools organized by the Popular Education and Action Project in

Toronto in 2009, where parts of this analysis were first presented. Mad props to all the amazing activists from the Ontario Coalition Against Poverty, No One is Illegal–Toronto, Coalition Against Israeli Apartheid, Socialist Project, and Toronto New Socialists who made those gatherings such powerful episodes of popular self-education. I have likewise benefited greatly from the opportunity to present some of these ideas at a variety of conferences, workshops, and seminars full of outstandingly thoughtful people. Foremost here are sessions organized by: *Historical Materialism* (at conferences in London and Toronto); the Left Forum in New York; Socialism 2009 and 2010 in Chicago; the Centre for Global Political Economy and the Labour Studies program at Simon Fraser University; the Society for Socialist Studies 2009 meetings at Carleton University; the Vancouver Socialist Forum; the International Development Studies Program at Trent University; the Ontario Public Interest Research Group at both University of Toronto and York University; *The Socialist Register* at a stimulating weekend workshop in Toronto; and the Great Lakes Political Economy Conference at Carleton University. I wish also to thank the wonderful activists with No One is Illegal–Toronto, UNITE HERE, Socialist Project, and Toronto New Socialists, who invited me to present my thinking in these areas to a variety of workshops and panel discussions.

I owe particular thanks to the editors of *Historical Materialism*, far and away the best English-language journal of critical socialist thought, for their invitation to submit an article, "From Financial Crisis to World Slump: Accumulation, Financialisation, and the Global Slowdown," based on my talk at their 2008 conference in London. That article, which appeared in 2009, provided me with an initial opportunity to develop some of my thinking about these issues at length. This book extends and develops ideas first broached in print there.

In the course of these occasions and in innumerable private conversations, I have received tremendous encouragement from Greg Albo, Alison Ayers, Himani Bannerji, Riccardo Bellofiore, Susan Buck-Morss, Johanna Brenner, Sebastian Budgen, David Camfield, James Cairns, Vivek Chibber, Aziz Choudry, Erin Chun,

John Clarke, Professor D of the Dope Poets Society, Ruth Wilson Gilmore, Todd Gordon, Adam Hanieh, Sarah Knopp, Michael Kuttner, Shahrzad Mojab, Colin Mooers, Fred Moseley, Amy Muldoon, Bertell Ollman, Leo Panitch, Charlie Post, Alfredo Saad-Filho, Alan Sears, Anwar Shaikh, Ahmed Shawki, Tony Smith, Hamid Sodeifi, Jesook Song, and Ellen Meiksins Wood. Many, many thanks to these incredible comrades and friends. I would also like to thank my father, who regularly reminded me that my hurried writing efforts would benefit from the occasional break for recreation.

My editor at PM Press, Sasha Lilley, first interviewed me about these issues for her marvelous series on KPFA Radio, "Capitalism and its Discontents." She then persisted in urging me to write this all up at greater length for publication. I am very pleased to have heeded her advice. I am also deeply grateful to Sasha for her sharp, intelligent editorial suggestions, which have greatly improved this work. Completion of this book was somewhat delayed— and necessarily so—by involvement in the protests against the G20 in Toronto in late June 2010 and the important defense campaign launched after police state tactics resulted in more than a thousand arrests. I want to acknowledge the courage of the thousands of protestors and detainees who challenged the G20, often braving police violence, arbitrary arrest and inhumane detention. While expressing my solidarity with all the detained G20 protesters, I wish to acknowledge one in particular, Syed Hussan, an exceptional organizer with No One Is Illegal–Toronto, who was released on bail the day I started the Conclusion to this book. While living together was forced upon us by the courts, I hope friendship and comradeship have been some small compensation for the indignities of house arrest. In the same spirit, I want to pay tribute to the steadfast commitment of my co-speakers at the June 28, 2010, protest rally outside police headquarters in Toronto: Irina Ceric, Debra Cowen, Taylor Flook, Naomi Klein, Abeer Majeeb, Farrah Miranda, Ben Powless, Judy Rebick, and Dave Vasey. Long may you stand up against injustice and oppression.

I owe huge thanks to some terrific friends who read parts of this text on incredibly short notice and offered me their wisdom and insight: David Camfield, Alfredo Saad-Filho, Charlie Post, and Hamid Sodeifi. This book is much better for their help.

Once again, my biggest debt is owed to Sue Ferguson, my partner in love, politics, childrearing, and more. Since those early conversations in New York, as Bear Stearns was collapsing, Sue has been an integral part of this project. She read every chapter in draft, offering greatly discerning comments on each one. Equally important, she helped keep me sane, or so I would like to think, as I scrambled to meet my deadline. Our boys, Liam, Sam, and Adam, were constant affirmations as to why I do this work. Their energy, exuberance, creativity, and wonderful humor keep me inspired. And they remind me that another world truly is possible. This book is dedicated to all of them, those incredible "Fergallys,"—Liam, Sam, Adam, and Sue—my co-conspirators in love and happiness.

The Mutating Crisis of Global Capitalism

"The global financial crisis of the late 2000s . . . stands as the most serious global financial crisis since the Great Depression. The crisis has been a transformative moment in global economic history whose ultimate resolution will likely reshape politics and economics for at least a generation." [1]

THOSE WHO LIVE THROUGH GREAT HISTORIC TRANSITIONS RARELY realize it at the time. This has something to do with the fact that, as the radical philosopher Georg Lukács once observed, it is exceptionally difficult to grasp *the present as history*. We tend to think of history as a record of past events, of things that are over and done with. We find it difficult to view our current moment as profoundly historical. Yet, the present is invariably saturated with elements of the future, with possibilities that have not yet come to fruition, and may not do so—as the road to the future is always contested. That is why, if we wish to make history, we "must be able to comprehend the present as a *becoming*."[2] One would think that it should be easier to see things this way during moments of profound crisis in our social and economic system, like that which broke out in 2008. As the tectonic plates of the global economy shifted, financial shocks rocked the world's banks, leveling many of them. Panic gripped money markets, stocks plunged, factories shut down. Tens of millions of people were thrown out of work; millions lost their homes. An extraordinary uncertainty shook the world's ruling class. The mood of the moment was captured in the confession by senior writers with the *Financial Times* that, "The world of the past three decades is gone."[3]

Within a year or so, however, candid statements like this disappeared from the mainstream press. The ruling class regrouped and regained its arrogance. It turned to the timeworn habit of denial—and tried to erase from memory the trauma it had undergone. But while amnesia may serve them well, it is not in the interests of those who seek social change. We need to remember. Among other things, we need to recall that the crisis of 2008 does signal the end of "the world of the past three decades." It represents the terminus of a quarter-century wave of economic growth—which I shall call the neoliberal expansion—and the transition to a protracted period of slump. It has also opened a new period of social conflict and class struggle. For our planet's rulers, this conflict takes the form of a war against indigenous lands, public services, unions, and communities of color. For the world's workers, it is expressed in factory occupations, general strikes, land seizures, street protests, and mass demonstrations for migrant justice.

To claim that we are living through a prolonged global slump is, of course, to fly in the face of the conventional wisdom propagated by governments, business and the mainstream media, all of whom claim that the world is on the path to recovery and prosperity. It is true, courtesy of the largest coordinated financial bailout in world history, that a halt was put to the domino-like wave of bank collapses. Giant auto corporations have been returned to profitability, on the back of huge concessions by the unions. Yet, even while every upturn in the economic statistics is greeted with giddy headlines the repeated waves of panic that roil financial markets indicate that things remain incredibly fragile. The passing of one crisis seems merely to be the prelude to the next: the end of the bank meltdowns was greeted by financial turmoil over Dubai's debts; no sooner had that passed than Greek debt rocked financial markets.

None of this is to deny that the Great Bailout averted the catastrophic collapse of the global economy. But it did so at extraordinary cost. Led by the U.S. Federal Reserve, central banks poured trillions of dollars into financial institutions while treasuries and finance departments pumped further trillions in stimulus money into their economies. All told, governments in the world's largest economies anteed up something in the order of $20 trillion—an amount equivalent to one and a half times the U.S. gross

domestic product—via a massive intervention without historical precedent.⁴

Through the financial equivalent of a complete blood transfusion, a stop was put to the bank collapses. But the consequence
was a colossal buildup in government debt. In medicine, a total
blood replacement is also known as an *exchange transfusion*. And
that is exactly what global banks received. Financial institutions that were collapsing under the weight of bad debts simply
exchanged their toxic assets for good money from central banks.
However, in order to come up with this cash for the banks, governments had to sell bonds in the financial markets. Yet government bonds are themselves a form of debt, loans that must be
repaid with interest. And the investors who make those loans
pay close attention to the capacity of borrowers to repay—even
when those borrowers are sovereign states. As a result, when the
immense debt burdens of a number of European governments,
like Greece, became public knowledge in early 2010, investors
shunned their bonds, setting off more tremors in world financial markets. The specter of government defaults traumatized
markets, forcing European states to dish out another $1 trillion
in bailout funds.

Greece, moreover, is no isolated case. Britain, Spain, the U.S.,
Ireland, Portugal, Italy, and many other states have become dramatically more indebted as a result of the Great Bailout. Public
debt in these countries is now above 60 percent of their annual
output (or gross domestic product)—and rising. Indeed, that is
what has most rattled investors: the realization that governments
have borrowed so much, and lost so much potential tax reve-
nue due to job loss, that public debt in these countries is set to
soar to as much as five times the gross domestic product within
a generation.⁵ It doesn't take rocket science to realize this is not
sustainable. Just as we do not expect wage-earners to be able to
handle debt loads on that scale, investors doubt the ability of
governments to do so as well. The prospect that sovereign states
might default sent a new wave of panic through financial markets,
compelling European governments to intervene massively once
more. Prudent gamblers will not bet against it happening again.

Moreover, while doubts about U.S. *federal* debt have not shaken financial markets, the same cannot be said for public debt held by subnational units, such as U.S. cities and state governments. Investors are getting increasingly unnerved by the spending obligations for pensions, roads, education, health care, and so on that these governments have assumed. With tax revenues declining, investors are becoming anxious about public defaults at these levels.[6]

In short, the bad bank debt that triggered the crisis in 2008 never went away—it was simply shifted on to governments. Private debt became public debt. And as the dimensions of that metamorphosis became apparent in early 2010, the bank crisis morphed into a sovereign debt crisis. Put differently, the economic crisis of 2008–9 did not really end. It simply changed form. It *mutated*.

With that mutation, the focus of ruling classes shifted toward a war against public services. Concerned to rein in government debts, they announced an age of austerity—of huge cuts to pensions, education budgets, social welfare programs, public sector wages, and jobs. In so doing, they effectively declared that working class people and the poor will pay the cost of the global bank bailout. These payments may well last a generation—producing higher rates of poverty, more disease and ill health, even more under-resourced schools, and greater hardship in old age. Consider the following. In response to financial market reactions to its debt, Latvia has fired one third of all teachers and slashed pensions by 70 percent. Ireland has chopped wages of government employees by 22 percent. The state of California has cut health insurance for nine hundred thousand poor children. And this is just the beginning. Commentators are predicting a "decade of austerity," ten years or more of huge cuts to public sector jobs and to the social services on which poor and working class people rely. Worldwide, an additional sixty-four million people will have been driven into poverty by the end of 2010 as a direct result of the crisis, according to the World Bank.[7]

Just as the crisis is mutating, so is neoliberalism. Originally nailing its sails to the ideological mast of "free markets," neoliberals have been humbled and embarrassed by their participation in the greatest government bailouts in history. So, they have shifted their argumentative grounds, emphasizing the harsh "necessity" of slashing government spending as essential to long-term economic survival. Neoliberal methods and practices remain central to this mutant neoliberalism, but its ideological justifications are being refashioned.

The ultimate purpose of all this is to preserve capitalism and the wealth and power of its elites. And so far the bailouts and their aftermath have decidedly served that end. As a columnist with the *Times* of London observes, "The rich have come through the recession with flying colours . . . The rest of the country is going to have to face spending cuts, but it has little effect on the rich because they don't consume public services."[8] The candidness of this statement is to be appreciated. But there is one error in this passage. These cuts do in fact have an effect on the rich: they help them. After all, they are essential to the massive transfer of wealth from the poor to the rich that funded the rescue of the world banking system, the bailout of corporations, and the salvage of the investment portfolios of the wealthy. So, when one U.S. economist observes that we have today "a statistical recovery and a human recession"—a point to which I return in the next chapter—we need to add, as one California teacher put it to me, that there is a statistical recovery *because* there is a human recession.[9] Put simply, profits have improved (the "statistical recovery") largely because working class people have paid for them, through layoffs, wage cuts, reduced work hours, and the decimation of social services. In the words of a poor rebel in Shakespeare's *Coriolanus*, "our misery" is the source of "their abundance; our sufferance is a gain to them."[10]

To compound today's suffering, the gigantic public service cuts now underway will further depress the world economy. Keep in mind that the tepid "recovery" from the Great Recession of 2008–9 was entirely driven by trillions in stimulus spending. But now, government incentives to buy cars or renovate homes are all expiring and public works budgets for highways, bridges and other infrastructure are being scaled back. As that stimulus ends and restraint becomes the order of the day, economic activity will decline. Indeed, as I write this section (in June 2010), government cuts are already driving Greece, Ireland, Britain, Spain, and other countries back into recession. Even the World Bank, which strongly advocates austerity, has openly conceded it will dampen growth. And the International Monetary Fund, responsible for overseeing the Greek cuts, estimates they will lead to an economic contraction of 4 percent in 2010 and an official unemployment rate of 15 percent the year after. Meanwhile, economists at the London School of Economics calculate that Britain's enormous cuts (around $170 billion) will reduce economic growth by 2 percent a year for up to a decade.[11]

Coordinated restraint and austerity could have similar effects on the world economy as a whole. Economist Paul Krugman argues that these policies will induce a "third depression" (the first two being 1873–96 and 1929–39). Describing the shift to austerity as a return to neoliberal economic orthodoxy that sees government debt as inherently bad, he asks, "And who will pay the price for this triumph of orthodoxy? The answer is, tens of millions of unemployed workers, many of whom will go jobless for years, and some of whom will never work again."[12]

All of these recessionary tendencies are exacerbated by system-wide deleveraging, i.e. major reductions in the amount of debt being carried by banks, individuals, and the public sector. Recognizing that banks melted down and millions of families lost houses because unsustainable debt loads crushed them, banks and households are now shedding debt, as are governments. But such deleveraging further depresses economic growth. After all, rather than spending all of their earnings, banks, corporations, governments, and individuals are using big chunks to pay back old debts. Money that would otherwise go into new investment, business loans, or consumer expenditures, thus goes instead to creditors. Aggregate spending by businesses and consumers moves correspondingly lower. Historically, such deleveraging episodes last at least six or seven years, and generate economic sluggishness.[13] But there is reason to think that this one might last longer, because it is *global* deleveraging that is now in motion. It is impossible, after all, for every economy plagued by excessive debt loads to export its way back to growth, as Japan did (albeit with only minimal success) following a debt crisis that began in the 1990s. *Some* economies may sustain export-driven growth today—China, Germany, and South Korea, for instance—but this will be at the expense of others.

This is one reason why it is so difficult to identify an engine of world economic growth at the moment. Europe, as we have seen, cannot play that role, as much of that region falls back into recession due to austerity-driven cuts. Japan, never having recovered from its crisis of the 1990s and more indebted than any large country, is incapable of carrying the global system on its back.[14] Meanwhile, the U.S. has showed the least improvement in job creation of any major economy—its sluggishness sends shivers down the spines of investors and financial analysts.

That leaves China as the one remaining hope for sustained recovery. Despite euphoric rhetoric here and there, such hopes are already being dashed. Having embarked on a stimulus program in 2008–9 that was proportionately much greater than what Bush and Obama did in America, the Chinese economy overheated massively. During the first three quarters of 2009, investment in fixed assets, like factories and the country's railway system, was responsible for an astonishing 95 percent of the country's economic growth and 45 percent of its GDP. This is a level without any historical precedent—and there was no way to sustain it. As investment poured into railway lines, apartment buildings, and new homes, commentators described a "forest" of empty office buildings, shopping malls, and housing developments around the country.[15] In the steel industry, where China had an excess capacity of between 100 and 200 million tons in late 2008, the stimulus program resulted in construction of 58 million tons of *new* steel-making capacity. The deputy director of the People's Bank of China acknowledged at the World Economic Forum that the country's excess capacity in steel equals 200 million tons, slightly more than the total output of the twenty-seven economies of the European Union in 2008.[16] So, while China's response to the Great Recession prevented a more dramatic economic collapse, it did so at the expense of a colossal over-accumulation of factories, mills, houses, shopping malls, and railway and subway lines, which could not be profitably used.[17]

As in every wave of overheated growth, substantial bubbles formed in China's stock and real estate markets. During 2009, stock prices rose more than 100 percent on the country's benchmark Shenzhen composite index.[18] At the same time, new home prices jumped between 51 and 68 percent in Shenzhen, Beijing, and Shanghai, while sales of cars, trucks, and buses, boosted by government incentives, rose 46 percent.[19] When China's banks then lent out more in the first week of January 2010 than they had in the entire month of November 2009, authorities finally moved to deflate the bubbles, raising reserve requirements and then ordering major banks to cease all new lending for the rest of the month.[20] Rather than comprise a viable basis for a sustained wave of expansion, China's growth since 2008 has heightened global problems of overcapacity while generating stock and real estate bubbles and greatly raising the risk that nonperforming loans will disrupt the bank sector.[21] The result is that Chinese authorities are reining in the economy at the same time such policies are being pursued in Europe and North America. World growth can only suffer as a consequence.

One of the clearest indicators of the deep recessionary tendencies in play at the moment is the contracting supply of money and credit. The latter expands whenever investment and spending are on the upswing. In contrast, the broad money supply in the U.S. has been falling persistently in defiance of claims for the end of the recession. According to the Federal Reserve Bank of St. Louis, commercial and industrial bank loans dropped every month from October 2008 into mid-2010. Broadly similar trends can be observed in the seven largest economies of the Global North.[22] All of this speaks of ongoing stagnation, not energetic growth.

It is these dynamics of the mutating crisis that I hope to capture with the term "global slump." Rather than describing a single crisis, the term is meant to capture a whole period of interconnected crises—the bursting of a real estate bubble; a wave of bank collapses; a series of sovereign debt crises; relapses into recession—that goes on for years without a sustained economic recovery. That, I submit, is what confronts us for many, many years to come. We are indeed living through "a transformative moment in global economic history," as the quote that opens this chapter suggests. And struggles over how it is to be resolved will almost certainly "reshape politics and economics for at least a generation." In a very profound sense, in other words, the present *is* history.

About the Arguments to Follow

The chapters that follow are meant as pieces of a puzzle, discrete parts that need to be connected for a comprehensive analysis of the global slump. Chapter 1 returns to the outbreak of the crisis in order to examine its titanic proportions and historical significance. In documenting the unbridled panic that swept ruling class circles, it lays the foundation for understanding what has happened since.

Chapter 2 then steps back to look at the twenty-five-year period of neoliberal expansion (1982–2007) that planted the seeds of this crisis. In developing this argument, I dissent from the views of many radical theorists (to be taken up later) who see the last forty years as one uninterrupted crisis, or a "long downturn." Instead, I show that the neoliberal period saw a quarter-century cycle of capitalist growth that transformed and expanded the world economy, ultimately producing a whole new center of world accumulation, based in China, while dramatically increasing the size of the world working class. The exhaustion of that cycle of growth now portends a prolonged slump.

Chapter 3 then locates the current slump in terms of the overall dynamics of capitalist accumulation and its propensity to periodic crisis. This involves looking at the interconnections among labor, markets, exploitation and competition in a capitalist economy. Some readers may find parts of this chapter demanding. But I hope they will also find that it clarifies how capitalism works and why economic crisis and the human suffering they create cannot be eliminated short of a radical change in the very bases of social life.

Chapter 4 takes up a crucially distinctive aspect of neoliberal capitalism: financialization. It seeks to show that, while the crisis is not about finance per se, the financial sector has indeed assumed a new significance in late capitalism.[23] Yet, although acknowledging the enormously increased role of debt and financial transactions, my account departs from explanations that restrict the focus to the deregulation of banking. Instead, I underline the historic transformation of world money that occurred after 1971, when the U.S. government ended the convertibility of dollars for gold, thereby launching an era of floating exchange rates for currencies. It is here that I locate the roots of the proliferation of exotic instruments such as financial derivatives, which figured so prominently in the financial meltdown of 2008.

Chapter 5 addresses the complex class and racial dynamics of the political economy of debt today. In this regard, I look at the tactics of predatory inclusion that, particularly in the U.S., drew poor people of color more fully into financial markets, and I analyze the processes of financial expropriation this involved. I then tease out the profound connections between debt and displacement, particularly in the Global South, and the processes of accumulation by dispossession they have involved. The chapter concludes by exploring the creation of displaced migrant workers as late capitalism's ideal precarious laborers.

Chapter 6 turns to the urgent question of resisting the global slump and the age of austerity. Drawing on examples of factory occupations against job loss, the inspiring general strikes in Guadeloupe and Martinique in 2009, the uprising of the people of Oaxaca, Mexico, against neoliberalism, and the urgent struggles of migrant workers today, it tries to chart pathways of resistance and anticapitalist transformation.

The conclusion then weaves together a number of these threads, reviews the state of the world economy and popular resistance, and underscores the truly transformative moment in which we live and act today.

★   ★   ★

Any book dealing with issues of political economy confronts a challenge. Throughout the history of capitalism, economic questions have been made deliberately obscure by the powers-that-be. Because economic analysis touches on such fundamental issues as the production, distribution, and ownership of the wealth of society, the ruling class cultivates economic illiteracy. Economics departments, financial analysts, and business economists use an inscrutable jargon, dressed up with charts, tables, and lots of mathematics, to convince us that only a select few can possibly comprehend these weighty matters. As I show in chapter 3, these High Priests of Modern Economics rely on quack theory and overblown rhetoric. Rather than producing knowledge of economic phenomena, they generate confusion and disinformation. That creates problems for them too, however, because their own nonsensical models are incapable of reading the actual dynamics of the capitalist economy—which is why they utterly failed to see the crash of 2008 coming.

This book is written in opposition to the mystifications of modern economics. I insist that the most basic issues of political economy are readily understandable by anyone who can overcome their trepidation about them. As much as possible I have avoided obscure or overly technical language. But I also refuse to talk down to readers. This is not *The Crisis for Dummies*. I have written it in the conviction that there is critical knowledge we need in order to understand the world in which we live. As a result, this book sometimes uses ideas and categories that may be new to many readers. It does so because critical knowledge involves subversive concepts that expose the ideological pretensions of capitalist thinking. But neither is this book *The Crisis for Ivory Tower Academics*. I see little point in encumbering a text with jargon designed to dazzle an in-crowd of scholars. My purpose here is to offer a book in which interpreting the world is joined to changing it. So, while introducing terms and concepts that will be new to some readers, I try to explain them as clearly as possible. To this end, I also offer a glossary of key terms.

I try to take the same approach to the use of numbers, tables, and charts. These too are entirely comprehensible, if the reader can overcome the memories of bad experiences in math class or the mind-numbing process of figuring out government forms.

Of course, some readers will come to this work with a lot of background knowledge, including in the literature of radical political economy. While I have not organized the text around the debates in this field, I do address them in the course of my argument. These controversies are important to clarifying what is happening around us. But they are not always accessible to as wide a readership as one would like. For that reason, more detailed discussion of these issues has been confined to endnotes. The reader particularly interested in these debates is advised to attend closely to these notes.

In the interest of promoting critical theory, I have also included an analysis of capitalism's inherent tendencies toward crisis. This forms the basis of chapter 3. While some issues are necessarily compressed there, I hope it will be of service to both the reader approaching these problems for the first time and to those who have some familiarity with debates in this field. Some readers may want to leave this chapter until they have read the rest of the text. Others may find it helpful to reread it after having gone through the whole book. My greatest hope is that readers will use this book, that they will discuss it, debate it, and adapt things I have said for the practical work of radical social change. More than a century and a half on, it remains the case that "the philosophers have only interpreted the world, whereas the point is to change it."[24] Rather than an injunction to stop analyzing the world, of course, this was instead an urgent reminder of the need to develop, share and mobilize critical analysis in order to remake our world. It is in that spirit that I offer this book.

CHAPTER ONE

The Great Panic of 2008

BEFORE THE DENIAL CAME THE PANIC. AND WHAT A PANIC IT WAS.

"I am really scared," U.S. Treasury Secretary Hank Paulson confided to his wife on September 14, 2008, as the Lehman Brothers investment bank disintegrated, sending shockwaves through global credit markets.[25] The next day brought Lehman's collapse, followed a day later by that of AIG, the world's largest insurance company. Before the month was out Washington Mutual would melt down, registering the biggest bank failure in U.S. history. Then America's fourth-largest bank, Wachovia, went on life support. A wave of European bank collapses rapidly followed.

So panicked and bewildered were global elites that Alan Greenspan, former chairman of the U.S. Federal Reserve Bank, informed a Congressional committee the following month that he was in a state of "shocked disbelief" over the failure of markets to self-regulate.[26] Small wonder. By the fall of 2008 the global financial system was in full-fledged meltdown. Worldwide credit seized up as financial institutions refused to lend for fear that borrowers would not survive. Stock markets plummeted. Global trade collapsed. Banks toppled. As shaken commentators invoked memories of the 1930s, two U.S. investment bankers openly compared the situation with the Great Depression.[27]

"Our economy stood at the brink," Tim Geithner, current U.S. treasury secretary, testified about those weeks. "The United States," he continued, "risked a complete collapse of our financial system."[28] Canada's finance minister, Jim Flaherty, echoed this view, stating that the world economy had hovered on the edge of "catastrophe."[29] Catastrophe, indeed.

Over the course of 2008, global stock markets plunged nearly 50 percent, wiping out about $35 trillion in financial assets. All five of Wall Street's investment banks simply vanished—*kaput*. But the disease did not stop with the U.S. economy. Banks went under in Ireland, Spain, Germany, the UK, Iceland, and beyond. Nor was the meltdown limited to finance. General Motors and Chrysler both went bust, only to be bailed out and taken over by the U.S. government. And across the meltdown, millions of people lost their jobs, and many of them their homes. Homelessness and hunger soared.

Unfolding into 2009, the crisis tracked the contours of Great Depression of the 1930s. The collapse of world industrial production, global trade, and stock market values was as severe as 1929–30, sometimes more so.[30] For the first time in seventy years, world capitalism seemed to have entered a crisis with no clear end in sight.

And for the first time in a very long time, the world's ruling class lost its swagger.[31] Arrogance and ostentation were displaced by fear and trembling. So severe was the capitalist crisis of confidence that in March 2009 the *Financial Times*, the most venerable business paper in the English-speaking world, ran a series on "The Future of Capitalism," as if that were now an issue. Introducing the series, its editors declared, "The credit crunch has destroyed faith in the free market ideology that has dominated Western economic thinking for a decade. But what can—and should—replace it?" The next day the paper's editors opined that "The world of the past three decades is gone." And one of its columnists quoted a Merrill Lynch banker who remarked, "Our world is broken—and I honestly don't know what is going to replace it."[32]

So palpable was the sort of fear expressed by Hank Paulson to his wife, so tangible the loss of confidence conveyed by Alan Greenspan's "shocked disbelief," that a small but important space opened up for real discussion and debate about our economic and social system. In this environment, even critics of capitalism occasionally found their views solicited by mainstream media.[33] "Marx is in fashion again," declared a Berlin book publisher, describing an uptick in sales of *Capital*, while in Japan a comic book version of Marx's greatest work sold tens of thousands of copies.[34]

It is not hard to see why the crisis generated interest in alternative social and economic perspectives. After all, for decades mainstream economics had denied that such an event was even possible. Clinging to the so-called Efficient Market Hypothesis (EMH), which insists that markets always behave rationally, the leading lights of the economic profession repeatedly proclaimed that systemic crises were no longer possible. "The central problem of depression-prevention has been solved," announced Nobel laureate Robert Lucas, in his 2003 presidential address to the American Economic Association. Meanwhile, the originator of EMH, Eugene Fama, haughtily dismissed those who predicted a financial crisis, telling an interviewer, "The word 'bubble' drives me nuts"—just as one of the greatest financial bubbles in history was exploding.[35] Backed by a profession that denied the possibility of economic slumps, David Lereah, former chief economist of America's National Association of Realtors, published one of the most absurdly titled books in a very long time, *Are You Missing the Real Estate Boom?: The Boom Will Not Bust and Why Property Values Will Continue to Climb through the End of the Decade—And How to Profit From Them* (2005). And the mainstream media, incapable of challenging the established consensus, turned the author into the foremost authority on housing prices, reproducing his views in hundreds of outlets, including the *New York Times*, the *Washington Post,* and the *Wall Street Journal.*

Little surprise then that the credibility of mainstream economics went up in flames as the crisis deepened. Not only could critics of free market nostrums now find a hearing, but books like *The Myth of the Rational Market* garnered widespread attention and favorable reviews in the *Economist*, the *Washington Post, Financial Times,* and beyond.[36] Not that any of this led to a fundamental rethinking within the mainstream itself. Instead establishment pundits, once they conceded that the economy was in crisis, endlessly proclaimed that it could not have been foreseen. It was a once-in-a-century event, they insisted, a bizarre aberration. "Everybody missed it—academia, the Federal Reserve, all regulators," Alan Greenspan recently claimed—though, as we shall see, this is anything but the case.[37] But by endlessly repeating these mantras, ruling class spokespeople and their media friends have been busily creating a structure of denial and mystification meant to close off critical inquiry into what actually happened—and why.

But just as denial is unhealthy for individuals, so it is for groups and societies. To deny or repress a traumatic experience means, as Freud taught us, to invariably repeat it.[38] And this is what global elites are in the process of doing. By denying the trauma of the meltdown and their own profound panic, by trying to wipe them from memory, they trap society in a repetitive cycle of trauma and repression. Of course, it is in their interest to do so; they profit from a culture that inhibits critical inquiry and analysis. But the vast majority—those who do not own banks and giant corporations, or multi-million-dollar stock and bond portfolios—need to understand the world in order to change it. And that requires confronting traumatic experiences—especially when jobs, incomes, housing, education, and pensions, not to speak of human happiness and well-being, are at stake. So, let us resist the denials and mystifications and probe the Panic of 2008 a bit more.

Why Hank Paulson was Scared

Hank Paulson had good reason to be scared on September 14, 2008. Global capitalism was in freefall, as one financial institution after another was taken down by "the most virulent global financial crisis ever."[39] With stunning rapidity, eight major U.S. banks collapsed, as did more than twenty in Europe, many of them to be taken over by governments. GM and Chrysler went bust, along with many parts suppliers. Tens of millions of people worldwide were thrown out of work. And no amount of government intervention seemed capable of calming the markets. Despite a full eighteen months of warning signs, from the collapse of hedge funds to huge losses at investment banks, government officials utterly failed to grasp the nature or severity of the crisis. On March 28, for instance, Fed chair Ben Bernanke calmly asserted that, rather than undermining the broader economy, mortgage-related problems were "likely to be contained." A few weeks later, the International Monetary Fund went further, issuing the astonishing claim that "global economic risks have declined . . . The overall U.S. economy is holding up well."[40] This was more than deception. It was also stupidity—as we shall see in chapter 4. Government leaders, just like world bankers, truly did not understand what was happening to the world economy. Yet, as the accompanying box, which tracks the First Phase of the crisis, demonstrates, the powers-that-be had received plenty of warning as to what was coming.

At this point, it should have been obvious that something was seriously amiss with the world's financial institutions. Indeed, it was obvious to a small number of critics and commentators, as we shall see. But because mainstream economics, armed with the Efficient Market Hypothesis, claimed that markets would quickly self-correct, government officials, bankers, and media talking heads kept proclaiming that all was well, or soon would be. To be sure, some of this was just the steady diet of lies and distortions that our rulers feed the people. But much of it was also their own stupidity, their incapacity to see that neoliberal capitalism was profoundly unstable and that its financial structure was coming undone. Had Paulson and the U.S. government brain trust at the Treasury and the Federal Reserve—which included Fed chief Ben Bernanke and then New York Fed president Tim Geithner—actually understood what they were dealing with, they would not have let Lehman collapse. For the disintegration of the New York investment bank triggered Phase Two of the crisis, by far its most virulent stage, sending shockwaves through the global economy that took down banks and at least one government.

The implosion of Lehman Brothers on September 15, 2008, was a truly spectacular event, without precedent in U.S. economic history. Seven years earlier, the collapse of Enron, worth $60 billion, had astounded commentators. But Lehman, valued at $635 billion only five days before it went under, was more than ten times the size of Enron and more than six times larger than WorldCom when it melted down some months after Enron. Most important, it was dramatically more interconnected with the world's financial institutions. The Enron and WorldCom failures were early tremors, shifts in the fault lines that signaled the quakes to come. The false calm that ensued was broken by the

Before the Collapse of Lehman Brothers:
Phase One of the Crisis

February 7, 2007: HSBC Holdings, the world's third-largest bank, announces a $10.6 billion loss on bad debts related to U.S. mortgage securities. The same day, America's second largest subprime mortgage lender, New Century Financial, informs investors of losses in the final quarter of 2006.

April 2, 2007: New Century Financial declares bankruptcy.

July 2007: Wall Street investment bank Bear Stearns shuts down two multi-billion dollar hedge funds after massive losses ($1.6 billion) on mortgage-backed securities, announcing that its collateralized debt obligations are worthless.

August 6, 2007: American Home Mortgage Investment Corporation files for bankruptcy.

August 9, 2007: BNP Paribas, France's largest bank, halts redemptions from three investment funds holding mortgage-backed bonds, leading to panic in European money markets.

Mid-September 2007: British bank Northern Rock seeks emergency support from the Bank of England, provoking a run on deposits.

October 24, 2007: Merrill Lynch announces its biggest-ever quarterly loss: $2.3 billion.

October–November 2007: Citigroup, one of the world's largest banks, declares losses of nearly $17 billion

February 17, 2008: British bank Northern Rock goes bust—taken over by UK government.

March 13–17, 2008: Wall Street investment bank Bear Stearns collapses, after cash reserves drop from $18 billion to $2 billion in a matter of days. The bank's shares, which had started the year at $173, now trade for a few dollars. The U.S. Federal Reserve backstops a takeover by JPMorgan Chase.

July 11, 2008: IndyMac Federal Bank collapses, the third-largest bank failure in U.S. history to that date. Fannie Mae and Freddie Mac, the world's largest mortgage lenders, lose half their value the same week.

September 5–7, 2008: As Fannie and Freddie disintegrate, the U.S. government takes them over, committing $200 billion to cover their bad debts.

wave of shocks that started in mid-2007. But Lehman's collapse was the Big One, a tectonic eruption that blew a gigantic hole in the world economy. If Lehman could go down, after 158 years as perhaps "the greatest merchant bank Wall Street ever knew," then no one was safe.[41] Worse, nobody—not Lehman's directors, not Treasury and Fed officials, not savvy investors—could calibrate the scale of the damage.

Because of the increasingly complex financial instruments that had emerged across the neoliberal era, an utterly opaque market had developed in which no one could figure out who owed what to whom. Derivatives, collateralized debt obligations, credit-default swaps, and similar instruments (all of which I explain in chapter 4) might have been profitable for a while, but they were obscure, deceptive and volatile. Built upon fantasies, deceit and nonsensical formulas, the values of these "assets" were impossible to calibrate, particularly as they melted down. "We have no idea of our derivatives exposure and neither do you," Lehman bosses told Treasury and Fed officials poring over their books as the firm expired.[42] As a result, no institution was prepared to lend to another, for fear that its borrower too would collapse and never repay. Worse, by this point, "Every major firm on Wall Street was either bankrupt or fatally intertwined with a bankrupt system," as one critic has noted.[43] As credit markets seized up for lack of lending, global financial institutions started to fall like dominoes. With every day bringing a new announcement of bank failures, it truly looked like the world economy would slip "into the abyss," as one White House aide later put it.[44] The accompanying box gives a sense of what the tumult looked like.

As multi-billion-dollar banks collapsed, even Hank Paulson understood that something was gravely, desperately wrong: "I'm worried about the world falling apart," he confessed.[45] Meeting with senior U.S. senators some days later, he implored them, "Unless you act, the financial system of this country, and the world, will melt down in a matter of days."[46]

Nothing like this had happened since the Great Crash of the 1930s. Within the space of just over four weeks, the U.S. had experienced its largest ever bankruptcy (Lehman Brothers), its largest

Phase Two:
Lehman's Meltdown Triggers Global Collapses

September 15, 2008: Lehman Brothers collapses. At $635 billion it is by far the largest bankruptcy in U.S. history.

September 16, 2008: The U.S. government bails out AIG, the world's largest insurance company.

September 18, 2008: Investment bank Merrill Lynch reveals losses of $50 billion on mortgage-related investments, while Citigroup announces similar losses of over $60 billion.

September 21, 2008: Wall Street investment banks Goldman Sachs and Morgan Stanley are turned into holding companies in order to access government protection. All five Wall Street investment banks have now vanished in the course of seven months.

September 25, 2008: Washington Mutual, with assets of $307 billion, goes bust, the largest bank failure in U.S. history.

September 29, 2008: Wachovia, the fourth largest bank in the U.S. collapses, and is bought up by Citigroup. Three European banks go under, as the British government seizes Bradford and Bingley, Germany bails out Hypo Real Estate; and Belgium and other countries rescues Fortis.

September 30, 2008: More European bank failures: France and Belgium bail out Dexia, while Ireland pumps $574 billion into its banking system. The U.S. government pumps $25 billion into General Motors and Chrysler, as the automakers teeter on the brink of collapse.

October 7, 2008: The government of Iceland takes over the country's two largest banks.

October 8, 2008: British government pumps $875 billion into ailing banks.

October 9, 2008: Iceland seizes the country's largest bank and shuts its stock market as the panic spreads.

October 10, 2008: U.S. stock markets finish their worst week since 1933.

October 13, 2008: Britain nationalizes RBS and HBOS in order to avert complete meltdown of the two mammoth banks.

commercial bank failure (Washington Mutual), the disappearance of Wall Street's two remaining investment banks, and the bailout of the world's largest insurance company. Europe, meanwhile, had endured a wave of toppling banks, resulting in takeovers or bailouts by governments in five countries. Still, the meltdown was far from over. Before the end of January 2009, AIG would be bailed out two more times, and both Citigroup and Bank of America would be rescued. That same month the government of Iceland was toppled by mass protests over economic policies that had destroyed that country's financial system. It was in this climate of continuing panic that the *Financial Times* began to query the future of capitalism.

After the Great Denial: Welcome to the "Decade of Pain"
Today, however, we are instructed to forget all of the above. Reflections on the future of capitalism have disappeared from mainstream media, including the *Financial Times*. The Great Panic has been replaced by the Great Denial. Having managed to halt the meltdown and generate a small economic bounce— thanks to the most massive global bailout ever undertaken—our planet's rulers are hurriedly sweeping their fear and panic under boardroom carpets. All is well with the world, they declare. The Masters of the Universe have saved the day, and capitalism once again reigns supreme. We were not at fault, they insist, because no one could have foreseen this crisis. It was a bolt from the sky, the financial equivalent of a "hundred year flood," in the words of Alan Greenspan.[47] And now that the flood has passed, so they claim, we can return to business as usual.

Yet, this is all a little too anxious and easy. While the meltdown has been halted, profound economic problems persist and new crises are already brewing. Perhaps sensing that the storms are far from over, the ruling class is at work shifting the very terms of debate. Rather than discuss what ails capitalism, it is devising a rhetoric designed to blame its victims. No longer are global banks or giant corporations at fault. Government officials and regulators need no longer be scrutinized for their failures to prevent lies, scams, and swindles—and the meltdown that accompanied them. No, the real culprits are poor and working class people who expected too much. Having bailed out the very banks and global corporations that created the crisis, political elites are now scapegoating its victims: poor racial minorities in the U.S. who were conned into taking out mortgages designed to explode, or Greek teachers and public employees who think they have a right to decent pensions after a lifetime of service. As they construct this discourse, our rulers hope to soften us up for "a decade of pain"—a period of high unemployment, falling incomes, and huge cuts to health care, education, and social-welfare programs.

"A decade of pain" is the term coined by the Institute for Fiscal Studies (IFS) in Britain to describe what faces ordinary citizens as a result of their government's massive rescue of banks and the $275 billion annual deficit it (and associated costs of the recession) has created. The IFS estimates that by 2017–18 the average British family will be more than $4,500 poorer, as a result of increased taxes or diminished social services, or some combination of the two, all to be imposed in order to eliminate the government deficit.[48] Other British commentators, from politicians to business analysts, have employed the expression "decade of austerity" to describe what is in store. But let's not quibble over the term, since pain and austerity are inseparable. Instead, let's look at what austerity—big reductions in public spending—will mean.

California is a useful starting point. In an effort to balance the books on the backs of the poor, the governor of the largest U.S. state, Arnold Schwarzenegger, has slashed billions from social spending. Fully $1 billion has been cut from programs that directly support the most disadvantaged, including funds for rural migrant clinics, temporary assistance to needy families, health insurance for nine hundred thousand poor children, and services dealing with domestic violence and maternal and child health. Altogether forty-five U.S. states are in deficit at the moment—and cutting frantically. Arizona too has scrapped its Children's Health Insurance Program, Ohio has slashed community mental health services, and Minnesota is eliminating health coverage for low-income adults. Some thirty-six states have chopped higher education spending, twenty-four have reduced services to the elderly and the disabled, and even more have attacked health care.[49] All of this is happening at a time when, as a consequence of the crisis, millions more will need such services after having been driven below the poverty line. Government agencies may have declared an end to the recession of 2007–9, yet the real unemployment rate in the U.S. is about 17 percent. For African-Americans and Latinos it is at depression levels, above 25 percent. Not surprisingly, use of food stamps is soaring. One in every eight adults and one in every four children in America are currently using food stamps in order to feed themselves. Incredibly, nearly half of all U.S. kids will rely on food stamps at some point in their childhood—a figure that rises to almost 90 percent for both black children and kids in single-parent households.[50] Meanwhile, over one million school-age children are homeless.[51] Yet, it is these people—children, the elderly, single-parent families, the homeless, the unemployed, and the under-employed—who will be hammered hardest by cuts to health care, education, and social assistance programs. Capitalism is attempting to right its ship at their expense, by punishing its victims for the system's latest crisis.

As we have seen, the U.S. is not unique in this regard, even if its situation is particularly shameful. Britain's decade of pain will involve sustained cuts to social spending—a long-term "strategic transformation" of the state, as one economic consulting group has put it—similar to the structural adjustment programs imposed on countries in the Global South in recent decades.[52] The Greek government, meanwhile, after having committed billions to banks, is savaging the poor by slashing billions from public spending. In order to bring its deficit under control, it has raised the sales tax to 21 percent, cutting public sector jobs, pay, and benefits while chopping pensions in half. Meanwhile, Latvia has fired one-third of all teachers and slashed pensions by 70 percent. Once held up as a shining example of the success of neoliberalism, the Irish government is savaging the public sector, cutting 10 percent from child benefits, 4 percent from welfare, and 22.5 percent from wages of public employees. But among the most obscene cases is that of the Canadian province of British Columbia (BC). After having doled out billions on the lavish 2010

Winter Olympics, the province turned around and introduced a budget that slams the poor. Attacking a program that had previously funded monthly nutritional supplements for low-income people suffering malnutrition, significant weight loss, marked neurological degeneration, and other severe symptoms, the BC government will henceforth require that people exhibit at least *two* such conditions in order to qualify. Not to be outdone, the government of Ontario, the country's largest province, used its 2010 budget to completely eliminate its Special Diet program for poor people with health problems.[53]

This, then, is where we find ourselves at the supposed "end" of the crisis. While banks and multinationals have been rescued, there is no bailout for working class people, who can only expect more "pain" for years and years to come. As corporate profits recover, jobs, incomes and social services continue to disappear. So blatant is the contradiction between what is happening to capital and what is going on with everyone else that even former U.S. treasury secretary Larry Summers acknowledges we are in the midst of "a statistical recovery and a human recession."[54] But the human recession hits some a lot more than others. As noted in the introduction, the compiler of the *Sunday Times Rich List* in Britain has observed, not only have "the rich have come through the recession with flying colours," but social service cuts have "little effect on the rich because they don't consume public services."[55] In other words, it is the working class and the poor who will pay for the crisis. Moreover, as I explain in the chapters that follow, the economy itself is fated to remain sluggish, incapable of generating robust growth. And by reducing employment and incomes, government austerity will intensify the economic slump, as the central bank of Greece has acknowledged.[56] Working class and poor people thus face a prolonged period of high unemployment and financial pain. Welcome to the global slump. How we got here, why things will not improve any time soon, and what we might do about a system that breeds human recessions—these are the themes of the chapters that follow.

CHAPTER TWO

The Day the Music Died:
Three Decades of Neoliberalism

"The American standard of living must decline."
—Paul Volcker, 1979[57]

THE SEA CHANGE WAS ANNOUNCED IN 1979. THAT WAS THE YEAR PAUL
Volcker, chairman of the U.S. Federal Reserve, proclaimed the
end of the Great Boom. Not only were the American people
counseled to no longer expect regular improvements in living
standards; they were also instructed to brace themselves for painful declines. And Volcker and the American ruling class had a
whole battery of weapons to insure it would happen. Strategically,
they cast their campaign as a moral crusade, a battle against a
people whom, they claimed, had become too complacent, too
ready to expect that life would just keep on getting better. People
were going to have to get used to living on less, much less—
Volcker and Company would see to that.[58]

The elite offensive was thus projected as a war against
laxity and laziness. Social program cuts, reduced wages, broken
unions—all of these were clothed as efforts necessary to bring
back the good old work ethic, the ostensible key to earlier prosperity. Working people would be taught once again that poverty
is the punishment for those who do not keep their noses to the
grindstone. Workers, of course, were anything but responsible
for the slowdown. The end of the economic boom of the post–
World War II era was a product of the same relentless drive to
accumulate that had initially sustained the expansion. By the
1970s, over-accumulated capital and declining profits had induced
a great seizing up of the capitalist economy.[59] Yet it was hugely
convenient to blame workers for the slump. After all, this made it
easier to administer Volcker's declared medicine—reduced living
standards. In truth, this was a pure and simple program for restor-

ing corporate profits—nothing more, nothing less. And it was joined to an offensive against the Global South, as an induced debt crisis became the lever for predatory invasions of economies in the Third World designed to pry open their markets, seize their assets on the cheap, and lock them into debt.

These were the early days of neoliberalism, the turn to a more virulent form of capitalism, which would result in a new wave of expansion—albeit with a growth pattern based on soaring social inequality, rising global poverty, and increased human insecurity.[60] These, as we shall see, have been hallmarks of neoliberal capitalism. But before investigating that, we need to attend to the crisis that Volcker and company encountered in the 1970s, and the draconian means they used to resolve it. And that means starting with the phenomenal postwar expansion of western capitalism, for it is there we shall find the seeds of the crisis that spawned neoliberalism.

Here I need to signpost key parts of my argument. There is a widespread tendency among radical political economists to say that western capitalism underwent a great boom for a quarter-century (1948–73), only to fall into a crisis or depression from which it has, for forty years, never recovered.[61] I dissent from central parts of this narrative. While agreeing that capitalism entered a deep slump in the early 1970s, I submit that a sustained (neoliberal) recovery began in 1982—a claim I will document below. To be sure, world capitalism did not attain the growth rates characteristic of the Great Boom that followed World War II—though China not only achieved, but actually exceeded those rates. But for twenty-five years after 1982, the trend line for profits was a rising one and the system underwent a sustained wave of expansion in which the world economy tripled in size and new centers of global accumulation, such as China, emerged. The world working class grew even more dramatically during this era, as we shall see. In tracking the sixty-five years since 1945, then, I submit that we observe the following pattern:

Sustained expansion (1948–73)

World slump (1973–82)

Sustained expansion (1982–2007)

World slump (2007–?)

With this sketch in mind, let us fill in the details.

The Great Boom and Its Unwinding

The world economy had never seen anything like the Great Boom of 1948–73. For a full quarter-century the dominant economies surged ever forward, generating jobs, robust profits, and rising incomes year after year. These were the golden years of western capitalism, and they have become such a powerful cultural marker that even many left-wing critics treat them as the norm. If capitalism is not replicating the Great Boom, then they declare the system to be in crisis. Yet, as we shall see, the golden years were anything but normal; they represent a period of unprecedented dynamism whose return seems highly improbable.

In the quarter-century after World War II, "The advanced capitalist nations as a whole grew three times as fast as in the interwar years and twice as fast as before World War One," notes one historian.[62] In the course of a mere twenty-five years, the output of the capitalistically developed economies—Europe, Japan, and North America—tripled.[63] For some parts of the capitalist core, spectacular growth rates were initially driven by the inevitable bounce-back from wartime destruction. But even when this is factored in, the sustained character of the expansion is arresting. Consider Western Europe, where at the end of the war the economy lagged a full half-century behind the United States. Riding the expansionary wave, it had closed the gap by 1973. Or ponder Japan, which had been a hundred years behind the United States in 1945. Astronomical growth—the Japanese economy expanded eight times over during the boom—closed that gap too in a mere twenty-five years. Much of this increase was propelled by great jumps in world trade, which doubled every ten years throughout the expansionary wave. As trade became more global, so did investment, spearheaded by U.S.-based multinational corporations that set up shop outside their domestic borders. Meanwhile, anticolonial movements in the Third World sparked a wave of decolonization that opened some space for development agendas in parts of the South, although these were hampered by a

new form of imperialism that reproduced economic dependence. But in unique circumstances, like those of South Korea, big
leaps forward in terms of capitalist development were possible.[64]

The most striking change, however, was the consistent rise
in the living standards of workers in the core capitalist countries.[65] Year after year, incomes went up, and cars, televisions,
and summer vacations became routine for millions of fully
employed workers in the North. To be sure, millions were left
out (or largely so), particularly members of groups subjected to
histories of racial oppression and marginalization—indigenous
peoples, African-Americans, immigrants of color, undocumented
migrants. But even some members of these groups made economic headway during the boom.

Improved living standards were underpinned by potent
increases in worker productivity. Between 1952 and 1973 output
per worker doubled, aided overwhelmingly by technological
innovations and new machines.[66] Employers could therefore raise
wages and still enjoy rising profits, so long as wage improvements
lagged behind productivity increases. This they did, thanks in
large measure to a huge expansion in the size of the working
class, which insured that employers always had large pools of
workers desperate for employment. With millions of Japanese
and European farmers departing the countryside to work in the
cities, and millions of migrant workers—from southern Europe,
South and East Asia, Latin America, the Caribbean, and parts of
Africa—setting out for work in the capitalist core, corporations
enjoyed a steadily growing labor force. Then, as the boom really
heated up in the late 1960s and early 1970s, a huge entrance of
women into labor markets served the same end. But by then the
engine of growth was starting to wind down.

The unwinding of the boom conformed to a familiar pattern of declining profitability and over-accumulation (as we shall
see in chapter 3). Indeed, the evidence for declining profits is so
overwhelming that radical political economists of varying per-
suasions, who can agree on little else, all accept that the profit
rate fell persistently from the mid-1960s until the early 1980s.
More than a dozen serious empirical studies show just this trend,

which is reproduced later in this chapter in figure 2.1.[67] While the reasons for this fall in the world profit rate are complex, a good case can be made that the basic mechanisms that Marx describes were at work. Marx, as we shall discuss in the next chapter, locates a contradiction in capital's need to mechanize in order to speed up labor and win the battle of competition. Yet, mechanization tends to make investment more "capital intensive," i.e. more reliant on machines and equipment, and correspondingly less labor intensive. Just this pattern can be observed across the Great Boom, when business spending averaged 4 percent or more per year. Moreover, this investment was heavily biased toward machinery—so much so that "the mass of means of production per worker more than doubled over the period. It was as though each worker was confronted by two machines where one had once stood."[68] But it wasn't only that the mass of machinery per worker rose.[69] In addition, the very technological basis of industry was regularly revolutionized, with new generations of machines and new production processes coming on stream, all contributing to persistent leaps in the productivity of labor. However, mechanization means a relative decline in the contribution of labor—and crucially profit-creating surplus labor—to each product. Everything else being equal, this can only translate into a falling rate of return on investment—as it in fact did.[70]

While profitability was turning down, over-accumulation was turning up in a classic pattern of over-investment. In fact, the pace of accumulation—the buildup of new factories, buildings, machines, equipment, office towers and so on—rose higher just as the slump approached. After averaging 4 percent throughout most of the boom, the pace of accumulation bumped up to an annual rate of 5.5 percent by 1970. With competition for sales and profits intensifying, firms frantically built up new capacity at an ever more rapid pace. Across the boom, these processes were most rapid in Japan, Western Europe, and South Korea, where entire industries were built virtually overnight. The Japanese economy led the way, with an accumulation rate of 12 percent, as business investment took an extraordinary 25 percent of gross national product. Output of steel rocketed, soaring from around one million tons in 1950 to 100 million tons twenty years later. Moreover, Japanese firms introduced the world's newest technologies, emerging as cutting-edge producers. By 1961, fully 40 percent of Japan's machine tools were less than five years old, making its productive equipment much younger than that of competitors like Britain and the United States. Riding a wave of technological innovation, Japanese corporations established themselves as world leaders: Sony in electronics, Toyota and Honda in cars, trucks, and motorcycles.[71] On its own, Japan's exceptional growth would have tipped the world economy into over-accumulation sooner or later. But Japan was not alone. Sustained growth in the U.S. and robust expansion in Western Europe meant that the day of reckoning would not be long postponed.

European rates of growth were not quite as remarkable as Japan's, but they were nothing to sneeze at. Automobile production, the leading manufacturing industry of the twentieth century, is a case in point. As firms such as Volkswagen, Fiat, Renault, BMW, Mercedes Benz, Saab, and others constructed new facilities, the number of cars on Europe's roads leapt from six million in 1950 to ten times that number by 1973. This in turn ramped up steel production and stimulated everything from heavy machinery to agriculture. But all good things must come to an end, they say—at least under capitalism. And by the early 1970s, the most sustained wave of expansion in capitalist history was bumping up against its limits. With excess capacity galore and declining profits, the world economy had entered a new period of global turbulence. Then, as we shall see, a frenetic wave of downsizing between the mid-1970s and the mid-1980s forced capitals to write off plants and equipment and, where they survived, turn to capital-saving innovations that drove up bankruptcies, even if they laid a basis for a restoration of profitability.[72]

A Decade of Crisis: 1971–82

In 1969, Paul Samuelson, author of the most widely used economics textbook in history, made one of the sorriest predictions of his often-boneheaded profession. No longer would the National Bureau of Economic Research have to track business cycles, he declared, for these were now a thing of the past.[73] Once again, history would make a fool of mainstream economics: in the following twelve years, world capitalism would undergo two deep, demoralizing slumps; and many countries, the U.S. included, would experience three.

The first hit in 1971, especially in the U.S. But a truly global slump followed in 1974. Over the course of the next two years, industrial output dropped 10 percent in the Global North. The American stock market lost half its value and the world system was rocked by the two biggest bank failures since the Depression, as Franklin National in the U.S. and Bankhaus Herstatt in Germany both collapsed. With recessionary forces kicking in, businesses rapidly cut back and layoffs mounted. The number of people officially unemployed in the major capitalist countries nearly doubled from eight to fifteen million. And now governments found themselves in a new bind: jobs loss and reduced economic activity were taking a bite out of tax revenues at the very moment that social assistance spending was soaring. This drove governments at all levels into deficit spending and sometimes into bankruptcy. In other cases, like Britain in 1976, emergency loans from the International Monetary Fund were used as the level to attack social service spending. By that point, the world's financial center, New York City, was officially broke and in financial receivership.

If proof were needed that times had changed, it was provided by the sight of Britain before the IMF or New York in bankruptcy court. For the first time in more than a generation, official jobless rates were heading toward double figures. Worse, a great burst of inflation considerably complicated the crises of this era.

This inflationary predicament was directly tied to the contradictions of Keynesian economics. Keynes, as I point out in the next chapter, had located the propensity of capitalism toward slumps in a psychological tendency for investors to hoard their wealth rather than spend it. The obvious remedy was for government to spend when capitalists would not. Yet, for much of the postwar period really sharp increases in government spending were difficult to execute. This had to do with the monetary arrangements established in 1946, known as the Bretton Woods system, under which all major currencies were tied to the U.S. dollar, which was itself linked to gold. But this system had broken down in 1971—an immense historical event whose implications I discuss at length in chapter 4. After 1971, with currencies no longer pegged to the dollar and gold, governments had much greater leeway to increase the money supply and spend their way out of crisis. And shocked by the first worldwide slump since the 1930s, they did exactly that.

Responding to the first signs of recession in 1971, governments immediately increased the money supply—by 12 percent in the core that year—in a bid to stimulate their economies. With things still looking wobbly, they further upped the ante. The U.S. government drove up the money supply by 40 percent between 1970 and 1973, while the British government oversaw a 70 percent increase in just two years. These expansionary initiatives certainly bought time, and produced a sharp mini-boom, but at the cost of ramping up inflation, as in this context, the expanded flows of money pushed up prices of everything from food and housing to oil, real estate, and gold.[74] At the same time, the decline of the dollar after it was detached from gold pushed sellers of commodities denominated in dollars to raise their prices in efforts not to lose income and purchasing power. In the context of inflation, a falling dollar, and speculative demand, producers of one raw commodity after another—copper, coffee, rubber, and more—were all able to raise their prices. Then, the world's major oil producing countries got in on the act, tripling the price of a barrel of oil. Contrary to mainstream claims at the time and since, oil price rises did not create the inflationary wave; they largely responded to it and to the falling value of the dollar.[75] As prices for everything from food to shelter rose, workers struck in huge numbers in an effort to keep up with the cost of living. Reacting to higher wage costs, employers responded wherever possible by raising prices in an effort pass on higher costs to purchasers. By then a vicious inflationary spiral was in play. In 1974, consumer prices rocketed up by 12 percent in the United States, 16 percent in Britain, and 23 percent in Japan. Still, governments kept trying to spend their way out of crisis, just as Keynes had advised, but in a context Keynes could not have anticipated. They pumped billions of dollars into their ailing economies and created millions of public-sector jobs—a million per year in the core between 1971 and 1983. Unable to generate the tax revenues to pay for all this, the dominant states ran persistent deficits, effectively printing money to pay their way—all of which further fed the fires of inflation.[76]

By the late 1970s, it was clear that Keynesianism could not get capitalism back on track. In fact, persistently high inflation was fuelling the very thing that worried Keynes in the first place: uncertainty. Keynes had argued, after all, that uncertainty about the future is what causes capitalists to save rather than invest. Yet, soaring inflation made the future ever more unpredictable. Not only did it cause them to worry that a given investment project might turn unprofitable, should inflationary costs wipe out gains; it also encouraged speculative investments in commodities—such as oil or gold—that looked set to rise faster than the general price level. Throughout most of these inflationary years, this was a sensible wager. In fact, the price of gold ripped through the stratosphere. From $35 an ounce in 1971, it leapt above $300 in the summer of 1979 before leaving earth's atmosphere that winter—at which point it was above $800 an ounce, or 2,280 percent higher than in 1971.

The gold mania of 1979–80 was also the moment that the inflationary spiral would be broken—as a result of the "Volcker Shock" administered by the Federal Reserve Bank of the United States. Though few knew it at the time, this was the turning point, the end of the inflationary crisis and the birthplace of global neoliberalism.

The Volcker Shock and the Birth of Neoliberalism

By the end of the 1970s the Keynesian era was over.[77] And it took a Keynesian to deliver the death blow. For Paul Volcker, elevated in August 1979 to the position of chairman of the U.S. Federal Reserve Bank, had always been a Keynesian rather than a monetarist.[78] Yet, he was first and foremost a pragmatic banker, and as the new Fed chairman he was about to do what conservatives and monetarists most dearly desired: deliver a monetary shock that would break the inflationary spiral.[79] In so doing, he plunged the world economy into a deep slump, kick-started a tidal wave of job losses, and created a Third World debt crisis. But these were small costs to pay in order to restore corporate profitability. Volcker had been clear from the start that this would require a decline in the American standard of living, though he might have added that the people of the Global South would soon have much worse inflicted on them.

To be sure, neoliberalism had its dress rehearsals before Volcker took the stage. Following the brutal overthrow of Chile's Socialist president, Salvador Allende, in 1973, the country's military dictator recruited a group of right-wing economists, known as the "Chicago boys," to restructure the Chilean economy. Liberals they may have called themselves, but the Chicago boys were only too happy to rush into the arms of a general who had ordered the murders of thousands while crushing democratic and civil rights in the process. Indeed, Friedman and his mentor Friedrich von Hayek had no qualms endorsing the brutal repression.[80] Collaborating with the IMF, these neoliberal economists, known as monetarists, set about privatizing public enterprises, opening the country up to foreign multinational corporations, and allowing these firms to ship as much wealth as they wanted out of the country. As these things often do, it looked good in the early going, until the 1982 debt crisis brought it all crashing down, as unemployment rocketed to 30 percent amid a 15 percent drop in GDP. To be sure, these Chilean initiatives were not the only neoliberal moves that preceded Volcker. So too did tight monetary policy by Germany's central bank and Britain's newly elected government led by Margaret Thatcher. Volcker was not the first, therefore, but he was the one who mattered most. For the U.S. still set the pace for the world economy. And Volcker was about to prove the point.

Not that it was smooth sailing for Volcker and his crew. They were improvising, flying by the seats of their pants, as they struggled to contain rising prices and wages. Consequently, the Fed had as many misses as hits with monetary policy in 1979–80, a lot of the misses proving that central banks are actually incapable of controlling the supply of money.[81] But once Volcker had twigged onto a mechanism that would produce sharp interest rate hikes, the hits came fast and furious. In no time, the Fed pushed short-term interest rates from 10 to 15 percent. When that proved insufficient to do the job, the central bank propelled rates steadily higher until they peaked at an astounding 20 percent. Meanwhile, the *real* interest rate—the rate of interest minus the rate of inflation—moved from negative territory in the mid-1970s to close to 9 percent. By keeping interest rates extraordinarily high for nearly three years, Volcker succeeded in knocking inflation down to 4 percent, while also knocking the floor out of the economy.

The key to the Volcker Shock was to reduce economic activity, and drive down prices, by making it prohibitively expensive to borrow money. Inevitably, as tighter credit reduced consumer spending and rising interest rates made it expensive to borrow, corporations sharply cut back investment. Indebted firms, facing huge interest payments, went broke in massive numbers. And ordinary consumers stopped taking out mortgages and car loans, put off by exorbitant rates. The economy was in the grips of a powerful contraction. For fully seventeen months the U.S. economy shrank, making 1980–82 the most prolonged slump since the 1930s. Manufacturing output fell by more than a tenth and the official unemployment rate went above 11 percent for the first time in forty years. The return of mass unemployment would on its own have had a traumatic effect on workers. But the U.S. government was intent on ratcheting the fear factor much higher. In August 1981, two years into Volcker's term at the Fed, President Ronald Reagan broke a national strike by air traffic controllers, firing all of them and crushing their union in the process. The shock of mass unemployment was thus joined to the trauma of union busting. And Volcker left no doubt as to the strategic importance of destroying the union: "the most important single action of the administration in helping the anti-inflation fight was defeating the air traffic controllers' strike," he later commented.[82] The reason for this is simple. It is an axiom of capitalism that "fear is the best motivator," as the author of *Profits Aren't*

Everything, They're the Only Thing puts it.[83] After all, if workers feel a reasonable degree of confidence, they will more powerfully resist the bullying and authoritarianism of employers and managers. Fear—for their jobs, their livelihoods, and the well-being of their families—typically serves to dampen rebellious impulses. And Volcker and company were in the business of instilling fear.

The results were incontrovertible: real wages in the United States dropped more than 10 percent between 1978 and 1983, and they continued to fall even as the economy recovered—a point to which we return shortly. Indeed, just to put the last nail in the coffin of the inflationary period, Volcker drove up interest rates again in 1983 and 1984, after a brief respite in response to Mexico's crisis. His successor, Alan Greenspan, later known as the easy-money man, actually continued Volcker's crusade and kept raising interest rates throughout the late 1980s, pausing only briefly in the wake of the stock market crash of 1987, before resuming his predecessor's course. The battle had been won. Wages and inflation were tracking down; profits were tracking up. The result, as Doug Henwood notes, was that "the central-bank-led class war succeeded in more than doubling the profit rate for nonfinancial corporations between 1982 and 1997."[84] The neoliberal expansion was clearly underway.[85]

This claim is surprisingly controversial, however, especially on the intellectual Left. As I have noted, there is a markedly unhelpful tendency in many radical analyses to treat the entire forty year period since 1970 as a "crisis," a "long downturn," or even a "depression."[86] Yet, as we shall see, such assessments miss the mark by a country mile. They either ignore, or thoroughly downplay the dramatic social, technical, and spatial restructuring of capitalist production that occurred across the neoliberal period, all of which significantly raised profitability, and led to a volatile but nonetheless real process of sustained capitalist expansion, much of it centered on East Asia. Grasping some of the central features of that process is essential to understanding the current crisis.

Because these claims are contentious, I want to spend some time documenting them. For, only if we have a clear picture of the last thirty years or so of capitalist development can we adequately assess the dimensions of the current slump. To that end, I shall first set down three markers, what we might call methodological guidelines, meant to direct our investigation of global capitalism over the past quarter-century. On the basis of these I will then offer three principal theses concerning the arc of expansion and crisis-formation that has characterized world capitalism during this period. Let me start with methodological principles.

Guidelines for Understanding the Neoliberal Period

I argue, first, that we need to treat the world economy as a totality that is more than the sum of its largest parts. This may seem mundane, but it is striking how many analyses focus on "the performance of the advanced capitalist economies,"—most frequently the U.S., Germany and Japan—and treat the world economy as largely an aggregate of these parts.[87] This is both methodologically flawed and empirically misleading.[88] However significant they are as points of concentration within the system, nation-states are not the fundamental units of analysis in critical political economy. Capitalism, after all, is a global system, and it is only at the level of world economy that all of its dynamics come into play.[89] Moreover, the core capitalist economies are far from the full story of the global economy in our era. Indeed, we miss much of that story if we ignore the phenomenal expansion across the neoliberal period of major East Asian economies, which have grown at three or four times the rate of the traditional capitalist core. This should serve as a reminder that any serious assessment of the global economy needs to focus on the process of worldwide accumulation.[90]

I argue, secondly, that an assessment of world capitalism cannot concentrate on national economic indicators. Capital does not invest in order to boost gross domestic product (GDP), national income, or aggregate national employment, or to maintain the highest possible rate of business spending. It invests in order to expand itself via the capture of shares of global profits (or surplus value).[91] But the capture of surplus value can—and does—happen in circumstances that are not optimal from the standpoint of the macroeconomic performance of national economies. Indeed, as I argue below, throughout the neoliberal era, capitals in the core economies of the world system have increased social inequality while also shifting investment outside their national economies in the search for higher rates of return. These policies have frequently produced more robust rates of capital accumulation in select regions outside the core, while contributing to slower rates of growth in the dominant economies.[92]

Third, the unique quarter-century long postwar boom (1948–73) ought not to be the benchmark against which everything else is deemed a "crisis." As we have seen, the Great Boom was the product of an exceptional set of social-historical circumstances that triggered an unprecedented wave of expansion. But prolonged expansion with rising levels of output, wages, and employment in the core economies is not the capitalist norm; and the absence of all of these is not invariably a "crisis." It is simply ahistorical to imagine that capital is in crisis every time rates of increase in world or national GDP fall below 5 percent per annum. Indeed, where wage compression characterizes a phase of capitalist expansion, this may be conducive to profitability while suboptimal in terms of the growth of living standards and annual rates of national economic growth. Nevertheless, as table 2.1 shows, while the neoliberal expansion (1982–2007) did not reach the heights of the Great Boom, it compares most favorably with every other phase of capitalist history.

Table 2.1 – Country, Regional, and World Economic Rates of Growth (annual average compound rate), 1870–2001

	1870–1913	1913–1950	1950–1973	1973–2001
Western Europe	2.11	1.19	4.79	2.21
USA	3.94	2.84	3.93	2.94
Japan	2.44	2.21	9.29	2.71
China	0.56	-0.02	5.02	6.72
World	2.11	1.82	4.90	3.05

Source: Angus Maddison, *The World Economy: Historical Statistics* (Paris: OECD, 2003)

This data demonstrates that world economic growth during the neoliberal period has been comparatively robust when judged against the overall history of capitalist expansion since 1870—with the obvious and predictable exception of the Great Boom. Indeed, the economies of Japan, Western Europe, and China all grew more rapidly during the neoliberal period than they had over the eighty years from 1870 to 1950. And China grew at a faster pace over the past thirty years than at any time since 1870. Put differently, over the past quarter-century neoliberal capitalism has performed at or above the norm. Indeed, the world economy tripled in size during this period (1982–2007). Unless one uses the Great Boom as the only point of comparison, there is simply no historical basis for declaring the neoliberal period to be one of sluggish performance, never mind some sort of prolonged downturn or crisis of the system.

Some analysts have pointed to the existence of sharp recessions across the neoliberal period (in both 1991–92 and 2000) as proof that the system had not escaped from the crisis of the 1970s.[93] Again, the *desideratum* seems to me to be faulty. The business cycle—boom, overheating, recession, recovery—is built into the operation of the capitalist economy and functions even when the system is highly dynamic. A period of crisis, however, like the 1930s or 1971–81 (which, to be sure, were themselves quite distinct) is characterized by the persistence of recessionary pressures—especially large drops in investment, output and employment—and, what is the other side of the coin, profound systemic difficulties in making the transition to a sustained recovery of profits and growth. The Great Depression, for example, saw two deep recessions (1929–33 and 1937–39) with a short-lived recovery in between. During the crisis decade 1971–81, the U.S. economy was hit by recessions in 1971, 1974–75, and 1979–81. The inability of the economy to maintain growth for more than three or four years before slipping back into a deep recession is clear evidence of enduring problems blocking the shift to a durable recovery. After 1981, however, the U.S. economy returned to a decade-long expansion, which even the stock market crash of 1987 could not derail. That wave was interrupted by a significant downturn in 1991–92, which was then followed by an eight-year expansion (1992–2000). The growth cycle of 2000–2007, while slightly shorter, was still longer than during the two crisis periods mentioned above. Like many expansions of its sort, it was sustained in considerable measure by credit expansion—an indication that the neoliberal growth wave was becoming exhausted.

In short, during the neoliberal expansion, the periodicity of the business cycle returned to something approximating its "classic" form, with recessions every seven to ten years, rather than every three or four.[94] Recoveries were more lasting and robust than they had been during the crisis decade 1971–81. It is true that Japan entered a protracted slump in the 1990s, and this is an important reminder that not all parts of the world system move in tandem. But the Japanese slump did not trigger a global downturn. Indeed, as we shall see, it was interconnected with China's robust growth during this period, which was significantly stimulated by a great wave of investment by Japanese-based firms in other parts of East Asia.

* * *

With these preliminary reflections in mind, I now want to turn to the neoliberal era of the past twenty-five years or so. My analysis will develop from three main arguments or theses.

Thesis one: Following the recessions of 1974–75 and 1980–82 and the launch of an offensive by ruling classes in the North against unions and peoples of the Global South, severe capitalist restructuring generated a new wave of capitalist growth, albeit a much more uneven and volatile one than occurred during the Great Boom. By attacking working class organizations and undermining states in the Global South; by raising the rate of exploitation and spatially reorganizing manufacturing industries; by generating huge new reserves of global labor (via accelerated "primitive accumulation"); through massive foreign direct investment, particularly in East Asia; by introducing new systems of work organization and labor intensification (lean production), and new technologies (robotics, computerization)—by all these means exploitation of labor was intensified, South to North value flows (or flows of wealth) were accelerated, and the rate of profit was significantly boosted from its lows of the early 1980s. In the process, new centers of global accumulation were created. To be sure, all of this entailed "global turbulence"—volatile restructuring, periodic recessions, heightened global inequalities, and national and regional crises.[95] But it has also involved a period of sustained capitalist expansion.

Thesis two: The upward trend in profit rates from the early 1980s underpinned a wave of capitalist expansion that began to falter in 1997 with the crisis in East Asia. The Asian Crisis signaled the onset of new problems of over-accumulation that shape the contours of the present slump. After that regional crisis, and even more so after the bursting of the dotcom bubble in the U.S. in 2000–2001, a massive expansion of credit did underpin rates of growth, creating profound sources of instability in the financial sector. So, while the entire period after 1982 cannot be explained in terms of credit creation, the postponement of a general crisis *after* 1997 can.[96] A decade-long credit explosion delayed the day of reckoning. But as the credit bubble burst, beginning in the summer of 2007, it ignited a major financial crisis, one that was bound to be severe given enduring processes of financialization throughout the neoliberal period. And because of underlying problems of over-accumulation that had first manifested themselves in 1997, this financial crisis triggered a powerful global slowdown.

Thesis three: Alongside and interacting with these changes, a wholesale reorganization of capitalist finance occurred, stimulated by a metamorphosis in forms of world money. The end of the Great Boom was punctuated by a collapse of the gold-dollar standard, the emergence of floating exchange rates, heightened financial volatility and uncertainty, and a proliferation of new financial instruments designed to hedge risk in a context of unstable monetary relations. These risk-hedging instruments opened up enormous new fields for financial services and profits, while also creating an inordinately larger sphere for speculation. Meanwhile, as financial gains radically expanded as a share of total profits, new credit instruments were created for both financiers and consumers. These transformations massively increased the sphere of purely financial transactions and contributed to a financialization of capitalism in its neoliberal phase—and in so doing laid down major fault lines that were sure to crack in the event of systemic pressures. Although I touch on these issues in this chapter, I shall treat them in a sustained way in chapter 4.

★　★　★

Building on this account of the neoliberal expansion and the unique crisis tendencies it created, I propose to examine this era in terms of three interconnected processes. Various analysts have done good jobs of highlighting one another of these processes. But rarely have they been brought together in an integrated analysis that captures the (contradictory) dynamics of the neoliberal expansion. So, while I treat each of the following developments discretely, it is vital to keep in mind that they are interconnected aspects of a total process. There is, moreover, a temporality to their interconnection, as industrial restructuring in the North tended to precede the full-fledged emergence of a new center of accumulation in East Asia. In what follows, I address these trends under the following headings: 1) labor's defeats and the new inequality; 2) industrial restructuring and lean production; 3) "primitive accumulation," China, and the spatial reorganization of global capitalism. In subsequent chapters I shall round out this analysis by investigating four other key aspects of our historical moment: financialization; privatization, enclosure, and accumulation by dispossession; finance and the new imperialism; and, finally, destruction of "infrastructures of dissent" and the remaking of consumer culture. But for now, let us turn to the three processes I have identified.

The Neoliberal Era 1: Labor's Defeats and the New Inequality

If the defeat of the air traffic controllers' union, PATCO, was a decisive turning point in the United States, it had its ugly parallels elsewhere. From the late 1970s on, governments and employers around the world launched a coordinated offensive to roll back union power, labor rights, and employees' wages, benefits, and conditions of work. Workers resisted these attacks, sometimes heroically. But the ruling class was bloody-minded and union leaderships were generally too passive and compromising to prevail. And where employers could not defeat workers on their own, governments turned to legislation, the courts, the police, and prison terms to do the trick. Mandatory wage restraints and trampled union rights became the orders of the day. The U.S. government's firing of striking air traffic controllers was part of a widespread revival of tactics only rarely deployed during the Great Boom: mass firings, jailings, and large-scale use of police to break strikes. In Canada, the government imposed compulsory wage controls in 1976 and then two years later jailed the president of the postal workers when his union, for a decade the most militant in the country, struck in defiance.[97] Similar methods would be employed on a much larger scale, supplemented by massive use of scabs and police, when Margaret Thatcher defeated Britain's National Union of Mineworkers in 1985, or in Bolivia the following year when troops were used to crush the tin miners union, long the backbone of labor radicalism.

In other cases, governments did not intervene so directly, instead aiding and abetting employers as they put in the boot. In 1978, German workers struck against employer plans to downgrade jobs, introduce new labor-displacing technologies, and lay down management-friendly work rules. Bosses retaliated with a massive lockout of two hundred thousand engineering workers, ultimately breaking the back of the resistance and forcing unions to sign a highly regressive contract in 1979. A year later, it was the turn of Italian unions, as workers at Fiat, following a defeated thirty-three-day strike, bowed to company demands for twenty-three thousand layoffs. As one major union after another fell to the employers' offensive, labor movements beat a desperate retreat. Union density—the percentage of workers represented by trade unions—declined dramatically and persistently in the U.S., Canada, U.K., France, Spain, and elsewhere, often calamitously in Latin American countries such as Chile, Peru, Bolivia, and Ecuador.[98] Management introduced tiered wage structures, with new recruits often making markedly less than those hired earlier, while "flexible" employment arrangements—part-time and limited contracts in particular—deprived workers of full-time wages and benefits. All of these trends contributed to painful drops in working class incomes. In the U.S. real wages were 15 percent lower by 1993 than they had been in 1978. Things were much worse in large parts of the Global South.

Chile was arguably the first neoliberal experiment, as we have seen. So, it is not surprising to learn that the compression of working class incomes was especially acute there, with workers' share of national income plummeting from 47 percent in 1970 to a mere 19 percent by 1989. The same pattern applied across the region, with huge hits to workers' incomes in countries like Ecuador, Peru, Argentina and Mexico.[99] Indeed, Mexico, which has enjoyed the "benefits" of a free trade agreement with Canada and the United States, saw wages for the best paid workers collapse 18 percent while the minimum wage plummeted 34 percent. Today, after fifteen years of free trade, 80 percent of Mexicans live in poverty and 0.3 percent of the population controls 50 percent of national wealth.[100]

Not surprisingly, sharp falls in wages in one country after another quickly produced the same pattern, boosting profits and the incomes of the rich. Indeed, one persistent trend across the neoliberal period has been for the distribution of wealth to get ever more unequal. Data from the United States are especially instructive in this regard. Detailed studies, which may actually underestimate the polarization, show a drop of 9 percent between 1973 and 2002 in average real incomes for the bottom 90 percent of Americans. Over the same period, incomes for the top 1 percent rose by 101 percent, while those for the top 0.1 percent soared by 227 percent. More recent updates demonstrate that household inequality in the U.S. has continued to worsen. And a recent report from the Organization for Economic Cooperation and Development charts similar trends, though not always quite so stark, for most major capitalist societies.[101]

But income statistics alone understate the real dimensions of inequality. Those fully emerge only when we factor in ownership of corporate wealth—stocks, bonds, and other corporate financial instruments. Whereas in 1991, the wealthiest 1 percent of Americans owned 38.7 percent of corporate wealth, by 2003 their share had jumped to 57.5 percent.[102] Similar trends are evident at the global level. In a world in which more than two billion people struggle to survive on $2 per day or less, the planet's wealthiest people—represented by the 16.5 percent of global households with $100,000 or more to invest—watched their assets soar 64 percent, to $84.5 trillion since 2000. The vast bulk of that wealth resides in the portfolios of millionaire households. Although they comprise just 0.7 percent of the globe's total households, these millionaire households now hold over a third of the world's wealth.[103] And it is these households, particularly in the conditions of renewed over-accumulation of capital since the late 1990s, who have ramped up demand for interest-bearing financial assets—a point to which we return in chapter 4.

As the United Nations *Human Development Report* indicates, the neoliberal period has seen an incredible increase in social inequality, which doubled in intensity between 1960 and 1990, and continued to rise afterwards. Table 2.2 shows the pattern clearly.

Table 2.2 – Share of world income received by the richest 20 percent of the world's countries relative to the share of the poorest 20 percent of the world's countries

1820 – 3:1	1960 – 30:1
1870 – 7:1	1990 – 60:1
1913 – 11:1	1997 – 74:1

Source: United Nations Development Program, *Human Development Report 1999*, 38

What is worse, these are national averages so they actually underestimate the real degree of inequality. Were we, for example, to take the richest people in the Global North and compare their incomes with those of the poorest billions in the Global South, the differences would be truly astronomical.[104]

When Paul Volcker set out in 1979 to insure that the American standard of living would decline, he could not have dreamed how successful he and his neoliberal cronies would be. Thirty years later, therefore, we live in a staggeringly more unequal world. And a decade of austerity will only make it more so.

The Neoliberal Era 2: Lean Production and Industrial Restructuring

As union resistance was pulverized, employers had carte blanche to reorganize work processes, introduce new technologies, downsize workforces, and speed up production in the quest for higher profits. And this they did, notwithstanding some radical commentary that suggests very little restructuring of capital has occurred since the crises of 1971–82.[105] In fact, wherever we look we find evidence of major downsizings, scrapping of old plants and equipment, and dramatic reorganizations of work processes and technology. In the first stage of restructuring the pace was set by widespread destruction of capital, as plants were closed and workers sacked:

> Britain lost 25 percent of its manufacturing industry in 1980–84. Between 1973 and the late 1980s the total number of employed in manufacturing in the six old countries of Europe fell by seven millions, or by about a quarter, about half of which were lost between 1979 and 1983.[106]

Similar processes were at work in the U.S. Taking the case of the domestic steel industry, we find that more than 350,000 jobs were lost by the end of the 1980s as large mills were shut or downsized and new technologies and work processes introduced. Deploying state-of-the-art techniques, new mini-mills—such as Birmingham Steel, Nucor, and Oregon Steel—established cost-advantages, viable accumulation regimes, and enhanced market share, as a radical transformation of the industry occurred.

Throughout the Great Boom, world steel output rose continuously, from 112 million tons to 704 million tons, almost all of it in the capitalistically developed world. Then, beginning with the recession of 1974–75, a contraction set in at the capitalist core, whose steel industries quickly lost about 100 million tons of capacity in the course of the first wave of downsizing. Throughout the 1980s, plant closures and layoffs continued, and employment at traditional integrated steel mills in the U.S. plummeted from over 520,000 in 1974 to 168,000 fifteen years later. Meanwhile, steel production kept rising in newly industrializing countries such as

South Korea and Brazil. By the early 1990s, a global reorganization of the industry was well underway, a process that intensified during the 1990s. Between 1997 and 2002, for instance, twenty-nine steel companies went bankrupt in the U.S. at the same time as a wave of buyouts and mergers reduced the number of firms. By the year 2000, the combined steel output of Brazil, China, South Korea, India, Taiwan, and Mexico was almost three times as large as U.S. production. Moreover, the technical foundations of the industry had been transformed, as huge, integrated mills using basic oxygen furnaces were replaced by mini-mills deploying newer technologies, from continuous casting to electric arc furnaces. And where large mills remained, like the Hilton Works of the Steel Company of Canada (Stelco) in Hamilton, Ontario, new processes of continuous casting were introduced while the workforce was more than chopped in half, plunging from over thirteen thousand workers in 1980 to barely five thousand sixteen years later.[107] Most decisively, across the globe, geographic relocation, wage-cutting, down-sizing, and new technologies contributed to a halving of the cost of making flat-rolled steel.[108]

The steel industry illustrates the basic dynamics at work in the transition to lean production systems during the neoliberal era. It is not simply that jobs went to the South, though in some industries this clearly happened. It is more that a severe process of restructuring occurred that involved an enormous downsizing of workforces and "leaning" of production systems everywhere. Geographic reorganizations, sometimes within the bounds of a nation-state, as in the flight of plants from the northern to southern United States, were one part of this picture. While industry-specific changes may have been in play in the case of steel, we observe a common pattern combining new technologies with old-fashioned employer tactics of speed up, contracting out, and undermining of unions. Production was made more "flexible" largely by making labor so—by tiering wages, altering shifts, increasing insecurity and precarious employment (casual, part-time, and contract work), and enhancing employers' power to hire, fire, and reorganize work. New technologies thus combined with old forms of precariousness to boost labor productivity. As Kim Moody observes, "Real flexibility in lean production lies primarily in the combination of information-age technology and worker experience with archaic forms of work organization, such as contracting-out, casualization, old-fashioned speed-up, and the lengthening of working time."[109] It was the concentrated offensive against the organized power of the working class that made possible these processes of downsizing, work reorganization, and technological renovation. No longer constrained by union power, capital pushed down real wages, shed labor, broke shop floor organization of workers, introduced robotics, computerized production systems, and other new technologies, and sped up and intensified work processes.

The cumulative effects of these processes were profound. In the first instance, they involved a sustained and significant rise in the rate of exploitation—the gap between workers' output and the value of their wages. Detailed calculations by Simon Mohun on the U.S. economy indicate, for instance, that after 1979, "The value of labor power fell for the remainder of the century (as productivity grew but hourly real wage rates for production workers did not), so that the rate of surplus value (the ratio of money surplus value to the wages of productive labor) increased by about 40%."[110] It was not just that wages were pushed down, therefore; it was also that speed-up and work intensification compelled workers to produce more per hour. And in conditions of labor retreat, such productivity gains were claimed almost entirely by capital, a trend that began in the late 1970s and kept intensifying across the neoliberal period. In fact, U.S. Bureau of Labor Statistics data reveal that labor productivity rose by an average of nearly 2 percent per year from 1979 to 2007, while real hourly compensation for workers edged up just a bit more than 1 percent a year.[111] Over a period of nearly thirty years, this involved a huge allocation to capital of new wealth created by labor. In Marx's terms, it signified an enormous increase in the rate of exploitation (or rate of surplus value). And rarely was the increase in surplus value greater than in American manufacturing, where during the 1990s productivity rose twenty times faster than wages.[112]

These processes were crucial to the sustained revival of profit rates after 1982, which is captured in figure 2.1.

Figure 2.1 Pre-Tax Rate of Profit in the U.S., 1964–2001

Source: Simon Mohun, "Distributive Shares in the US Economy, 1964–2001," *Cambridge Journal of Economics* 30, no. 3 (2006): 348.

As figure 2.1 shows, the average rate of profit rose persistently from 1982 to 1997, reversing the trend line of the previous eighteen years (1964–82). It then began a downward movement in 1997, which seems to have been reversed for a time after 2001, though data here must be treated with care given the widespread phenomenon of fictitious profits based on financial manipulations and accounting fraud.[113] But there can be little doubt that the doubling of the U.S. profit rate between 1982 and 1997 that Henwood identified was very real. Concerted attacks on workers' power and intense industrial restructuring, hallmarks of neoliberalism, did boost corporate profitability after the recessions of 1974–75 and 1980–82—not to the levels of 1950–64, to be sure, but substantially enough to move the global economy out of crisis for a quarter-century. Equally important as the defeat of labor and industrial restructuring in this regard was the geographic reorganization of world capitalist production.

The Neoliberal Era 3: China, "Primitive Accumulation," and the Spatial Reorganization of Global Capitalism

As part of the intense reorganization of capital that emerged across the global recessions between 1974 and 1982, multinational corporations increasingly resorted to foreign direct investment (FDI) as they restructured throughout the North—which is still the site of most foreign investment—while also seeking out strategic low-wage sites of investment. To be sure, foreign direct investment into the South began from quite low levels and its importance in the early going could not be compared with that of industrial restructuring at home. But by the 1990s, it was coming to be of decisive importance, particularly in East Asia.

The acceleration of foreign investment took off as a response to the crises of the 1970s. During the four years of Jimmy Carter's presidency (1977–81), American banks and multinational corporations tripled their foreign investments, a trend that would only accelerate over time.[114] While Japanese- and German-based capitalists were slower to make the shift, when they did so in the mid-1980s, they quickly made up for lost time. In the four years 1985 to 1989 alone, foreign direct investment by Japanese firms tripled. From 1991 to 1995, foreign investment in manufacturing rose another 50 percent as Japanese corporations sought to reduce costs and boost profits by way of building regional production chains that could take advantage of cheaper labor in Taiwan, South Korea, China, and Malaysia in particular.[115] As a result, the share of manufacturing output produced abroad by Japanese multinationals soared, as did trade between Japan and its East Asian neighbors, who were increasingly linked through regional commodity chains. Indeed, by 2000, Japanese capital had 772 production facilities in China alone. This outsourcing to China was clearly linked to a domestic loss of more than two and a half million manufacturing jobs between 1992 and 2001, when Japanese manufacturing employment dropped from 15.7 million to 13 million.[116] By early 2001, as one reporter observed,

Toshiba Corporation stopped making television sets in Japan, turning to its factories in China to supply the home market.

> Soon after, Minolta Co. announced that it was phasing out
> camera production in Japan and would import from Shanghai
> instead ... several other Japanese manufacturers announced
> plans to import bicycles, motorcycles, buses and cell phones
> from their Chinese factories.[117]

While Japanese capital has aggressively pursued a regionally-based "globalization" strategy, both U.S.-based and German-based capitals have adopted similar policies, with their own regional specificities. American multinationals have channeled more investment into Mexico and Central and South America than have their rivals, but for the past decade China has taken center stage. German capital, meanwhile, has moved forcefully into lower-wage regions of Central and Eastern Europe, as well as East Asia. Indeed, foreign direct investment by German firms quadrupled from 1985 to 1990 and doubled again by 1995.[118]

The key incentive for multinational corporations from the core to relocate production facilities to parts of the Third World is found in the huge reserves of cheap labor in parts of the Global South, which make possible dramatic reductions in wage costs. Across the neoliberal period intense processes of primitive accumulation—enclosure and privatization of land in order to develop plantation farming, mining, eco-tourism, logging, giant dams, urban real estate projects, and so on—have driven hundreds of millions of people from the land, turning them into propertyless proletarians.[119] I explore many of these processes in chapter 5. But what matters critically here is that these hundreds of millions of displaced people comprise an enormous labor reserve, available for exploitation by global capital. In fact, the quarter-century 1980–2005, saw a quadrupling of the world's so-called "export-weighted" global labor force, an estimate of working class size based on exports to world markets. Most of this growth occurred after 1990 and about half of it took place in East Asia, where the working class increased nine-fold—from about 100 million to 900 million workers. South Asia too saw significant growth in both manufacturing and the number of industrial workers. In fact, of a global labor force of roughly three billion people, more than half today live in East and South Asia combined.[120]

As accumulation by dispossession intensifies on a world scale, and hundreds of millions leave the land, we are witnessing one of the great migrations in world history—one that registers a demographic shift in which, for the first time ever, a majority of humankind will live in cities and towns, rather than the country-side.[121] And nowhere is this transformation more massive than in China, the world's most populous country, which is "in the midst of the largest mass migration the world has ever seen."[122] Perhaps 150 million Chinese peasants have already left the coun-tryside for work in urban areas, and something approaching twice that number may join them by 2050. These migrant workers represent a huge precarious proletariat. Under China's *hukou* (household registration) system, rural migrants lack the legal right to reside full-time in the cities. Although they fill nearly three quarters of all manufacturing jobs, China's migrant work-ers are deprived of access to social services, their children do not have the right to attend public schools, and they are crammed into substandard housing.[123]

So mammoth is China's working class, today at 750 million, that it is one and a half times larger than the labor force of all the thirty rich countries of the OECD combined. The country's *sur-plus* labor force alone is three times larger than the entire man-ufacturing workforce of the OECD countries.[124] This is a key reason why, after thirty years of market-driven growth, wages in China's manufacturing industries are only around 5 percent of the U.S. level. The following table illustrates this point, while also highlighting why multinational corporations based in the Global North have been so eager to relocate investment in parts of the South.

It is this reality—gigantic reserves of cheap labor—that is one key to capitalist globalization in the neoliberal area. To be sure, cross-border investment from one country in the North to another still leads the process; about two-thirds of all for-eign direct investment stays within the capitalistically developed world.[125] This is a straightforward result of the development of regional production and distribution sites across the North by multinational firms. But it is also the case that in response to the

Table 2.4 – Manufacturing Workers' Wage Rates in Selected Countries

Country	Monthly wage as a percentage of U.S. wage
United States	100
Japan	91.4
South Korea	80.4
Argentina (2001)	28.9
Czech Republic	21.1
Chile	14.9
Turkey (2001)	14.8
Mexico (2004)	11.8
Peru	8.2
China (2004)	4.9
Philippines (2004)	3.4
Indonesia (2001)	1.9
India (2003)	0.8

Source: International Labour Organization, *Yearbook of Labour Statistics*, 2006

crisis of profitability of the 1970s, capital not only attacked unions and living standards in the North; it also devised elaborate strategies to profit from cheap labor in strategic sites in the South. A significant spatial reorganization of global capitalism ensued, with industries such as textiles, electronics, furniture-making, and steel becoming centered outside the core nations. As we have seen, in 1975 steel production in the developing world was utterly insignificant on a global scale. Yet, by 2000 the steel industry in China, South Korea, Brazil, India, Mexico, and Taiwan together produced three times more steel as did the U.S. industry—a stunning transformation accomplished in a generation.[126] Much of this had to do with state-driven or joint-venture industrial policies designed to build up steel-making capacities. And we need to remind ourselves that much of the Global South remained outside this process. Nonetheless, this geographic restructuring of world capitalism created new centers of world accumulation, a fact that is sorely missed if we concentrate simply on the countries of the old capitalist core. The pace and scale of this shift are captured in data on capital formation—the creation of new facto-

ries, mines, mills, and office complexes, along with new machinery and equipment. In the space of merely six years, 1990–96, for
instance, total capital formation in East Asia (excluding Japan)
jumped by nearly 300 percent. Over the same period, capital formation increased by 40 percent in the U.S. and Japan and a mere
10 percent in Europe.[127] A structural shift of immense importance
was reshaping the world economy. And China has been its pivot.

China's growing centrality to the global economy has to do
with its role as a crucial hinge in global supply chains, in which a
given commodity is produced through synchronized labor processes in multiple countries. The production of a personal computer, for instance, involves more than 1,000 discrete acts of labor,
typically conducted in ten to twenty countries. A "Japanese" computer, to take one example, is frequently the product of work
performed in the U.S., Singapore, Japan, Malaysia, South Korea,
and China, among other national sites. But generally about a
quarter of the labor is performed in China by low-wage migrant
workers.[128] And it is this—China's vast reserves of cheap labor
inserted into a draconian system of repression and control—that
has made it the world's manufacturing hub.

China's turning point came in 1978, when its leaders dramatically embraced the market as the key mechanism for organizing economic life. Land was privatized, state enterprises sold
off, social services like healthcare virtually eliminated, managers
given greater powers to fire and discipline workers, and workers' right to strike abolished. Special Economic Zones were created, where foreign multinationals would be welcomed—and
these areas were massively expanded over time. By the early
1980s a steady flow of foreign investment began to transform
the economy. That flow increased persistently throughout the
1990s, especially as the Chinese government became more recep-
tive to wholly foreign-owned firms. Then, after the Asian Crisis of
1997, to be discussed below, it turned into a torrent. By 2002 China
was the world's largest recipient of foreign direct investment,
which had increased fifty times over in just seventeen years, from
$1 billion to $50 billion per year between 1985 and 2002. In one
sector of the Chinese economy after another, the world's larg-

est corporations have now set up shop: IBM, Motorola, General Motors, Intel, Samsung, Philips, Hewlett Packard, Volkswagen, Toyota, Siemens, AT&T, Panasonic, Nokia, Daimler-Chrysler, General Electric, JVC, and hundreds of others. By 2000, in fact, almost four hundred of the world's five hundred largest corporations were producing electronics, cars, pharmaceuticals, telecommunications equipment, petrochemicals and much, much more in China.[129]

As China pulled in growing shares of global capitalist investment, its real GDP increased by a factor of twelve between 1978 and 2005, and annual rates of capital formation—the share of gross domestic product going to business investment—hit 45 percent, a historically unprecedented level that surpassed even those of Japan, Taiwan, and South Korea during their boom years.[130] All of this has established China as *the* major new center of world accumulation, one that is redrawing the very geography of global capitalism. To be sure, China's growth trajectory is also throwing up significant contradictions and instabilities, as we shall see. Nevertheless, the country's economy has been moving up the value-chain and becoming increasingly sophisticated. So, while it is true that the Chinese economy is home to much of the world's low cost manufacturing, dominating industries such as footwear, clothing, sporting goods, and toys, it is equally true that China has in recent years joined the ranks of the world's largest exporters of electronics and information technology hardware.[131] Furthermore, a growing number of multinational corporations are building major research and development facilities in the country.[132]

The decline in the share of world manufacturing done in the Global North since 1990 (from 85 to 73 percent) is almost entirely the result of China's rising share—which has jumped from two to 18 percent.[133] Linked by production chains to the international operations of hundreds of multinational corporations, China has been undergoing an industrial revolution and its landscape is being frenetically transformed as more than one hundred thousand miles of roads, thousands of miles of rail lines, huge airports, hundreds of skyscrapers, and unfathomable amounts of new housing and office space are thrown up. Table 2.5 gives some sense of China's significance as a center of world manufacturing: by 2002 the country had more than twice the number of manufacturing workers than the world's largest industrial nations, the G-7 (the United States, Germany, Japan, Britain, France, Italy, and Canada) combined.

Table 2.5 –Number of Manufacturing Workers in China and the G-7 Countries (2002)

China	G-7 Countries
109 million	53 million

Sources: Judith Banister, "Manufacturing Employment in China," *Monthly Labor Review*, July 25, 2005; and Bureau of Labor Statistics, *Comparative Civilian Labor Force Statistics: Ten Countries, 1960–2004* (Washington, D.C., 2005)

Here we get a powerful indicator of the significant weight of manufacturing in East Asia (outside Japan), and in China in particular.[134] These figures are especially striking when we remember that state-owned enterprises in China shed around 35 million workers during this period.[135] The fact that by 2002 there were twice as many manufacturing workers in China as in the G-7, where the number has been in steady decline for decades, is indicative of major structural shifts that have taken place in the global economy throughout the neoliberal period. Without grasping the central importance of these transformations, we fail to understand not only key dynamics of the system in recent decades, but also crucial features of the new period of persisting crises. But before turning to that issue, let us also register just how much China's boom has conformed to the neoliberal pattern. After all, China's growth is not without its brutal contradictions and instabilities, which strongly conform to the neoliberal model. I will explore issues related to accumulation by dispossession in China in chapter 5. For the moment, let us consider the enormous increase in social inequality.

As the *Economist* magazine has observed, while the share of national incomes going to wage and salary earners has been falling worldwide, "nowhere has the drop been as huge as in China."[136] Between 1990 and 2005, labor income, the total earnings of Chinese working people, plunged from 50 percent of gross domestic product to a mere 37 percent. This represents a dizzying shift in of the distribution of wealth between workers on the one hand and corporations, bankers, and the rich, on the other. As everywhere throughout the neoliberal period, increased social inequality in China has produced a new geography of apartheid as the wealthy segregate themselves from the masses by means of gated communities and luxury consumption zones revolving around expensive nightclubs, high-end restaurants, designer shopping malls, theme parks, and elite private schools. China's 250,000 millionaire households, making up only 0.4 percent of the population, now control 70 percent of the country's wealth. Meanwhile, 100 million people live on a dollar a day or less; only 4 percent of the population has access to public healthcare—which has contributed to both an HIV pandemic and the 2003 SARS crisis; and tens of millions of migrant workers from the countryside lack basic rights to housing and social services. According to the Asia Development Bank, China is now the second most unequal country in the region.[137] These growing social contradictions have produced a pattern of intense social protest—strikes, riots, land struggles, and more. So far, however, these movements have remained largely episodic and localized, though how long that will be so is clearly something that deeply worries China's rulers, especially in light of the much more coordinated wave of strikes that swept manufacturing plants in May and June of 2010.[138] Also worrying them are the tendencies toward over-accumulation and declining profitability that have become central features of China's market-driven development. These tendencies are not unique to China; instead, they shape the very trajectory of global capitalism today.

East Asia and Global Over-Accumulation: Growing Contradictions of Neoliberalism

"'The China Price.' They are the three scariest words in U.S. industry." So wrote *Business Week* in a 2004 Special Report.[139] Worldwide, prices for manufactured goods have been falling persistently since the mid-1990s, directly related to the dynamics of the Chinese economy, particularly its low wages and pell-mell accumulation. In fact, the so-called consumption deflator, which measures price changes for consumer goods, shows that price changes for U.S. consumer durables—electronics, appliances, cars, and more—began to decline in the autumn of 1995. Similar indices used by the United Nations and the European Union show absolute declines in prices for manufactured goods generally since 1996.[140] In other words, by the mid-1990s, manufacturing firms around the globe were facing a downward trend in prices for the goods they produce, something that tends to depress profitability in late capitalism. Indeed, if we look back at Figure 2.1 we see that the rate of profit in the U.S. turned down in synchrony with prices.[141] While commentators are typically quick to identify low Chinese wages as the driver of this process, this is only part of the story. For it is also the case that as Chinese wages exerted downward pressure on prices, so did emerging problems of over-accumulation in a whole range of industries. To take just one example, it has been observed that the entry of new semi-conductor firms from Taiwan into the world market contributed to significant over-capacity that forced companies to cut prices in efforts to stay afloat. Overcapacity in dynamic random access memory (DRAM) hit 18 percent by 1997, the year of the Asian Crisis, dramatically driving down prices.[142] In conditions of global overcapacity, after all, some firms will not have enough sales to justify the factories that have been built, the equipment that has been purchased, the parts that have been bought and the wages already paid—and this drives all competitors to cut prices in a scramble to hold on to sales and revenues. Such pressures of over-accumulation were a key cause of the 1997 Asian Crisis, when Thailand, Malaysia, South Korea, the Philippines, Indonesia, and other economies in the region suffered a massive contraction.

Most commentators treated the Asian Crisis of 1997 as simply a matter of global flows of finance (which exited the region en masse at the time). To be sure, such flows were a major contributor to the regional meltdown, as we shall see. But these financial outflows reflected severe pressures of over-accumulation of capital, as I argued at the time.[143] The investment boom in East Asia—with business spending rising to 40 percent of GDP—had created enormous excess capacity in computer chips, autos, semiconductors, chemicals, steel, petrochemicals, and fiber optics. "A persistent trend to overcapacity," observed the World Bank at the time, had induced "price wars and intense competition."[144] While extremely high domestic rates of accumulation drove these buildups in capacity, enormous flows of *foreign* investment greatly exacerbated the trend. As a case in point, investment by Japanese firms in Thailand, where the crisis first broke, shot up more than sixteen times in the course of five years (1986–91).[145] In addition to factories, there was frantic building of airports, highways, shopping malls, and hotels. By the early 1990s an overheating economic expansion was being fuelled by waves of speculative investment that drove real estate and stock prices sky-high. So long as quick profits were being made, the hot money kept on coming. But, as prices for manufactured goods started to fall in 1995–96, it became increasingly obvious that the boom was unsustainable—too much productive capacity had been built relative to market demand, sales, and profits. As the first investors headed for the exits, a stampede followed. Whereas foreign investors had pumped up to $95 billion into the economies of Thailand, Malaysia, South Korea, the Philippines, and Indonesia during the 1990s, the tide promptly reversed in 1997, producing a net *outflow* of $20 billion. As foreign money fled, currencies plummeted, trade crashed and the region underwent a traumatic convulsion. At the most devastating point in the meltdown, ten thousand South Korean workers were losing their jobs every day.

The 1997 Asian Crisis was the first great crisis of the globalization period. It indicated the winding down of the neoliberal boom that had started in 1982 under pressures of over-accumulation and declining profitability. Little surprise, then, that the crisis took place in the world's new center of accumulation, East Asia. It then sent out aftershocks—collapses in Russia and at the Long Term Capital Management hedge fund in the U.S. in 1998, in Brazil in 1999, throughout the U.S. dotcom sector in 2000, and in Argentina in 2000–2001—that were offset, as we shall see in chapter 4, by powerful stimulative actions by world central banks and a frenetic shift to investment in China. But notice had been served. The neoliberal expansion was on its last legs—and the actions of central banks would only postpone the unwinding, at the cost of inflating asset bubbles whose bursting would shake the world financial system.

Rather than just the latest installment in a forty-year crisis, then, what happened after 2007 represents the closing of one period and the opening of another. It is a ruptural development, a qualitative break from the previous quarter-century. People dedicated to radical change need to understand this transformation in all its novelty. That also requires grasping the new world of global finance that has defined the neoliberal order. But before turning to that issue, it will be helpful to review the fundamental contradictions that repeatedly generate capitalist crises.

CHAPTER THREE

Manic Depression: Capitalism and its Recurring Crises

*"Even if the crises that are looming up are overcome
and a new run of prosperity lies ahead, deeper
problems will still remain. Modern capitalism has
no purpose except to keep the show going."*
—Joan Robinson[146]

RATHER THAN A ONCE-IN-ONE-HUNDRED-YEARS EVENT, AS ALAN Greenspan claims, a great crisis like that of 2008–9 happens with striking regularity. "Great depressions recur," Charles Kindelberger reminds us in his major study of the Great Depression of the 1930s.[147] To be sure, each crash is unique. But this does not make them random events. On the contrary, as a host of major political economists have long recognized, growth in a capitalist economy invariably generates great breakdowns in the system.[148] As a result, capitalism goes through booms and slumps just as people inhale and exhale. Cycles of expansion and contraction are thus hardwired into capitalism; they are an organic reflex of the system. At the same time, some crises are much deeper and more prolonged than others—we can think of the depression of 1873–96 in these terms, as well as the great slump of the 1930s. But although every cancer is different, the disease has certain common features. And the same is true of the recurring contractions of the capitalist economy.

Of course, the mother of all crises was the Great Depression. When the current slump broke out, many commentators made direct comparisons with that era. Knowingly or not, they were raising the question posed by Hyman Minsky in his book, *Can "It" Happen Again?*[149] By "it," Minsky meant a devastating and enduring breakdown of the capitalist economy like that of the 1930s. But there can be no serious answer to that question unless we have a reasonable sense of what actually happened during the Great Depression of 1929–39, and of its fundamental causes.

When 1929 came around, deep recessions were nothing new to world capitalism. But the scale and ferocity of this violent global spasm was without precedent. In the United States, gross national product declined by one third in the first four years of the downturn, while industrial production was halved. Unemployment rolls ballooned as the number of people out of work swelled from 1.5 million to 12.8 million. Business investment almost disappeared, plunging by 88 percent. Banks collapsed, as did real estate and stock markets. Half of all farmers fell behind on their mortgage payments, with hundreds of thousands being foreclosed on in a single year. And the U.S. was not alone. In the world's second largest industrial economy, Germany, industrial production dropped by half in the first three years of the slump. At the depth of the Depression (1932–33), fully 44 percent of German workers were unemployed. Meanwhile, half of all U.S. banks collapsed while major financial institutions in Europe imploded. In a six-month period in 1931 alone, eighteen national banking systems went on life support. World trade underwent a dizzying freefall, contracting by 60 percent. And for economies reliant on sales of agricultural commodities—from Argentina to India to Paraguay—the results were catastrophic. As world trade collapsed, prices for wheat and tea dropped by two-thirds, while the cost of raw silk plummeted to one-quarter of its previous value. Dramatic declines in prices for everything from coffee to rice devastated many poor countries of the Global South.[150]

The Depression of the 1930s was thus a truly global slump. Any economy intertwined with world markets was powerfully affected. Yet, contrary to many popular images, it is not the case that all economic activity ground to a halt. There were in fact bursts of considerable economic growth throughout the 1930s. In fact, the U.S. economy actually expanded by 5 percent or more in twenty quarters over the decade. Each time, the cheerleaders declared that the slump was over and recovery at last underway. And time after time they had to eat their words. For, interspersed with these quarters of growth, were thirteen quarters of contraction that undid the preceding months of growth.[151] So, while short "recoveries" were possible, a wave of ongoing and sustained growth was not. After touching bottom in 1932–33, the general economic trend was upward for four years. Then came a crushing new recession in 1937, and the world economy again spiraled downward, relinquishing much of the ground it had just retaken. It speaks volumes about this system that only the arrival of war and rearmament in 1939 restored capitalist prosperity.

Over-Investment, Speculation, and Slumps:
Lessons from the 1920s

One defining feature of every capitalist boom is the absurd outbreak of triumphalism that accompanies it. We live in a "new economy," pundits proclaim, a perpetual motion machine of ever-expanding economic activity. Recessions are a thing of the past, the chorus chants, an ancient demon now vanquished. Just as such voices were heard repeatedly prior to the meltdown of 2008, so they bleated out their convictions on the eve of the Great Crash of 1929. Capitalism had "mitigated" its "childhood diseases," opined economist Alvin Hansen at the time. Not to be outdone, the month of the Great Crash, October 1929, economics luminary Irving Fisher declared, "I expect to see the stock market a good deal higher than it is today within a few months."[152] Fisher was ever so slightly off the mark: it would take twenty-five years before stock prices would again see those heights.

Ludicrous forecasts are part of the manic mentality that grips investors in the late phases of a boom. And from 1925 to 1929, the U.S. and international economies were certainly booming. In that four-year period, world mining and manufacturing output grew by almost 20 percent. U.S. electricity generation more than doubled during the decade, and a wave of expansion swept sectors like automobile manufacturing. Profits soared as union-busting and anti-labor laws constrained workers, while immigration and movement from farms to cities and towns created a labor surplus for business. With profits rising, businesses feverishly built factories and invested in new technologies, all in the expectation of yet greater profits to come. New factories meant more products—

more cars, washing machines, refrigerators, and radios. Following Henry Ford's introduction of the assembly line at his company's Detroit area plants in 1914, auto plants roared and the number of motor vehicles registered in the U.S. tripled in a decade. A booming auto industry boosted one sector after another. By 1929, more than half of all strip steel produced in the U.S. was going into cars, as were 20 percent of all tin and nickel, and three-quarters of all plate glass and rubber. "An industry that had barely existed fifteen years earlier . . . now dominated the economy."[153]

But where was the demand for all these cars, appliances and new homes coming from? After all, more than 90 percent of Americans saw their incomes *fall* during the boom of the 1920s, just as they would in the expansion of the 1990s.[154] In an era of union-busting and anti-labor laws, income distribution became more unequal than ever before. But early twentieth-century capitalism had a solution: debt. Or, perhaps we should say, it had a short-term fix. With incomes falling, many purchases of cars, homes, washing machines, and the like were undertaken with consumer credit, which doubled during these years. Expanding credit in turn fuelled a massive real estate and housing boom whose epicenter was Florida. With millions of homes going up and millions of cars hitting the roads, a wave of euphoria washed across society. Everything is possible, pundits declared, helping to inspire speculative activity in every sphere imaginable. Grandiose investment projects were the order of the day—witness Chicago's Art Deco–style Board of Trade Building and Civic Opera House, or New York's Rockefeller Center and Empire State Building. All designed in the late 1920s, these buildings came to completion after the crash, often languishing for lack of demand. Indeed, the world's tallest building of the time quickly acquired the moniker, Empty State Building.[155]

But it was in the stock market that the mania went truly, utterly wild. Between May 1924 and the end of 1925, stock prices rose by 80 percent. After pausing in 1926, the upward march resumed the next year. Then, "early in 1928, the nature of the boom changed. The mass escape into make-believe, so much a part of the true speculative orgy, started in earnest."[156] The stock market rose more than 30 percent that year. There was nothing in the economic "fundamentals"—profits, average incomes, employment—that could possibly justify such a leap, but this did not matter. There were fortunes to be made and not a moment to lose. In the summer months of 1929, stock prices rose by a full 25 percent, in a matter of three months almost equaling their inflated gains of the previous year. To maximize their winnings at this casino, more and more investors financed stock purchases with borrowed money. Such loans now catapulted upward at a pace of $400 million a month with nary a thought for how they would be repaid if stock prices fell—for this was truly unthinkable. Then, of course, the unthinkable happened: the great bubble began to deflate, following a decline in factory output that had begun some months earlier. On October 23, a market drop surrendered all the gains that had been made over the previous four months. The next day, panic selling began, only to be halted by a meeting of the nation's largest bankers who claimed to have everything in hand. But the reassurance was short lived. The fall resumed in earnest the next week, and on Tuesday, October 29 the bottom dropped out, as the market gave up all the gains of the previous year. Now the New York bankers themselves lost their shirts, and a full-fledged rout was on. The rest, as they say, is history.

Because the stock market crash provides such a dramatic tale, touching ancient themes of hubris and its comeuppance, it has held center stage in accounts of the Great Depression. But thoughtful economic historians have regularly reminded us that the slump began elsewhere—in the collapse of the investment boom of 1925–29. For, what drove the economy on the way up was the same engine whose failure sent it crashing down: business investment. As one economic historian rightly notes, "Excess investment was the key ingredient in the rotten apple that brought the 1920s boom to an end."[157] Put simply, corporations had massively invested in electrical goods plants, auto factories, steel mills, railroad lines; in fact, they had over-invested. They had created way more productive capacity than they could profitably use. Between 1925 and 1929, for instance, the number of manufacturing establishments in the U.S. grew by twenty-three thousand. More than this, the size of plants had grown enormously, as had the productivity of the workers they employed. Ford's River Rouge plant, completed in 1928, on the eve of the crash, was the largest in the world. But more important than size was labor productivity: it took ninety minutes to make a Ford Model T chassis, down from twelve hours just a few years earlier. By 1929, the average American autoworker produced ten times as many cars as he had twenty years earlier.[158] For a time, raging over-investment and soaring output were masked by the hiring generated by building and construction projects and then, increasingly, by the doubling of credit that enabled consumers to purchase the cars, washing machines and houses that were pouring onto the market. Yet, this simply meant that over-investment was joined to an unsustainable debt buildup—an utterly toxic combination, as we learned again in 2008. But in the heat of excitement, the false prosperity underpinned an insane stock market bubble. When that bubble finally burst, as it had to, it appeared as if it were the cause of all the distress, when, in fact, it was a mere effect of a classic cycle of over-investment.

The over-investment boom of the 1920s had actually started to depress profits by 1927–28.[159] Companies had built too many factories, laid down too many railway lines, produced too many cars, built too many homes, created too much electrical generating capacity—at least from the standpoint of profitability, which, as we shall see, is all that matters under capitalism. As earnings fell, firms cut back investment and the dividends they paid to shareholders. With profits declining, investment turning down, and layoffs beginning, rising stock prices were nonsensical. After all, a stock is ultimately a claim to a share of corporate profits (in the form of dividends). If the latter are falling, it is absurd to pay more to get a share of them. That is why the stock market crash was inevitable. And just as stock prices cannot forever keep rising when the profits they earn are falling, neither can investment. When profits turn down, so must the entire capitalist economy, even if there is something of a time lag. This is a basic law of capitalism, one that repeats itself in every major crisis of the system. Let us see why.

Economic Instability in a Profit System

That capitalist economies are prone to destabilizing swings from boom to slump is something that a number of political economists have understood. Some, particularly Karl Marx and John Maynard Keynes, have also grasped the degree to which the rhythms of the capitalist economy are set by patterns of business investment. Whereas mainstream economics tries to portray individual consumption as the pivot of the capitalist economy, the evidence clearly shows that "investment spending is the variable that explains . . . the business cycle."[160] Keynes, however, offered a largely psychological explanation of cyclical changes in investment, based on shifts in expectations that induce a propensity to save (a "liquidity preference") that undercuts economic growth.[161] Irrational worry about the future, he suggests, makes capitalists start to hoard their wealth, rather than invest it. The great originality of Marx's theory rests on his insistence that an economy driven by production for profit is systemically irrational. In their scramble for profits, he contends, capitalists are compelled to over-invest (or over-accumulate); yet in doing so they undermine profitability within the economy as a whole. It is not a psychological flaw that drives capitalism into crisis, therefore, but the very dynamics of an economy based on production for the market in order to maximize profit.

Marx saw that the capitalist economy is the first in human history that revolves around producing goods for sale on the market. Of course, many societies throughout history have used markets for the exchange of some goods, particularly luxuries. But only in capitalist society do people acquire the overwhelming bulk of all the goods they consume—their morning tea or coffee, their housing, their clothing, entertainment, transportation, the food that sustains their households—by purchasing them from a market seller.

Prior to the rise of capitalism, most people worked the land and, thanks to access to lands that belonged to the whole community, produced almost everything they consumed. They wandered common lands and fields to collect wood, straw, mud, and rocks to build and heat their dwellings. They grew crops and raised livestock on their own plots and on communal fields. They made their own clothes, furniture, soap, and candles. They gathered firewood, berries, and herbs from the forests. They fished and drew water from the lakes, ponds, rivers, and streams, which all members of the community could freely use. In all these ways, they had direct access to the means of life. This is not to say that life was easy. Nor is it to say they were free from exploitation—in fact, they generally had to pay rent and taxes to landlords, priests, chiefs, and/or the state. Nevertheless, outside periods of drought or warfare, most people could count on having food and shelter thanks to their possession of land (either as tenants or small owners) and to the vast amounts of land—including forests, fields, rivers, and lakes—that were held in common, as the collective property of the community.

Capitalism ended all that by dispossessing peasants and privatizing common lands. As landlords and rich farmers sought to build large profitable estates, peasants were driven from their plots and forced to seek work for a wage. Land was concentrated into great farms worked by landless laborers hired to produce a "cash crop" for sale on the market. And the vast common lands, embracing millions of acres in England, were enclosed and turned into private property of wealthy landlords. Landless and unable to produce for themselves, people had no option but to enter market exchange—transactions between buyers and sellers—in order to make ends meet.[162] Of course, groups could occasionally survive by squatting on land and/or stealing from the rich—the stuff of enduring legends, like that of Robin Hood—or through seizing ships and living in pirate communities that lived by looting.[163] But heroic and inspiring as such communities of squatters and pirates were, these options were usually not available to the vast majority, who had to seek a buyer for their labor in order to earn wages with which to purchase the necessities of life.[164] In many parts of the world, perhaps most dramatically in China at the moment, we can see similar processes at work, as millions of peasants are dispossessed of land and turned into propertyless laborers who migrate to urban areas in search of work.

With the rise of capitalism, people thus become market-dependent.[165] Lacking economic self-sufficiency, the ability to produce the goods of life for themselves, their very survival came to depend on the market—on whether they could sell their labor for a wage. Worse, millions of people during the rise of capitalism—Irish boys, English convicts, poor youth from India and China, Scottish Highlanders, indigenous peoples of the Americas, and, more massively and more brutally than any others, kidnapped Africans—actually became market objects themselves, bought and sold as commodities called servants or slaves. In tandem, millions of indigenous peoples were driven from their lands and slaughtered, or worked to death mining gold and silver for their colonial masters.[166] By one means or another, the capitalist market economy was brutally imposed on millions.

In such a system, all basic economic activities become market-regulated; the market determines who prospers and who starves. For millions this can mean being purchased as a commodity—and we need to remind ourselves that far from disappearing, forms of bondage and enslavement have grown during the neoliberal period.[167] And for the rest, the majority of the poor, market pressure means coercion and insecurity: should you fail to find a buyer for your labor, you run the risk of being unable to buy the goods of life. No longer is human survival based on working land possessed by your household, clan, or tribe; it now revolves around buying and selling. The market thus becomes an ever-present part of our daily lives, the central regulator of our well-being. Capitalism allows us no other way of living but to purchase the goods of life on the market. And you can purchase these only if you can sell something that provides the cash with which to buy goods. For the vast majority lacking independent wealth, this means selling your ability to work, your labor.

But what drives such a market economy? What is the point of producing goods for exchange on the market rather than for your own use? Why should business owners make investments that bring huge amounts of grain, cell phones, cars, steel, and DVDs to the market?

Mainstream economics can provide no answer here because it pretends that consumer demand determines what is produced in a capitalist economy. It thus imagines that capitalism is governed by production for human use. Yet, the mere fact that millions of houses sit empty while millions of people are homeless shows that usefulness is not the issue. However much homeless people might have use for these houses, the market dictates that you get what you pay for, not what you need. Let us turn away, then, from the mystifying pronouncements of mainstream economists. Instead, let us attend to a blunt statement by a former CEO of U.S. Steel Corporation. Explaining why his company was closing mills and laying off thousands, he remarked, "U.S. Steel is in business to make profits, not to make steel."[168] Rarely is the reality put with greater clarity: under capitalism, use is irrelevant; profit is king. Capitalist enterprises have no particular attachment to what they turn out, be it flat-rolled steel, loaves of bread, or pairs of blue jeans. They produce these things if, and only if, they think they can make a profit in doing so. When they invest in a bakery, the real goal is not to produce bread; when they buy a garment factory, the objective is not to turn out jeans; and when they build a steel mill the purpose is not to turn out steel. For capitalists, bread, jeans, steel, and everything else are merely means to an end: profit. This is what it means to say that capitalism is a system of production for exchange, rather than for use (i.e. for direct consumption). Capitalists are ultimately indifferent to the use values of the things they bring to market; they have no inherent interest in the durability of steel, the warmth and texture of coats, or the taste and nutrition of bread. Rather than these concrete, useful qualities of things, what matters to capital is a purely abstract property of the commodity, its capacity to turn into money. Put in the terminology Marx developed, it is the value, rather than the use value of goods, that ultimately matters for capital.[169]

By "value," Marx refers to a commodity's property of abstract exchangeability with money and all other goods. For in the capitalist economy, goods that share no common physical or chemical properties—from tables and blue jeans to Big Macs and haircuts; from computers and airplanes to coffee and vacation cruises—are nonetheless capable of exchanging with each other or with money. But this can only mean that the market is measuring them according to some abstract metric, some standard of measure separate from their concrete characteristics. The market thereby reduces them to some number, treating them all as units of the same thing. The capitalist economy thus involves the victory of quantity over quality; all qualitatively different things must be reduced to quantitative units of the same thing (measured in money). Somehow, the market must be capable of reducing Big Macs and blue jeans to the same standard of measure and then quantifying them, one being valued at, say, $3 and another at $45. In this case, the market would be informing us that fifteen Big Macs equals one pair of a particular brand of blue jeans. But how is such an equation even possible? How can radically different things, which satisfy entirely different needs, be interchangeable? How can they all be converted into numbers on the same scale? Clearly, this cannot have anything to do with physical properties—what do a hamburger and a pair of blue jeans, or a computer and a haircut share? It must have to do with the fact that all of these things are products of human labor. Of course, each act of labor—from preparing and cooking a hamburger, to cutting, sewing and stitching denim into jeans, or washing and cutting someone's hair—is quite distinct. But they are all expenditures of the general human capacity to exert muscles, energies and brain cells to create or produce something. Even if all commodities come into being through different acts of concrete labor, they nonetheless all share the property of being products of the generic act of human labor, or what Marx calls abstract labor, i.e. labor as a general power abstracted from all its specific forms. And just as the capitalist market system evaluates all commodities in abstraction from their concrete form—in order to determine their abstract exchangeability with each other and with money—so the market also reduces all acts of labor to the same metric, treating each work process, from baking to welding to haircutting, as interchangeable, as just different ways of producing money, the abstract representative of market value. Once again, everything—including acts of labor—is quantified, reduced to a set of numbers.

Capitalism is thus governed by the value abstraction, by the drive not for specific things, but for the one abstract thing—money—that is exchangeable with all. Bread, steel, water, houses, blue jeans, books, computers, and cars count for capitalist firms only as potential sums of money. The specific human needs they satisfy are ultimately irrelevant to the drive to accumulate wealth. What matters is that the numbers—the amounts of sales and profits—should grow. This is why firms will invest in producing bombs or bread, cigarettes or vitamins—it doesn't matter which— as long as it looks likely to generate abstract wealth, measured in money. The same, as we shall see, is true of financial "assets," like mortgage-backed securities, no matter how loaded they may be with toxic junk. All that matters is that these goods represent potential sums of expandable wealth. Whether their purchase is good for humankind is irrelevant. In the words of one Canadian investment manager, "A business doesn't have any feelings. Its DNA is to make money."[170] That is why corporations will pollute the environment, destroy the ozone layer, and sell cancer-causing products. In an economic system based on profit, these consequences are irrelevant so long as the firm is making money.[171] From a capitalist point of view, all goods are entirely interchangeable—they are merely repositories of abstract wealth. The question of food illustrates this particularly clearly.

In recent years, traders in raw commodities claim to have rendered a variety of commodities interchangeable. They insist they have mastered the art of shifting them from one function to another, all in an effort to maximize exchange value, earnings, and profits. The same raw goods can, they say, be readily converted into food, fuel, plastics, and more, depending upon their profitability. Corn, for instance, can be eaten or used for biofuel. Of course, the more it becomes biofuel, the less food there is on the market, the higher food prices go, and the more people starve. But this is irrelevant to the capitalist business system. As one commodity trader explains,

> . . . we don't care what commodity you buy. We call it bushels-to-barrels-to-BTUs convergence. Take corn: it can now create heating and transportation . . . And you can use petroleum to create plastics or to create fertilizer to grow food—suddenly we are indifferent to what commodity we are buying to meet our demands.[172]

But while capitalist firms are indifferent to the concrete good being produced and to its uses, the vast majority of people are not. It matters enormously whether the corn being grown will be used for food, rather than as fuel that propels trucks or heats factories. In 2007, for instance, less than half the grain produced in the world was eaten by people. The global grain harvest that year was 2.1 billion tons, but just one billion of that went to human consumption. The rest went to producing biofuels or animal feed.[173] So, while a billion people teetered on the brink of starvation, most of the world's grain was diverted away from them—because that was the more profitable thing to do.

And this allows us to understand the perverse logic of an economy based upon production for profit. As a rule, when capitalists enter the market, their purpose is entirely foreign to the motivations of most people. For most of us, money is a means to get commodities that sustain life. We sell a commodity (usually our labor), get money in return, and use that money to buy commodities to consume. Put as a simple formula, we are regularly engaged in the cycle C-M-C, where C represents commodities and M stands for money.[174] The whole point of engaging in the market, therefore, is to procure the commodities that make life possible. But things are very different for a capitalist enterprise. For a business, the operative formula is M-C-M'. The capitalist begins with money (M) then buys commodities (C), such as machines, raw materials, and labor-power, with which to produce new commodities (like bread or jeans) that are sold for money (M'). Money, not commodities for consumption, becomes the end goal of production. But that only makes sense for a capitalist if the second sum of money is bigger than the first, which is why it is designated as M'. Otherwise the capitalist would be simply going through the whole cycle of investment only to come out with the same sum of money with which he began. Clearly something else is going on: the drive for profit, the drive to accumulate greater wealth.

But this drive for profit is not a mere personal idiosyncrasy of an individual investor. Capitalists, after all, inhabit a competitive environment. Each owner of a bakery, every investor in a garment factory, every CEO of a steel mill is competing with many others. Each is trying to bring to market a product of equal quality at less cost. That is the only way to be sure of sales and profits. And this means that profits must regularly be plowed back into the company in order to buy the latest technology, machines, and equipment. Only in this way can the company become more efficient, capable of producing the same good (or an improved one) more quickly and cheaply. But such investments are not possible without making profits; they can only be paid for if the company earns more than it spends. As a result, competition for sales compels each firm to minimize costs and maximize profits. And because the source of all profit is unpaid work, or as Marx prefers, surplus labor, if profits are to rise then labor must be sped up and intensified, its productivity (output per hour) increased.[175]

However, the capitalist drive to maximize profits encounters two powerful obstructions: workers, and other capitalists. Workers, after all, have an interest in improving their wages and benefits, and in minimizing the physical and psychological stress of their working lives—and thus in resisting efforts to squeeze profits from them. To the extent to which they are successful in these respects, they limit the productivity and profitability of the firm. Meanwhile, other capitalists have an interest in taking markets and sales from their competitors. So, in an economy in which buyers are finite, capitalists in the same markets are locked in conflict for market share. Both of these constraints impose an imperative on each and every capitalist to invest in new technologies that break through workers' resistance, speed up work, and get an edge on the competition.

While new technologies are not the only way to improve productivity and profitability, they are far and away the most effective one. It is certainly possible to speed up production simply by forcing workers to do more per minute of labor. But this strategy has severe limits: the physical capacities of workers are not infinite (they cannot do each and every task increasingly faster without breaking down or making mistakes), nor is their willingness to accept speed-up. But machines can often overcome both of these limits. They can be used to automate and reconfigure tasks so that workers produce more; and by replacing large numbers of workers with machines they can increase unemployment and insecurity, a key tactic in weakening workers' resistance. In recent decades, automation, robotics, and computerization have been used for just these purposes. New technologies also assist capitalists in the competition for market share, because they make it possible to produce a good or service more quickly—and therefore at less cost. Recall, for instance, how Ford's assembly lines reduced the hours necessary to assemble a Model T chassis from twelve to one and a half. Such productivity improvements are crucial because the firm that can produce basically the same good or service at a lower price stands the best chance of seizing market share from its rivals. This is why, everything else being equal, commodity prices tend to fall over time.[176] One need only think about what has happened over the last ten or twenty years to prices for personal computers, digital cameras, laptops, cell phones, and so on to see this point.

The pressure to maximize sales and profits in order to afford large investments in new technologies (and new factories, mines, mills, and offices) is unending. As soon as one firm has an even newer system of machinery, yesterday's new technology is on the verge of becoming obsolete; economic survival requires its rapid replacement. And so, capitalists come under incessant pressure to maximize profits in order to accumulate new means of production.[177] This is the reason the system is characterized by frenetic growth—at least until a crisis comes, which itself will have been caused by the very process of feverish growth. Because the company that stands still is the one that will lose the competitive race, each is driven to expand incessantly. Yet, capitalist growth is not about better meeting human needs; it is about doing whatever is necessary to beat the competition. As a result, each cycle of growth requires yet another—a mad rat race without pause. This is not a matter of choice for the entrepreneur; it is a commandment of the system. In a memorable passage, Marx mocks capitalism's religion-like injunction to expand: "Accumulate! Accumulate! That is Moses and the prophets."[178]

This analysis demonstrates that the capitalist market system comprises a machine that no one controls. Every agent must conform to its imperatives. Fail to turn an adequate profit and an enterprise will not survive. The market thus operates like a computer program with its own rules—and those rules often lead to great crashes. As one European banker puts it, "We are a bit like an airline pilot who knows he is going to crash but whose computer controls no longer respond. The computer follows its own rules, that's what the market is like."[179] In his marvelous novel of the Great Depression, *The Grapes of Wrath*, John Steinbeck brilliantly represents this logic. Explaining why banks and owners were taking land back from tenant farmers, one character in the novel explains,

> A man can hold land if he can just eat and pay taxes... But— you see, a bank or a company can't do that, because those creatures don't breathe air, don't eat side-meat. They breathe profits; they eat the interest on money. If they don't get it, they die the way you die without air, without side-meat.[180]

So, while a person can treat land as a means of life, a capitalist must treat it as a means of growth, of profit-making. It is not enough that the land (or factories) provide survival; it must provide ever-growing amounts of wealth. And this constant drive to expand is at the very heart of economic crises of the sort that hit in 2008. For, as every capitalist firm invests in order to lower costs, boost sales and increase profits, they all build factories, offices, mines, mills, hotels, and shopping centers at a manic pace, all the while retooling their facilities with new equipment and technologies. This produces an economic boom in the early going. Then, as things start to falter, companies borrow to finance additional investment, while pressing governments to lower interest rates so that consumers can keep borrowing and buying too.

But why do things start to falter? Why does capitalist growth undermine itself? Here, Marx argues that the process of capitalist expansion creates both over-accumulation and declining profitability.

Over-Accumulation and Declining Profits

Over-accumulation is another way of describing what we earlier dubbed over-investment. It emerges at a point where, relative to demand backed by money, there are simply too many factories and too much equipment producing the same good, be it bread, jeans, or cars, and too many service companies do things like opening restaurants or selling trips to the Caribbean. In such circumstances, some of these firms become entirely unprofitable; they are not earning enough to pay rent and salaries, to cover the costs of their raw materials and equipment, or to pay back loans to banks. They may frantically borrow for a while to stay alive, but inadequate revenues eventually drive them to bankruptcy. This is the point at which over-accumulated capital finds itself in a crisis situation. As all this has been going on, the rate of return on investment—or the rate of profit—has typically been turning down for another reason, one having to do with the contradictory effects of mechanization.

Recall that mechanization is necessary to speed up production and win the battle of price competition. Recall too that labor is the source of profit.[181] So, here we encounter a contradiction—for the very thing that improves the competitiveness of the firm also undermines the rate of profit. After all, mechanization means that some tasks previously done by workers are now done by machines. Consequently, a larger share of business spending will go to machinery and equipment, and a smaller share to labor. Put differently, the amount of labor hired declines per unit of investment. In mainstream terms, investment becomes more and more "capital-intensive."[182] In the U.S., for instance, we can see this trend in the postwar period when, for the one hundred largest firms, the amount of money invested in equipment per worker doubled between 1949 and 1962.[183] But this means that, everything else being equal, the source of surplus value and profits— living labor—tends to become a smaller component of business expenditure over time. Ironically, then, mechanization enables firms to lower costs in the struggle to stay alive, while simultaneously reducing the share of business spending that hires the only force that can create profits—workers. It follows with arithmetic certainty that, as the ratio of labor to total investment declines, so the ratio of profit to total investment will tend to fall.[184] This does not mean that all firms suffer a fall in their rate of return; in fact, the most efficient (and typically most highly mechanized) companies may boost their market share and their profits, typically at the expense of their less efficient rivals.[185] But it does mean that there will be a tendency (not an iron law but a tendency) for the rate of profit to decline system-wide. So, while mechanization is very much in the interest of the innovators, it has more contradictory results for capitalism as a whole.

One of the reasons that, following Marx, I have described this as a tendency is that mechanization also tends to cheapen the costs of machines, something which should offset declining profitability. And ultimately it will. But this tends to happen only in the course of big crises and intense competition over prices and market shares, as those with older and more costly machines and equipment struggle to survive. However, as profitability starts to decline, and firms cut prices to hold on to market share, capitalists with older and less efficient technologies often find that they can no longer operate with that equipment, even if it has not been paid off—it is just not competitively viable to do so. As a result, they are compelled to scrap older machinery, even if they are financially obliged to keep paying it off. This means they have to absorb big losses, as a result of ditching equipment that has not even been paid for; and this then drives down profits even more dramatically.[186]

It is not the case, therefore, that mechanization depresses the rate of profit in an automatic and straight-forward way. In fact, as we have seen, it frequently improves profitability for capitalist innovators. But, by displacing labor (at least in relative terms) in favor of new technologies, it puts downward pressure on profits and makes the least efficient capitalists increasingly vulnerable to competition and economic slumps. When the latter arrive, and the rate of profit drops, often dramatically, these firms are highly susceptible to being bankrupted. Over time, such bankruptcies help to restore profitability for the remaining firms and lay the basis for a recovery. But that cannot happen without the wrenching suffering and hardship of a system-wide economic contraction.

Whenever both of these trends—over-accumulation and declining profitability—are at work, capitalism is heading for a crisis.[187] But how severe such a crisis will be is also significantly determined by the degree to which the financial sector has inflated during the boom, and how fragile this has made the whole banking and credit system.

Finance, Credit, and Crisis

"Money makes the world go around." Only in capitalist society could such an adage take hold. For, only in capitalist society is money literally the difference between life and death. While this is palpably, frighteningly true for the poorest members of humankind, it is also the case for giant corporations, even if their death is of a very different nature. As we have seen, the cycle of capitalist production and exchange (M-C-M') begins and ends with money. For capital, things are valuable not for their intrinsic properties, but for their monetary worth. Moreover, for corporations it is literally true that you need money to make money. And often, the only way firms can finance the massive investments necessary to keep up with the competition is by borrowing money. For this reason, modern capitalism could not function without a highly developed credit system, involving banks, stock exchanges, and other financial institutions. This credit system makes it possible for capitalists to finance spending on a scale that would not be possible from their retained earnings alone. But in order to borrow, firms have to pledge a share of future profits in exchange for investment funds in the here and now. And the future profits pledged must both repay the original loan (the principal) plus a flow of regular interest payments. But because the only thing creditors receive in the here and now is a promise to pay—be a stock, a bond, or some other kind of promissory note—that represents a claim to a share of future profits, they are accepting forms of fictitious capital. As opposed to actual buildings, machines or stocks of goods, paper promises are fictitious precisely because the profits they pledge to share may never materialize. What holders of these "financial assets" possess is in fact a debt, a legal IOU. But should the debtor go under, the loan itself may never be fully repaid, if at all.[188]

As claims on *future* wealth, rather than actual stocks of commodities or means of production, fictitious capitals are inherently risky. And things get riskier with the growth of financial markets in which these paper claims to future profits are themselves bought and sold as commodities. Financial assets then become fictitious commodities. And, during periods of speculative excitement, they often command enormously inflated prices relative to the future profits they might reasonably be expected to claim. During the dotcom boom, for instance, shares of some new firms soared to hundreds of times their actual earnings. In early 2000, the price of a share of Cisco Systems was 160 times higher than the company's earnings. Put differently, if you purchased a Cisco share it would take you 160 years of divided payments at year 2000 rates of return to get back your investment. Clearly, no reasonable investor would make such a wager—unless their investment was purely speculative, based merely on the bet that someone else will pay even more for the stock. This is what happens when the "irrational exuberance" of a stock market bubble is in play. Many investors start to buy stocks (and other financial assets) not because of the profits the company in question is making, but simply because they expect the price for the paper asset itself to rise. In short, they are engaged in *purely* speculative buying and selling.[189] But at some point, the reality of underlying profits (or lack thereof) will take over, just as it did in 1929. Then economic reality strikes back with a vengeance and speculative fever turns to panic, as it did in the case of Enron stock, which plummeted from $90 to 36¢ a share, in the process wiping out $60 billion in fictitious capital owned by shareholders, during the company's 2001 meltdown.[190]

In a crisis, then, the over-accumulation of means of production (factories, machines, buildings, and so on) is amplified by a massive over-accumulation of fictitious capitals, of paper claims to future profits in the form of stocks, bonds, collateralized debt obligations, and more, which are sure to be savaged during a crisis. And because dumping financial assets is a lot easier than selling a company, crises often break out most violently in just these areas. As investors realize that the party is over, they scurry to sell off paper claims before their "value" evaporates—as they did with stocks in 1929 or more recently with mortgage-backed securities. At this stage of the game, the financial crisis frequently becomes the center of the storm, as it did in 2008, when banks collapsed and world stock markets lost almost half their value. Having created a precarious fault line throughout the system, financial over-accumulation produces profound collapses. This is why, "At first glance . . . the entire crisis presents itself as simply a credit and monetary crisis,"[191] even though it is the overall decline in profitability that is the ultimate source of the slump, just as it was in 1929.

But no crisis of capitalism is permanent. Even the Great Depression eventually ended—albeit only as a result of war and immense human suffering. Because the latest crisis will also involve a decade or more of unconscionable hardship, under-standing the mechanisms capitalism uses to get out of crisis is an intellectual task of the greatest urgency.

"Creative Destruction": How Capitalism Rights its Ship by Sinking Others

"Creative destruction" is the term Joseph Schumpeter once used to describe the dynamic processes of capitalist growth and con-traction. Through destruction—such as shutting down plants, scrapping machinery, eliminating jobs—capital eventually estab-lishes the basis for a new cycle of growth. Schumpeter's term contains a powerful insight about the violent binges capitalism requires to resolve a crisis. But it is also involves an obfuscation. For "creative destruction" can all too easily call forth images of the tortured artist, the great genius who destroys a canvas in order to bring forward a work of immense power and human meaning. Capitalism's destructiveness is anything but so heroic. Its spasmodic collapses involve wanton and terrifying binges of sheer mayhem. In their wake, people are rendered homeless, disease rates ramp up, children suffer and die, and epidemics of physical and psychic trauma are unleashed. We ought never to lose sight of the human dimensions of such events.

Nevertheless, it is true that crises are a mechanism for restoring capitalist growth. This is because, as Marx argued long before Schumpeter, the principal means capital has for overcoming over-accumulation and declining rates of return is the destruction of "excess capital," by bankrupting those firms that cannot attain adequate sales and profits.[192] Even though it means a deep economic contraction—a recession or depression—eventually such a crisis should restore conditions for renewed investment and growth. But, because destruction of capital means massive financial losses for firms and their investors, and massive layoffs for workers, the immediate effect is severe economic trauma—collapse of businesses and of financial institutions that lent to them, huge drops in workers' capacities to buy goods as job loss mounts, and the downward spiral all this sets in motion. Equally important is that crises contribute to driving down workers' wages. As layoffs and unemployment and poverty climb, employers gain a huge power advantage when it comes to setting pay levels. Every crisis in the history of capitalism has thus involved a decline in real wages.

By shutting down factories, offices, mines, and mills, crises purge excess capital from the economy. At the same time, they reduce costs for surviving firms. Not only do wages fall, so do prices for raw materials and other components. They also make it easier for these companies to buy up assets like buildings and machines on the cheap from bankrupted firms. Most importantly, by driving competitors out of the market at the same time as costs are lowered, they make it possible for surviving corporations to introduce whole new technologies and production systems that contribute to improved profitability. We have seen in chapter 2 how such processes worked themselves out in the restructuring of the steel industry in the late 1970s and early 1980s.

Financial crises are often the key mechanisms through which such destruction of capital takes place. Utter collapses in the prices for a firm's stock can be the means by which a corporation is driven under or bought up. As investors pull their money out, wobbling firms lose their credit-worthiness and are unable to borrow. Should such crises happen on a large enough scale, a full-fledged panic will ensue in which credit—lending by banks and firms to one another—seizes up across the economy. At this point, the center of the storm becomes stock and money markets. During such a wave of destruction, Marx noted,

> The chief disruption ... would occur in connection ... with capital *values*. The portion of capital value that exists in the form of future claims on surplus-value and profit, in other words promissory notes on production in their various forms [such as loans, shares, and bonds—DM], is devalued simultaneously with the fall in the revenues on which it is reckoned ... The chain of payment obligations at specific dates is broken in a hundred places, and this is still further accompanied by a breakdown in the credit system, which had developed alongside capital. All this therefore leads to violent and acute crises ... [193]

As capitalism ages, however, crises must get more and more destructive to do the work of restoring conditions for expansion. As the units of capital, the corporations and banks at the heart of the system, get ever larger, they have greater resources for obstructing their demise. By operating at a loss, merging with rivals, rolling over bank loans and so on, they can often cling to life in circumstances that would drive smaller firms into bankruptcy. At the same time, governments frequently step in to aid such firms—as the U.S. and European states did with automobile corporations and major banks in 2008-9—on the grounds that their collapse would be catastrophic to the economy. Ironically, however, by keeping large companies afloat, these tactics inhibit the destructiveness required to get the system expanding again. Studying just such phenomena in 1931, the Russian economist E. A. Preobrazhensky argued that these new capitalist dynamics create a "thrombosis in the transition from crisis to recession," i.e. that they suppress the system's destructive tendencies.[194] The result is a stretching out the crisis—by making it longer, if less severe. In short, by inhibiting the destruction of capital, recessions are made less brutal—but also less effective. In fact, one of the extraordinary things about the Great Depression is that even a decade of slump with average unemployment of 20 percent or more could not get the system back on its feet. Only world war, with its barbaric destructiveness, laid the basis for a new period of growth.

Our world had never before seen anything like the unrelenting mass destruction of World War II. The human devastation was unprecedented: tens of millions killed, much greater numbers rendered homeless and displaced. Yet, perversely, the economic destruction wrought in the war's wake did the trick. Japan lost a quarter of its factory buildings and a third of its machines and equipment. Almost 20 percent of Germany's capital stock was destroyed, while a quarter of Italy's steel industry was wiped out.[195] By these means the problem of over-accumulated capital was resolved—in the most barbaric way imaginable. Next, insurgent labor had to be put in its place. Through the war years, anti-fascist and democratic sentiments had combined with anger about wartime hardship and suffering to produce a postwar labor upsurge across Europe, the United States, and East Asia. Mass strikes, occupations, and union organizing were everywhere. In Japan and South Korea, U.S military occupation put recalcitrant workers back in their place, while in the United States anti-union laws, like the Taft-Hartley Act of 1947, helped break the back of working class insurgence. Finally, by the end of the 1940s, with over-accumulation resolved, labor repressed, and rates of profit restored, a new boom was in the making, stimulated by the need to rapidly rebuild Europe and Japan. That boom would be the most sustained expansion in the history of capitalism. But when it came undone, the stage was set for the era of neoliberalism, whose great crisis defines the moment in which we now live.

CHAPTER FOUR

Financial Chaos: Money, Credit, and Instability in Late Capitalism

"On August 15, 1971, the world of international finance was changed forever."[196]

AN ESCALATING FINANCIAL PANIC ANNOUNCED THE ARRIVAL OF THE Great Recession of 2008. As banks toppled and prices of financial assets plummeted, bank lending ground to a thundering halt. This is always disastrous for capitalism, as the flow of credit—the lending and borrowing of funds—is utterly essential to the daily operations of the system. Each and every day thousands of corporations and banks need to borrow in order to conduct business. So, as the flow of credit seized up, the economy suffered cardiac arrest. This led many pundits to dub the panic a "credit crisis." Yet the drama of the credit seizure has frequently led commentators to see the entire trauma in exclusively financial terms. It is thus worth reminding ourselves that the existence of a financial meltdown was nothing terribly unique to the Panic of 2008. As we have seen, Marx observed in the 1860s that "At first glance . . . the entire crisis presents itself as simply a credit and monetary crisis."[197] He went on to insist on the need to get beyond first glances in order to grasp the deeper dynamics at work, which I reviewed in the previous chapter. Regrettably, much discussion of the Great Recession has failed to do this, choosing to interpret the slump as a strictly financial event. This bias owes something to the inherent disposition of mainstream economics to focus on the sphere of exchange—the buying and selling of goods and money—at the neglect of production and accumulation of "hard" assets, like factories, buildings, and equipment. But, more than this, it also has to do with a series of transformations of neoliberal capitalism often grouped under the catch-all term, financialization.

Without a doubt, finance—the creation of debts (loans) as a means of profit-making—has been spectacularly lucrative in recent decades. Rarely in the history of capitalism have transactions related to debt loomed larger in the modern economy. This is reflected in the growing profitability of financial institutions. If we go back to 1973, for instance, financial returns made up just 16 percent of total profits in the American economy—a level that remained steady until the mid-1980s. By 2007, however, financial gains had soared to fully 41 percent of all U.S. profits. And because these profits derive overwhelmingly from loans, their stupendous rise could only mean one thing: mounting levels of indebtedness throughout the economy. And soaring debt loads have been a central feature of the neoliberal era. During Alan Greenspan's tenure as chairman of the Federal Reserve (1987–2005), for instance, total debt in the U.S. quadrupled from slightly more than \$10 trillion to \$43 trillion. Mainstream commentators customarily blame over-eager consumers for this ballooning of debt—and it is true that U.S. consumer borrowing relative to GDP doubled between 1980 and 2007. But the leader of the debt pack was the financial sector itself. In fact, during the same period that consumer debt doubled in relative terms, financial sector debt *quintupled* as a proportion of U.S. GDP, rocketing from 25 percent in 1982 to 121 percent in 2008.[198] In other words, banks were boosting their lending by themselves borrowing more and more (from other banks and "shadow banks," like hedge funds). Borrowing was thus fueling borrowing, as finance and the debt economy seemed to be the new engines of economic growth.

As consumers borrowed more than ever via mortgages, credit cards, lines of credit, car loans, and so on; as financial institutions turned out waves of exotic debt instruments like collateralized debt obligations and asset backed securities; and as banks themselves went on a borrowing binge in efforts to finance more business, many commentators talked of a financialization of the economy. To be sure, important transformations were at work. But too often they were portrayed in terms of the birth of a new economy driven by knowledge, information, and symbolic assets (like brand images), rather than the old-fashioned hard kind. No longer, pundits claimed, would companies need to build production facilities and purchase equipment—that old material world had been eclipsed. Henceforth, enterprises would simply need to use their imaginative powers to create images and symbols: logos, brand names, ads, and so on.

Seduced by rhetoric about "virtual" corporations, Enron president Jeffrey Skilling even proclaimed that the energy company of the future "won't be based on pipes and wires and generating facilities; it will be based on intellectual capital." So, when entering into the fiber optics business, Enron officials mocked companies like AT&T for building actual telecommunication networks. Instead, Enron simply bought access to the networks of others, short-circuiting the development of actual infrastructure.[199]

Just as businesses swallowed the new economy hype, so did trendy social theory. "Money is the only genuine artificial satellite," declared French cultural theorist Jean Baudrillard. Having become "utterly detached from production and its conditions," money was now said to enjoy "a truly astral mobility . . . it rises and sets like some artificial sun." In an economic universe dominated by signs and images, Baudrillard claimed, we are witnessing "The end of labour. The end of production. The end of political economy." [200]

While most radical critics resisted such hype, it became common to view late capitalism in terms of the rise to prominence of a new group of financial parasites who simply exploited the rest of us through their control of money and credit. Some commentators located a "financial coup" at the end of the 1970s, which enabled bankers to gain ascendency across government and society, and rewrite the rules of finance.[201] To be sure, widespread financial deregulation did take place at this time. But the story of powerful bankers seizing the reins of capitalism and remaking it in their interests is decidedly unhelpful. Among other things, it falls prey to the illusion that powerful men (and the odd woman) actually direct the way our society develops, determining what happens as if they were changing channels on their television sets. Yet capitalism is an alienated system that, like Frankenstein's Creature, takes on a life of its own. No one can actually control it, even if relations of power allow some to profit from it, and massively so. In fact, if the dominant class truly controlled things, it is hard to see why debilitating economic crises would ever occur. What interest could they have in causing multitrillion dollar bank and stock exchange collapses? So, if we genuinely want to understand the deep roots of financialization, we need to peer below the surface in order to locate the unintended structural shifts to which human actors adapted.

At first blush, an analysis of financialization may appear to be a purely academic exercise. It is not. If, for instance, we imagine that it is banks that rule late capitalism, then radical politics might legitimately focus its economic sights on taming, regulating, and controlling finance. We might then picture the struggle as one between the parasitic and the productive (the latter of whom include owners of manufacturing firms). If on the other hand, financialization represents a transformation within a capitalist economy that (contra people like Baudrillard) still depends on exploiting labor in workplaces—be it cleaners in office towers, farm workers in fields, data processors in packed cubicles, sewing machine operators in back street sweatshops, or autoworkers on giant assembly lines—then opposition to banks must be joined to a politics that challenges all the sites of capitalist exploitation.

None of this is meant to deny that late capitalism is financialized in distinctive ways and has, therefore, significant tendencies toward asset bubbles and financial meltdowns. And we need to explain why this is so if we are to provide a persuasive account of the complex interconnection between financial circuits and the exploitation of labor. To this end, I offer below a unique account of financialization, one that recognizes real historical changes without falling prey to the idea that the financial sector is thoroughly dominant today. My analysis begins by examining a series of systemic changes within post–World War II capitalism whose center point was a radical transformation of international money.

The Day World Finance Changed Forever

For most of capitalism's life, money has been linked to commodities—usually to a precious metal like gold or silver. To be sure, paper moneys have also been widespread. But the stability of money—crucial if investors are to predict the prices that will guide investment decisions—has usually been secured by having some way of converting paper money for precious metal. Across the key decades in which a capitalist world economy was institutionally consolidated—the 1870s and 1880s—the majority of dominant economies followed Britain's lead on to the gold standard (under which currencies were legally tied to gold). Many others took this step before the nineteenth century was over. By the final decade of the nineteenth century, all major currencies could be exchanged for gold, and gold could be demanded in settling accounts between nations. This international gold standard operated until the 1930s, when it disintegrated under the impact of the Great Depression. But during its period of operation, it had provided a remarkably stable price system.[202] After World War II, the major powers agreed to create a new dollar/gold standard, under which the U.S. dollar would be the world's main international currency used for the conduct of world trade. But the dollar was in turn pegged to gold (at a rate of $35 per ounce of the previous metal), while all other currencies were tied to the dollar at fixed rates of exchange. This arrangement, known as the Bretton Woods system, after the New Hampshire town where it was approved, operated with a considerable degree of stability from 1945 to 1971.[203]

A dollar/gold standard was the only reasonable choice in 1945. For, by the end of the war, the American economy exercised an unprecedented dominance over the world system. While Europe and Japan had suffered massive losses in productive facilities as well as lives, the U.S. economy was unscathed. When war commenced in 1939, the American economy was half the size of Europe, Japan, and the Soviet Union together. But after its wartime boom, as factories churned out steel, aircraft, tanks, electrical goods, bombs and more, it emerged by war's end as larger than all these others combined. American-based manufacturing accounted for fully half of world output at the end of World War II. This meant that virtually every nation needed both U.S. goods and the currency with which to pay for them, the dollar. But in capitalism, nothing ever stands still. And by the mid-1960s, new trends were reshaping the global system—trends that would create industrial rivals to the U.S. and destabilize the role of the dollar.

During the sustained post–World War II expansion of capitalism, other capitalistically developed economies of the North grew much more quickly than did America, constrained as it was by massive military spending. The Japanese and German economies, for instance, boomed at a much higher rate than did America. As table 2.1 from chapter 2 shows, between 1950 and 1973, the U.S. grew at an average rate of just under 4 percent per year. Meanwhile, Western Europe grew a bit faster, while Japan barreled ahead at double the American pace. It wasn't long before German and Japanese steel firms were seizing growing shares of the American market; and it wasn't long before Volkswagen and Toyota grabbed more and more car sales throughout the United States. In fact, by 1968 the American economy imported more cars than it exported. The same thing happened in electronics, chemicals, business machines, and more. During the 1960s, imports into the U.S. expanded at twice the pace of American exports. Then, in 1971, the U.S. was rocked by its first postwar deficit in trade with the rest of the world.

The shift in world trade flows overlapped with big deficits in the U.S. current account—the balance of inflows and outflows of money as well as goods. The combined outflows for foreign direct investment and for U.S. military spending for bases and weapons around the world created a structural imbalance: year after year, more money flowed out of America than flowed back in. And by the early 1970s, as more goods were flowing in than out, the shortfall (the trade deficit) also had to be covered by dollars. But with ever-larger numbers of dollars leaving the U.S. every year, many of them making their way to central banks overseas, the likelihood of a run on the dollar increased. After all, America's major trade partners were now accumulating dollars they did not need. So rapid was the growth of foreign dollar holdings that they doubled between 1968 and 1971 alone—from $150 billion to $300 billion. By the early 1960s, U.S. dollars overseas exceeded the country's gold reserves.

All these dollars washing around the world stimulated the emergence of the so-called Eurodollar market, a unique space, unregulated by the U.S. or any other state, in which dollars could be lent and borrowed. The Eurodollar market was especially attractive to American multinational corporations, which could often raise money there on better terms than at home. In the early days, most banks trading in these "stateless" dollars were legally based in London, though over time institutions in the U.S. and elsewhere got into the action by setting up offshore branches in places like the Bahamas and the Cayman Islands. In reality, Eurodollars were held in the U.S. itself, but they were entered into ledgers and computers as the assets of offshore banks to escape American regulators. Thus, as this sector grew throughout the 1960s, states lost effective control of an increasingly large and influential financial market, one that had grown from around $10 billion in deposits in the mid 1960s to something two hundred times larger by 1984.[204]

The impact of all this was momentous. For it is here that we find the structural foundation of financialization and the liberalized and deregulated markets that accompany it. It is not the case that deregulation occurred first, followed by a financial explosion. Instead, the flare-up of unregulated markets came first—with the massive growth of an unregulated offshore market. Government deregulation of finance sought to catch up with this changing reality. As regulators followed the trend they removed restrictions that banks and corporate borrowers disliked in an effort to attract financial business that was flowing outside their jurisdictions. In the U.S., for instance, the Depository Institutions Deregulation and Monetary Control Act was not introduced until 1980, well after the Eurodollar market had developed. In Europe major pieces of liberalizing bank legislation were passed toward the end of that decade.

Although 1971 was a turning point, the contradictions of the dollar / gold standard had built up over many years. As early as 1958, the U.S. gold stock had declined by $2.3 billion, as foreign central banks and financial institutions cashed dollars in for gold. In 1968, the American government limited the right to demand gold for dollars to foreign central banks. But even that did not stop the outflow of gold. Until Nixon took the greenback off gold in 1971, the U.S. continued to lose a billion dollars worth of gold per year.[205] By that year foreign holdings of dollars, at $300 billion, were more than twenty times greater than all the gold the U.S. government possessed. Once the reality of the 1971 American trade deficit set in, the rush to convert dollars into gold went through the roof, reaching an annual rate of $35 billion that summer as rumors built that Nixon would suspend convertibility.[206] By that point it was a question of when, not if. Before long the U.S. state would be out of gold—and with that would come a full-fledged dollar crisis. Better, insisted a few of the president's advisors, to strike first. Still, breaking dollar/gold convertibility remained unthinkable for many. Told of the Nixon plan, one Treasury official put his head in his hands and groaned, "My God!" And the day of Nixon's announcement, staff at the International Monetary Fund circulated an obituary notice which read in part, "R.I.P. We regretfully announce the unexpected passing away after a long illness of Bretton Woods . . ."[207] Although U.S. officials initially claimed the move was temporary, by 1973 it was clear that there would be no return to gold. The world of money had radically and irrevocably changed.[208]

Unstable Money, Volatile Finance

For the first time in its history, capitalism operated with officially de-commodified money, a global currency regime lacking any tie to an underlying commodity. No longer did money bear a direct link to past labor embodied in a commodity. With Nixon's declaration, global finance lost its anchorage in gold (or any other commodity) and became a pure and simple national credit-money system (or fiat money system). All other currencies, which had been linked to the dollar, likewise became unhinged and began to "float" in value, often swinging wildly in the course of a few weeks or months. In fact, during the period after 1971, exchange rate changes among currencies became three times more volatile than they had been under Bretton Woods.[209] World money had begun to operate, in the words of the West German Chancellor, as a "floating non-system."[210] *Float* may be too benign a term, however, for the great gyrations that shook financial markets. Over the course of the 1970s, for instance, the U.S. dollar dropped by 30 percent or more against other major currencies and other major currencies rose by corresponding amounts or more. In this volatile global environment it was increasingly difficult for firms, particularly those operating multinationally and doing business in multiple currencies, to predict the costs of investments, or the scale of their earnings. Faced with this new world of exchange rate volatility, investors, banks, and speculators rapidly expanded markets that would allow them to buy and sell currencies on an around-the-clock basis. And this explosion in foreign exchange trading only added to the uncertainty, as investors rapidly sold off falling currencies while piling into rising ones. Not surprisingly, currency trading quickly became far and away the world's largest market.

As table 4.1 indicates, the daily turnover in foreign exchange (forex) markets amounted to $15 billion in 1973, just as we were entering the new world of de-commodified money. Twelve years later, the daily foreign exchange turnover had jumped ten times to $150 billion, a figure that shocked many commentators at the time. Another ten years on, even that figure looked paltry as daily foreign exchange trading soared to $1.2 trillion. Yet, the steep rise in currency trading was far from over; by 2004 the daily volume hit nearly $2 trillion, and by 2007 it had surpassed $3.2 trillion.

Table 4.1 Daily Turnover in Foreign Exchange Markets, selected years 1973–2007

Year	Amount
1973	$15 billion
1980	$80 billion
1985	$150 billion
1995	$1.2 trillion
2004	$1.9 trillion
2007	$3.2 trillion

Source: Bank for International Settlements, *Triennial Central Bank Survey*, multiple years

One way of getting a sense of the relative size of foreign exchange markets, is to consider their relationship to world trade. In 1973, the daily value of currencies traded was twice that of daily world trade in goods. By 1995 it was seventy times greater—a clear indication that most foreign exchange trading is purely speculative, rather than meant to facilitate the actual trade of goods and services.[211]

But looking at the massive trading in traditional foreign exchange markets does not reveal the true dimensions of the financial explosion set off by the move to floating currencies. For outside of standard foreign exchange trading, an even larger over-the-counter market in currency related instruments (derivatives) soared from $1.2 trillion in 1992 to $4.2 trillion fifteen years later—or a trillion dollars larger than traditional foreign exchange.[212] The development of these derivatives has exacerbated the risk associated with the volatile world of floating currencies.

As monetary instability became the order of the day, so did new forms of "risk management." After all, firms that operated multinationally now confronted the risk that profits made in a particular national market might be wiped out by devaluation of the local currency. A German multinational, for instance, that made a 10 percent return on its U.S. sales and operation would record only two-thirds of that profit at the home office if the dollar declined by a third against the mark (or today the euro). Global businesses thus began to search for "hedges" against currency fluctuations, turning to complex financial instruments known as derivatives, which are meant to provide protection from financial and currency volatility. Indeed, the timing here couldn't be clearer: trade in derivatives known as financial futures began in 1972 when the Chicago Mercantile Exchange created the International Money Market; business in currency futures (purchase of currencies at a certain rate at some future point in time) commenced the next year as did the Chicago Board Options Exchange. During the 1980s, options on currencies were also introduced on the London Stock Exchange and the London International Financial Futures Exchange. Currency hedging thus drove the dramatic growth of derivatives after 1972.

I shall explain unique features of derivatives in more detail in a moment. But, first, let us recall that as necessary as new instruments to hedge risk were in a world of floating currencies, the growth of these instruments also enhanced the space for purely speculative transactions. Only a sharp increase in speculation can explain how it was that by the mid-1990s the *daily* volume of currency trading was equal to the average *monthly* volume of trade in goods and services. By the late 1990s, in fact, the global foreign exchange trade was more than ten times larger than the world's annual gross domestic product.[213] So, while currency trading became vitally important in an era of heightened monetary instability, it also increasingly became an end in itself. If traders could accurately predict which currencies were likely to rise and which to fall, they could reap enormous profits without ever undertaking the long-term risks associated with building factories, buying machines, hiring workers, constructing supply and distribution chains, and so on. Currency markets thus seemed to offer a capitalist utopia in which money breeds money; it seemed to be a question of guessing which currencies would be winners and which losers. The extraordinary growth of foreign exchange trading thus drove the financialization of late capitalism. And here derivatives figure prominently.

It is worth noting that derivatives themselves were not new to the neoliberal world of fully de-commodified money. But for a long time their use had largely been confined to agriculture. American farmers, for instance, at the beginning of the planting season for grain, might want to guarantee themselves last year's price of, say, one dollar per bushel. Meanwhile, a grain merchant, convinced that rising demand would drive the price higher, might be more than willing to contract to receive grain at a future date (after the harvest) at that price. So, the two parties could enter into a futures contract, agreeing to a transaction in the future at a price set today. The farmer would receive an income guarantee, the merchant a chance to reap great profits if, for instance, grain prices rose to $1.40 per bushel. The farmer could also purchase an option to sell at this price in the future. This would not require that he sell to the grain merchant at $1 a bushel, but it would give him the option to do so if that price looked attractive.

These contracts are known as derivatives because, although no actual commodity exchange takes place at the time they are negotiated, their terms are *derived* from prices of real commodities. Crucially, such derivatives are designed to provide protection against uncertainties. The farmer could be confident that it was worth sowing and plowing the fields, while the grain merchant could be sure of having product to sell at a given price. Risk had thereby been offset. But in principle the same thing could be done in a world of monetary and financial uncertainty. So, from the early 1970s on, financial derivatives took off precisely because they reduced risk due to financial volatility. To take the example used earlier, the U.S. office of the same German multinational we have described could purchase a contract giving it an option to sell U.S. dollars at a set rate to the German mark, thus preventing a loss of profits in the event that the dollar should fall. So, if the dollar declined by 10 percent, the company would have locked in the right to sell dollars (the currency in which it received its U.S. profits) at their old price, 10 percent higher, and thus protected their profits when converted to euros. In the event of the dollar rising or staying steady, the firm could choose not to exercise that option, and merely pay the cost of the contract— thus giving a straight profit to the option seller. But if the dollar were to fall, the German company would have protected its U.S. profits for a relatively small price. Similarly, a firm that expected interest rates to fall in one country and rise in another could purchase a swap contract by which it literally swapped the (higher) interest rate it expected to pay in one country for the (lower) rate it anticipated elsewhere, and vice versa in the case of interest-bearing securities.

Note here that while the term "derivative" refers to a financial contract whose price is supposed to be derived from some underlying asset, in fact, most of the underlying prices are predictions as to future values. Just like the price of a bushel of grain in six months, the future values of currencies have become highly unpredictable. In addition to the explosion of foreign exchange trading, therefore, the period from 1973 on saw a tsunami-like wave of transactions in financial derivatives related to currency and financial uncertainty. Derivatives markets quickly eclipsed those in stocks and bonds. By 2006, more than $450 trillion in derivative contracts were sold, massively exceeding the $40 trillion of sales in global stock markets, or the $65 trillion that moved through world bond markets in the same year.[214]

Unintentionally, then, the breaking of dollar-gold convertibility and the move to floating exchange rates—the development of the so-called "floating non-system"—had tremendously financialized late capitalism. Immense profits could now be made by finding gaps between prices in different markets—between, say, interest rates in one economy and those in another—and capitalizing on the mismatches. Similarly, great profits could be made by betting correctly on the direction of future assets, for example, by accurately predicting the rise or fall in prices for oil, gold, the euro, or the direction of Japanese interest rates. As a result, new financial instruments were endlessly generated, all designed to make it possible to place such bets. While central bankers and mainstream economists extolled all of this as demonstrating the growing efficiency of global markets, many critical political economists recognized that powerfully destabilizing tendencies were emerging.

Debt, Securitization, and the Financial Crash

In the meantime, other changes in the neoliberal economy were producing a financial explosion. Two trends were crucial in the early stages. One was the continuing rise in the number of dollars that circulated outside the United States. The second was the sharp rise in the global money supply across the 1970s, as governments sought to stimulate economies that kept sliding into recession (1970–71, 1974–75, 1980–82). Much of that money inevitably found its way into banks. But what were banks to do with such funds when corporations, afflicted by declining sales and profits, were throttling back on investments? After all, corporate demand for loans was not keeping pace with the growth in the money supply. As fortune would have it, global banks discovered that many governments in the Third World were eager to borrow, particularly oil-importing nations stung by the quadrupling of the world price for "black gold." Western banks were only too happy to lend to these ready customers. Between 1968 and 1980, total Third World external debt went up twelve times, from $47.5 billion to more than $560 billion. But then the Volcker Shock did its dirty work in the Third World. As interest rates soared from 6 or 7 percent to 20 percent, many governments in the South could not make their debt payments. In 1982, Mexico informed Washington that it was broke. Over the coming months, states like Brazil, Poland, Argentina, and Chile too found themselves on the verge of default. This spelled disaster for the banks. The largest of them, the likes of Chase Manhattan, Bank of America, and Citibank, had huge loans outstanding to Brazil, Argentina, Venezuela, Chile, and others. In fact, by 1982 the nine largest U.S. banks had Third World loans twice the size of their total bank capital.[215]

Enter the International Monetary Fund, the World Bank and the U.S. government, all of which orchestrated a solution that bailed out the banks, opened up Third World economies to structural adjustment and transferred wealth from the South into the hands of investors and financial institutions in the Global North. Debt now served as a means for neoliberalizing the Global South, a process we shall track in the next chapter.

In the meantime, banks in the West, having soured on lending to Third World states, sought out new business. Given the trends of the neoliberal era, they did not need to look far. For the planet's richest households, whose incomes were shooting to the stars, were on the prowl for profitable outlets for their excess wealth. With interest rates trending down after the Volcker Shock finally broke the back of inflation, the wealthy wanted better returns than they could make from conservative interest-bearing investments, such as government bonds. The same was true for the managers of pension and mutual funds. And bankers were only too happy to accommodate, conjuring up a slew of exotic financial instruments that promised higher returns. The age of securitization was upon us.

In a nutshell, securitization consists in taking debt—mortgages, corporate loans, credit card debt, student loans, it doesn't matter what—and repackaging it as a "security" that can be purchased. Because mortgages are the largest loans most people will ever take out, and because securitization started in this sector, the term is often directly associated with mortgages. But in fact securitization actually applies to any debt that is repackaged and sold off. Stocks, of course, are the most long-standing of such securities. They too are a kind of debt, since in purchasing a share in a company I am giving it a loan in the hope of getting some of the firm's future profits (a dividend). The same principle applies if I buy a collateralized debt obligation (CDO) based on credit card debt. Here, I am effectively buying a share of, say, one thousand different credit card balances. I am now guaranteed a steady stream of the interest payments due on these debts—provided the original borrowers do not default. And because the rate of interest on credit cards is much higher than on government bonds, these new debt instruments became insanely popular, not only to the millionaire households of the neoliberal era, but also to large institutional investors like pension and mutual funds. The result was that a securitization mania swept finance, radically transforming banking in the process.

Traditional models tell us that what banks do is collect deposits and make prudent loans. So a bank branch might take in the deposits of one thousand people and forty small businesses in its locale, and it might make hundreds of loans, for mortgages, spending by small businesses, and car purchases. In order to make lending decisions, the bank tries to get to know its community, to evaluate credit-worthiness in order to finance viable borrowing. In the process, it profits by lending at a higher rate, say 5 percent on average, than the rate it pays for deposits, say 2 percent. Securitization radically changes this model of banking.[216] Instead of making loans, like a twenty-five-year mortgage, and holding them on its books, a bank now makes the loan and, for a fee, sells it off to an institution that specializes in creating "financial products," such as mortgage-backed securities. In this system, banks move loans off their books almost as fast as they make them, collecting a fee every time they sell them to an investment bank or similar institution. In the process, they take themselves off the hook in the event of default. No longer is the mortgage (or credit card, or student loan) originator stuck if the borrower defaults. That risk is now passed on to the new owners of these debts, wealthy individuals and institutions who have purchased these debt-based securities. Securitization also means that a growing share of bank profits derive not from years of interest payments on mortgages and the like, but from the fees they make by selling such loans to investors. This gives banks a huge incentive to increase the volume of loans they make, because they no longer carry the risk—unless they are foolish enough to buy some of these loans themselves, which, as we shall see, many were.

In this environment, the financial institution that created a hitherto unknown debt security could reap tremendous profits. This was true, for instance, of Salomon Brothers, the bank that originated mortgage-backed securities. But very quickly Salomon, like any financial innovator, encountered imitators. As a result, the fees it could charge fell off under pressures of competition from other banks. This created an incentive to find ever more exotic securitized instruments. It also generated a powerful inducement to speed up trades and increase their scale. If the margin of profit was small and fleeting, then ever-larger trades done ever more quickly seemed the way to go. Here, computerized trading programs provided a solution, as they could respond to price signals by sending massive buy and sell orders in microseconds. For this purpose, complex mathematical models were constructed, designed to instruct computers as to which shifts in prices for currencies, stocks, bonds and more should be met with orders to buy and sell. Throughout the 1980s, therefore, banks added computing power at a frenetic pace, increasing their budgets for computers, software and telecommunications equipment by 19 percent a year—four times faster than U.S. automakers.[217] Twenty-four-hour electronic trading exchanges, with names like Globex, Soffex, Cats, and Fox came on stream, providing automated platforms for the buying and selling of stocks, bonds, currencies, futures contracts and so on. A high-tech "Money Grid" came to dominate global finance, consisting of "satellites, fiber-optic cables, and computer chips, all of it tamed and fed by complex financial theories and streams of electricity."[218] The financialization of capitalism in recent decades, then, has been driven by an outpouring of new securitized debt instruments joined to arcane mathematical formulas and massive computing power. Those who got it right could make immense fortunes. But if the formulas were flawed—and, as we shall see, they were profoundly so—then tremendous havoc could be unleashed, as it was in 2007–8.

Not that 2007–8 was the first time the whole Money Grid looked as if it might collapse. But each previous time the system had trembled, central banks were able to stabilize things, and the money machine kept on churning out profits. Yet, it was clear—or it ought to have been clear—that the computerized Money Grid regularly produced *asset bubbles*, great speculative waves that drove prices for financial assets far above what any rational economic analysis could justify.

The first of these bubbles formed in the mid-1980s when a coterie of "corporate raiders" floated junk bonds to raise funds with which to take over existing corporations. That bubble burst with the stock exchange crash of 1987 and jail time handed out to a number of the most fraudulent raiders, like Michael Milken of Drexel Burnham. The next bubble, inspired by the so-called "Internet Revolution," began inflating in the 1990s, as investors poured money into stocks and bonds for new dotcom firms that had never turned a profit. The price to earnings ratio on U.S. stock markets doubled in five years, hitting forty-four in 2000—meaning that it would take forty-four years of current earnings to make back the cost of a share. And ratios were much higher for dotcom firms—160 times in the case of Cisco Systems, as we have seen. When the dotcom bubble burst in 2000–2001, the 280 stocks on the Bloomberg U.S. Internet Index lost $1.755 trillion in seven months. Over the course of two and a half years, fully $5 trillion in market value would be wiped out.[219] The Nasdaq index went into freefall. Having peaked at over 5,000 in March 2000, it plummeted to 1,114 by October. Along the way, the U.S. economy suffered its largest-ever corporate bankruptcies at Enron and WorldCom—the largest, that is, until Lehman Brothers came along. Then, from 2000 on, as Federal Reserve Chairman Alan Greenspan repeatedly cut interest rates in response to the dotcom recession, the lethal bubble in real estate began inflating.

Fearing the effects of the dotcom collapse, Greenspan had first cut interest rates in January 2001 to 6 percent. For more than two years he just kept cutting, driving them down to the historic low of 1 percent by 2003. In so doing, he created ideal conditions for a real estate boom, because the cost of mortgages was so inviting. But nothing like the six-year-long mortgage mania would or could have happened had it not been for the insatiable appetite of banks for new financial instruments.

Although securitization of mortgages had been around since the 1970s, it did not really take off until the early 1990s. By then, every form of debt, from credit cards to auto loans, was being securitized. But the sheer, unbridled explosion occurred from 2000 on. In that year, the amount of debt Wall Street bought, packaged, and sold equaled $1 trillion dollars. Five years later, the number was $2.7 trillion, a 270 percent increase in half a decade. And the stuff was going global, as banks in Germany and pension funds in Japan lapped it up. Lehman Brothers, which had moved massively into the business, saw its foreign sales of securitized debt soar by 600 percent.[220] The appetite of banks was voracious; month in and month out they wanted to buy more and more debt that could be repackaged and sold off. But there was no way of creating enough securitized junk unless whole new strata of the U.S. population could be sold mortgages. This meant that ways had to be devised of persuading poor, African-American, and Latino households to take out housing loans. This is where subprime and other nonstandard mortgages came into play. If poor people could be talked into taking out a home loan at a teaser rate, then the mortgage could be repackaged and sold off while it was still affordable. Later the interest rate would shoot up—as, inevitably, would default rates. But by then the financial institution that made the loan would have been paid off, and the securitized version of the loan would be in someone else's hands.

In fact, however, few banks were quite this deviously intelligent. Many of them, seduced by absurd mathematical models that we shall investigate shortly, actually believed in the toxic junk they were selling and held onto huge quantities of it. They too would be ravaged when the explosion came.

Let's note something absolutely crucial here. Contrary to a myth peddled by mainstream commentators, it is not the case that poor people came to the banks to misrepresent their economic circumstances and recklessly take on loans they could not afford. Instead, banks went hunting for new clients—someone, anyone they could persuade to take out a mortgage. Then bankers and mortgage brokers fiddled the numbers and offered teaser rates to persuade people to sign. Along the way they deceived and manipulated. Once again, the racialized dynamics of U.S. capitalism were in play here, something to which we return in the next chapter. It was, in other words, the unquenchable thirst of banks for ever more mortgaged-backed securities that drove the mania. As a consequence, whereas in 2000 there had been $130 billion in subprime mortgage lending in the U.S., $55 billion of which had been packaged as mortgage bonds, by 2005 banks made $625 billion in subprime loans, more than $500 billion of which was securitized. In five years, in other words, bonds based on subprime mortgages had grown by nearly ten times, to half a trillion dollars in a single year.[221] Still, like a junkie whose habit just keeps getting worse, Wall Street wanted more and more of the stuff. And if there were not enough poor people who could be duped, swindled, and sweet-talked, there was a new gadget that might be deployed: the credit-default swap (CDS). With bonds based on CDSs, Wall Street crossed the line into sheer insanity—profitable insanity at first, until the earthquake came.

At the most basic level, a CDS is a sort of insurance policy. Say that you own $1 million in General Motors bonds (in which case you are unlikely to be reading this book) and you are worried the company might default, thereby wiping out your investment. For a price, say $20,000 per year, a financial institution might agree to "swap" this default risk. For that fee, in other words, the company would sell you a CDS, agreeing that in the event of a GM default it would be on the hook to make good all your losses. Of course, there is no incentive for any firm to take on that risk unless they believe that the chance of a GM default is fairly low—and the higher that risk gets, the more they will charge for a CDS. Between 2000 and 2007, as pundits talked of an endless "Goldilocks economy" that got neither too hot nor too cold, prospects of significant default risk were held to be extraordinarily low. As a result, companies like AIG, the world's largest insurer, sold CDSs on mortgage-backed securities to anyone interested. Slowly, however, it dawned on a handful of contrarians that the U.S. real estate boom was completely out of step with historical trends.

For a hundred years after 1895, after all, housing prices had risen in tandem with inflation. They kept their value, but they didn't gain much of anything. Then from 1995 to 2007 they rose 70 percent faster than the Consumer Price Index, generating paper gains of $8 trillion for U.S. homeowners. This was a radical departure from the historic pattern—and obviously unsustainable. To make matters dicier, by 2006 more than 40 percent of all mortgages were "nontraditional," pushed onto people with troubled credit histories. But the banks were anything but troubled. They just kept securitizing the stuff, passing it off to investors around the world as a great deal while keeping great swathes of it for themselves. A handful of contrarians smelled the fumes of an impending meltdown, however. And they had a new weapon to bet against the mania since it had become legal in 2000 for investors to buy credit-default swaps on assets they didn't own. In other words, if you thought GM would go bust or mortgage bonds would fail you could buy "protection" against a risk you did not actually hold.[222] This meant that those who did not buy the real estate hype could make colossal wagers on the collapse of the American mortgage market. Precisely that is what happened, to the tune of billions upon billions of such bets by speculators, including a few inside the large Wall Street investment banks.[223]

CDSs on mortgage bonds had another perverse use. So insatiable was the appetite for mortgage-backed securities that Wall Street was having trouble producing enough of the stuff. In other words, housing loans were not being created fast enough to produce the mortgage-backed collateralized debt obligations (CDOs) that investors wanted. Why, reasoned the rocket scientists on Wall Street, should we not create synthetic CDOs, financial instruments that actually held no bits of real mortgages, but merely a package of credit-default swaps based on (or "derived" from) mortgages. In this case, an investor would "own" bets that mortgage holders would not default. So long as they did not do so, or at least not in large numbers, the holders of CDS-based bonds would get a cut of the fees that CDS purchasers paid. But should defaults mount, the holder of the synthetic CDO would quickly discover that what they really owned was a policy requiring them to compensate mortgage-bond holders for their losses. But until that day of reckoning arrived—which it did with explosive force in 2007–8—Wall Street gloried in having created a new "asset" to sell to investors who wanted in on the housing boom.

The extraordinary thing here was that, theoretically, there was no limit to the number of CDSs that could be generated on a mortgage-backed security. As long as someone wanted to buy insurance on these securities and pay the annual fees, which the seller would pocket, the market was unlimited. In fact, things eventually reached the point where by 2006 CDSs on mortgage bonds were eight times larger than the actual value of the bonds themselves. It was as if an infinite economy had been created in which endless numbers of people could buy a synthetic CDO derived from mortgages without actually owning any mortgages at all. This was fine so long as they simply pocketed the annual fees. But it also massively increased the size of the hit that would come should mortgage defaults ever take place on a large scale. A collapse of mortgage-backed securities to the tune of half a trillion dollars, for example, would result in losses eight times that size, i.e. $4 trillion.[224]

As we shall see in a moment, the creation of all this paper—an explosion in fictitious capital—also tremendously increased the risk to the banks that bought the mortgages and held them in "warehouses" (a variety of special banking entities) while it was packaged, priced and sold. If the moment came when the music stopped and all the chairs disappeared, the banks would be left holding billions of dollars worth of junk that could not be moved. Yet, so convinced of the inherent value of the stuff were the banks, that most actually wanted to hold tons of it— to devastating results.

The key problem for the banks (and shadow banks like hedge funds) was the classic capitalist dilemma of the falling rate of return. Too many banks were turning out too much of the same stuff, and profit margins were falling.[225] The almost universal response was for banks to increase leverage, i.e. to finance more and more of their business with borrowed funds, as this made it possible to expand the scale of their operations (to sell more units of junk) as a way of countering falling rates of return. In 2001, Merrill Lynch's leverage ratio was 16:1; in other words, it had borrowed $16 for every dollar it held in bank capital. By 2007 Merrill's ratio had doubled to 32:1. Morgan Stanley was at 33:1, as was Bear Stearns. Lehman Brothers stood at 29:1, and its leverage would eventually reach a mind-numbing 44:1.[226] Leverage on this scale dramatically increases the risk of bankruptcy. If creditors demand back just 3 percent of the loans of a company leveraged at 33:1, that firm will be effectively broke. Precisely this is what happened to Bear Stearns, Lehman Brothers and other banks in 2008. Moreover, it was not merely the U.S. financial industry that got caught up in the mania. Driven by their own real estate bubbles, banks in countries such as Britain, Iceland, Spain, South Korea, and Ireland went on even more manic lending sprees, driving overall debt levels even higher than in the U.S.[227]

And here we need to insist on something that is widely ignored in mainstream narratives of the crisis. The latter tend to blame the meltdown on the over-indebted consumer, the working class person who took on ever-rising levels of debts. Yet, as we have seen, it was the banks that pushed people to borrow, especially as interest rates fell from 2001 on. More than this, however, financial institutions took on debt at a much faster rate than did individuals. While consumer debt relative to GDP was doubling in the U.S. between 1980 and 2005, for instance, financial sector debt was more than quintupling, rendering the system ever more fragile in the event of an economic shock.[228] In short, bank debt (or leverage) was at the heart of the financial crisis.

Many critics have blamed bad risk management for these problems. To be sure, this was a huge issue, as we shall see. But the problems ran deeper. They grew out of systemic pressures that reduced banks' profit margins. With smaller returns on each "product," like a CDO, banks sought to compensate by selling more. Like any business, they had to borrow more to spend more—and this meant more leverage. And in an intensely competitive environment, bank borrowing just kept rising. When confronted by one of his partners about this bank's insane leverage ratio, Richard Fuld, chairman and CEO at Lehman, retorted: "Growth, growth, growth . . . That's what we want and need," as if he was mimicking Marx's satirical dictum, "Accumulate! Accumulate! That is Moses and the Prophets!"[229]

Many critics have similarly blamed banks for deliberately foisting toxic waste on unsuspecting investors. Again, there is truth to this. Deceit and manipulation were certainly widespread. But an exclusive focus on these misses the larger issue: banks actually believed their own formulas; they stuck by their idiotic risk assessment models and bought and held billions upon billions of the very mortgage-backed securities that would very nearly topple the world financial system. In short, as one commentator has noted, "there were more morons than crooks."[230]

"More Morons than Crooks": Risk, Number Fetishism, and the Global Meltdown

To get a sense of the sheer stupidity of Wall Street and of banks across the world, consider just how much toxic junk they kept on their own books. Of course, banks held onto some mortgage-backed securities for technical reasons that had to do with how the stuff was packaged. Most of this was classified as "super-senior" debt and considered to be risk-free. When the crash came, the giant bank UBS had $50 billion in this type of mortgage junk on its books. Other banks, such as Citigroup, were so confident in the stuff they were peddling that they included "liquidity puts" in the deals, which required them to buy the junk back in the event that markets for mortgage-backed securities ever froze up. Citi ended up having to repurchase $25 billion worth of toxic waste that had lost two-thirds of its value, resulting in losses of more than $16 billion. Astonishingly, some banks kept buying mortgages and trying to package and resell them even as the market was clearly collapsing. Lehman had about $80 billion in such securities that it could not move when the crash came. And other banks continued to sell credit-default swaps on mortgage backed CDOs—in other words, continued to take on all the default risk—even as the market was turning down. A single trader at Morgan Stanley, for instance, took on $16 billion in subprime mortgage risk between September 2006 and January 2007, when the steady rise in mortgage default rates was common knowledge. And then there is the extraordinary case of AIG, which sold $400 billion worth of credit-default swaps on mortgage-backed CDOs, and subsequently needed $175 billion from the U.S. taxpayer in order to survive.[231]

All of this demonstrates that there were indeed "morons" at the highest levels of the world's banks. More than this, it indicates just how moronic were the mathematical models these institutions used to measure risk. Extraordinary as it may sound, each and every one of these banks had invested tens or even hundreds of millions of dollars over the years in quantitative analysts, computer systems, and mathematical trading and risk assessment models. Not only did all of these fail the test of the market meltdown; they made matters dramatically worse.

Modern mathematical risk management techniques really took off amid the heightened volatility of the era of floating exchange rates, when investors turned to derivatives to minimize risk. But, as we have seen, these instruments not only assisted firms in reducing risk; they were also deployed for aggressive strategies of speculation which greatly *increase* risk by way of large, leveraged and computer-driven bets as to the movements of future prices for virtually anything. The immense speculative (and hence destabilizing) possibilities of derivatives reside in the way in which they monetize temporal shifts. We have seen how derivatives involve bets as to future values—of currencies, interest rates, stocks, bonds, etc. In this respect, they mirror the new world of global money. If, previously, money had some tie to values based on past labor (embodied in gold, which was stockpiled in treasuries and central banks) today it is largely linked to fictitious capitals, such as U.S. federal debt, denominated in bills and bonds sold by the U.S. Treasury. As a result, capitalists now try to price money and other paper assets in terms of future values, by calculating their anticipated prices at some point down the road—a day, a week, a month, and so on.

But how can future price movements be predicted? Modern financial theory thought it could answer this question by wedding formulas based on random movement in the physical world to the equilibrium assumptions of the Efficient Market Hypothesis, according to which all prices are rational reflections of actual value. It follows that, because existing prices are rational, the small, random movements that prices undergo will always tend to gravitate toward a stable center. Anything else would mean that existing prices are not rational—and this assumption is precluded from the start. Tracking price fluctuations, the mathematical models used in finance economics predict that small movements will soon be offset by predictable counter-movements back to earlier prices. Armed with such assumptions, these models construct a classic bell curve, which shows prices always tending toward the existing norm. If you plot the height of a thousand adults, the vast majority will be grouped quite closely together. Even the addition of a very short or tall person to your sample will barely budge the curve. Mathematical finance assumes the same thing about prices—they will always stay around the current norm. In so doing it takes models based on the physical world and assumes that financial markets will show the same regularity and stability.[232] But note: if the economic universe is not so stable and regular as assumed, then the models will completely malfunction in the event of a crisis, and the sharp swings in values and prices it brings. Put differently, mainstream economics has no inherent capacity to make sense of full-fledged breakdowns in equilibrium. Radical political economy, on the other hand, expects economic crises. But this is because it does not expect markets to be inherently stable, efficient, and rational. However, mainstream economics and its quantitative analysts ("quants") refuse to acknowledge the possibility of phenomena that violate the predictions their equilibrium models generate. Indeed, after the stock market crash of 1987, two quants offered a proof that it was statistically impossible—i.e. that what had happened could not have happened![233]

So, as banks were ramping up their leverage and accumulating billions of dollars worth of mortgage-backed CDOs, the quants kept running calculations of risk showing that all was well. Based on a concept known as Value at Risk (VaR), these calculations reduce all the various risks in the economy to a single number. And this means in essence that modern risk management operates with a notion of abstract risk.[234] Just as capitalism reduces all concrete acts of labor to abstract labor, just as it treats all unique use values as reducible to abstract value (measured in units of money), so it measures all risks as if they were just quantities of the same thing, risk in general. Indeed, the very essence of financial derivatives is that they try to price all possible risks on a single metric. This means that each and every risk—from the adverse effects of climate change on Florida's orange crop, to the likelihood that Evo Morales's government in Bolivia will nationalize the hydrocarbons industry, to the possibility of a housing crash in the U.S.—has to be computable as a certain quantity of (qualitatively undifferentiated) risk in general. Only in this way can modern financial techniques commodify risk, i.e. set a price for every conceivable purchasable asset based on the "amount" of risk it embodies.

So widespread have these models become that VaR is now the fundamental tool with which financial institutions and investors assess the riskiness of their investment portfolios. Over the past decade, in fact, it has also been the basis upon which banks set their own capital requirements. Using a set of models that share a common mathematical framework, VaR is supposed to measure literally any asset under any and all conditions. Crucial to the operation of VaR assessments is the assumption that all points in time are essentially the same and, therefore, that tomorrow will be just like yesterday and today. As a result, the timeframe upon which VaR measures are constructed rarely extend beyond a few weeks. Even "long-view" assessments, known as "histori-cal VaR," typically deploy data that stretch back only one or two years. In the summer of 2007, for instance, such models utterly discounted the possibility that house prices in the U.S. might stop rising steadily, never mind decline. After all, they had not done so during the recent past, the time period whose data were plugged into the models. Indeed the models used by the ratings agency Standard and Poor's, which declared toxic CDOs to be high quality (or AAA) investments, could not even accept a neg-ative number—in other words, they literally could not acknowl-edge the possibility that housing prices might ever decline.[235] Inherent in such models, therefore, is the reification of time, its treatment as a purely quantitative variable. It is as if time is always continuous and repetitive, and qualitative breaks or ruptures in the temporal continuum are inconceivable. By deploying reified, mathematical concepts of space and time joined to assumptions of market equilibrium, the models that guided derivative pricing and risk management were doomed to implode the moment a crisis emerged. In fact, the computerized trading programs kept telling firms to buy as the market started falling, thus massively amplifying losses in the midst of a full-fledged market meltdown.

It is especially shocking to realize that the writing in this area had long been on the wall. In 1998, for instance, world markets were rocked by the collapse of Long Term Capital Management (LCTM), a multi-billion dollar hedge fund that was run by two Nobel Prize winners, Myron Scholes and Robert Merton. Using Scholes's celebrated formula for derivatives pricing, LCTM made a massive bet that blew up in August 1998 when the firm lost a staggering $1.9 billion in a single month. Only a colossal inter-vention by fourteen global banks, orchestrated by the Federal Reserve, contained the system-wide damage. Two years later, Enron collapsed, largely as a result of horrifically bad derivatives deals. But still banks trudged on, clinging with religious fervor to their mathematical models and denying that a crisis was possible. When huge losses shook hedge funds in August 2007, the quants insisted that it was a once-in-ten-thousand-years event. Then it just kept happening—in complete defiance of the models—all the way through 2008, until $35 trillion in world stock holdings had evaporated. By this time even Alan Greenspan had to concede that "the whole intellectual edifice" of modern financial economics had "collapsed."[236]

More than an esoteric theory had collapsed, however. So had life savings, jobs, hopes, dreams, and more. Where the quants normally saw numbers and the zigs and zags of lines on charts, real human suffering lurked. Occasionally, even someone from Wall Street could get a fleeting glimpse of the underlying reality, as did the Lehman trader who wrote:

> Where I once stared at the zigzagging line, and just thought, *Up, down, win, lose, profit, crash, problem, solution, long, short, buy, sell*, now I see mostly people. Because every movement, up or down, has a meaning...
>
> I find myself thinking of the families of the people I knew so well... how lives were devastated, life savings obliterated.[237]

But the devastation experienced by Wall Street traders, which is all this commentator could grasp, does not even scratch the surface. Beyond Wall Street, people who have never bought a stock, eaten a $200 meal, or sent their children to a private school have known suffering and hardship on an inconceivable scale throughout the neoliberal era. The great fortunes of the neoliberal era were made at their expense. Now the Masters of the Universe will be coming for more—more of their labor, their hopes and dreams, their land and their natural resources. What kind of world emerges from this global slump will very much depend upon how successfully they resist these assaults.

CHAPTER FIVE

Debt, Discipline, and Dispossession: Race, Class, and the Global Slump

"Modern high-tech warfare is designed to remove physical contact: dropping bombs from 50,000 feet ensures that one does not 'feel' what one does. Modern economic management is similar: from one's luxury hotel, one can callously impose policies about which one would think twice if one knew the people whose lives one was destroying."
—Joseph Stiglitz, former chief economist for the World Bank[238]

AMONG OTHER THINGS, THE CAPITALIST MARKET IS A DISCIPLINARY system. By depriving people of access to the means of life except via money and the market, it creates the basis for modern work discipline. Function as an efficient, disciplined laborer, it decrees, or face the dire consequences: unemployment, poverty, and the insecurity, ill health, and hardship these entail. With these threats, capitalist market dependence tends to inculcate in workers the basic habits necessary to regular exploitation: time management (showing up to work regularly and on time); obedience (following the dictates of employers, managers, and supervisors); industriousness (working flat out); and financial responsibility (paying one's bills promptly and in full). Of course, workers regularly resist these impositions in a whole variety of ways, from coordinated collective responses (like strikes and slowdowns or participation in mass political protests) to small-scale acts of resistance, such as hidden defiance or shared jokes about puffed-up supervisors.

All of this is another way of saying that capitalism involves not just specific economic mechanisms, but a whole system of social relations. At the heart of these relations is the dispossession of the workers—the fact that they do not possess means of production (land, machines, or workplaces) that would allow them to produce the goods of life on their own. As a result, capitalism is a system of market compulsion in which laborers are compelled by the threat of hunger and poverty to sell their labor to an employer. That is why the employing class can appropriate the goods and services workers produce. As the owners of the means of production, capitalists have the legal right to claim workers' products. And because of this, workers find themselves regularly in a state of dispossession, lacking means of production with which to produce on their own. Capitalism is thus a system of alienation. What workers produce is taken from them, appropriated by those who own but do not labor. The very process of work is also an alienated one—controlled, dictated, and regulated by managers, supervisors, and foremen working for the owners. On top of all this, capitalism does its best to alienate the workers from one another, to keep them divided and fragmented so as to inhibit their ability to act in unified, collective ways.[239]

Such a system of social relations also involves certain cultural forms of life—habits and behaviors that must be instilled in people in order to reproduce these alienated social relations. From an early age, workers are taught discipline and obedience. Consider, for instance, that the two main social institutions regulated by the sound of bells are factories and schools. It is at school that children are first taught to regulate their lives by the clock, to defer to authority, to do what they are told. As part of deference to authority they are instructed that teachers are never to be questioned, police are to be glorified, and politicians, the rich, and the "stars" of the entertainment industry are to be treated as gods rather than mortals. The children of the poor—especially children of the racialized poor, along with girls and queers—have their "inferiority" hammered into them. Coming from poor neighborhoods, "the wrong side of the tracks," being of darker skin, having a "deviant" sexuality, not being a "man"—all of this is stigmatized. And lacking the clothes, cultural resources, manners, and "breeding" of the rich, working class children soon learn that they do not belong at the top. By treating such children as stupid, uncultured and deviant our society injures their dignity, frequently damaging their sense of self.[240] All the while it instructs them that the complicated business of running the world ought to be left to their "betters." Then, as yet another line of protection, the dominant institutions mock independent thought and critical inquiry, while penalizing and criminalizing defiance and rebellion. In all these ways, capitalism uses families, schools, the media, and criminal justice to inculcate the cultural practices and norms that keep the system ticking over.

In important measure, neoliberalism was a response to a perceived weakening of all these mechanisms—economic, social, and cultural—meant to impose and inculcate market discipline. After the Great Depression and the labor upsurge of the 1930s and '40s, working class pressure had compelled governments to introduce modest protections against unemployment and poverty. But as the Great Boom wound down, neoliberal pundits claimed that unemployment insurance, social assistance, and commitment to "full employment" had removed workers' fear and insecurity. They further declared that the social movements of the 1960s— civil rights, Black Power, women's liberation, indigenous radicalism, labor militancy, gay and lesbian activism, Third World liberation struggles—had undermined respect for authority and fostered a criminal rebelliousness. And they vowed to fix all this.

On the economic front, the Volcker Shock—and similar policies in countries from Britain to Bolivia—were designed to make employment more precarious, through mass layoffs, factory closures, public sector job cuts, and the replacement of full-time by part-time work. Alan Budd, chief economic advisor to former British prime minister Margaret Thatcher, was surprisingly forthright about all this. "Rising unemployment," he argued, "was a very desirable way of reducing the strength of the working class . . . What was engineered—in Marxist terms—was a crisis in capitalism which re-created a reserve army of labor, and has allowed the capitalists to make high profits ever since."[241] In short, generate unemployment and you will curb workers' powers of resistance. By fostering job insecurity in these ways, a new political climate was engineered, one designed to buttress market discipline. Through the media and the pronouncements of politi-

cians, a cultural atmosphere was created that disparaged noncon-
formity and rebellion while extolling obedience and respect for
those in power. A law and order regime, to be discussed below,
threatened those who challenged authority. TV shows glorify-
ing cops became the rage. In all these ways, people were warned
of the severe risks involved in standing up to dictatorial managers, organizing a union, or going on strike. Do any of the above,
came the message, and you could easily be replaced. All of which
reminds us that, notwithstanding the force of economic coercion
imposed by market dependence, capitalism has always required
an intricate web of social, political, and legal coercion organized
in and through the state.

Fundamental to intensified state coercion was a get-tough
"law and order" regime that was backed up by increasingly militarized policing. Poor communities of color suffered an invasion of ever more brutal and intrusive policing; radical political
movements were infiltrated and harassed, their members frequently jailed on trumped up charges and, in the case of groups
like the Black Panther Party, chillingly murdered. Schools in poor
communities were subjected to heightened surveillance and dramatically increased police presence (in the U.S. this has included
jails in schools). And on the street level, those who hang around,
gather on corners, and generally do not lead the disciplined lives
of the neoliberal era are immediately suspect and liable to be
confronted by police, their very mode of life deemed suspicious.
Not that any of this is new. But it was a return to (and an intensification of) older forms of keeping poor, working class people in
line. Once again, it was truly a *neo*-liberalism, the revival of policies and practices that had characterized capitalism in its early
(classically liberal) phase.

During the rise of capitalism in Britain, for instance, workers
who were dispossessed did not automatically accept the harsh
regimes of wage-labor. They could regularly be found squatting
on common lands, where they hunted, fished, picked berries,
gathered firewood, built shelters, and occasionally stole from the
rich—just the images we have from traditional Robin Hood stories. Sometimes they formed traveling bands of peddlers, trou-

badours, entertainers, and itinerant laborers, crisscrossing the countryside in groups, frequently sleeping in the open air. And in some places and times they simply occupied public space to request alms from their neighbors.

Britain's rulers were both unnerved by the independence of these crowds and determined to crush their survival strategies. One way or another, industrial work discipline would be imposed upon these rowdy, boisterous, self-reliant communities of dispossessed people. And so the ruling class erected a system of draconian legislation that licensed beating, whipping, branding, chaining, severing of ears, and imprisonment for those who begged, stole, or were of "idle" disposition. In all these ways, observed Marx, "were the agricultural folk first forcibly expropriated from the soil, driven from their homes, turned into vagabonds, and then whipped, branded and tortured by grotesquely terroristic laws into accepting the discipline necessary for wage-labour."[242] To be sure, when capitalist market relations become widely normalized, states do not regularly have to behave in such blatantly brutal ways to keep their work forces in line. Much can be left to the quiet violence of the capitalist economy in which dispossession (owning no productive assets except for one's ability to work) compels people to submit to the unyielding disciplinary regimes of wage-labor.

But while much can be left to market discipline, not everything can. That is why law, police, prisons, and direct force remain omnipresent. Indeed, the intensified disciplinary regimes of the neoliberal period—punitive laws against panhandling or sleeping in parks, widespread incarceration of those found with small bits of drugs, harsher street-level policing and jail terms, and ever more people stuffed into prisons—are sharp reminders that the coercive powers of the state will be regularly mobilized every time the "work ethic" and social discipline seem to be waning.

Essential to such efforts are strategies meant to make it less and less possible to survive outside the labor market. Typically, these strategies have been couched in terms of making our streets safer, as if unemployed youth, lacking meaningful facilities in which to gather for conversation and recreation, are the problem.

In California, a mid-1980s Task Force on youth gangs defined the problem of unemployed youth on the streets as "street terrorism." And the 1988 law it spawned bore the ominous title Street Terrorism Enforcement and Prevention (STEP) Act.²⁴³ In Ontario, Canada's largest province, an exceptionally mean-spirited neoliberal government borrowed the same rhetoric. Having cancelled all social housing and cut welfare rates by 22.6 percent, it introduced a so-called "Safe Streets Act" meant to protect ostensibly endangered citizens from panhandlers and "squeegee kids," who wanted to clean their car windshields for a small price. The perceived threat had nothing to do with public safety or fear of clean windshields, but much to do with efforts to criminalize social groups who sought out alternatives to wage-labor. Among other things, people who do not conform with the disciplines of wage-labor violate the spatial relations of the neoliberal city. Street people, panhandlers, squeegeers, and others tend to gather in public space; they put their own distinctive stamp on parts of the city. In so doing, they collide with the sanitizing mission of neoliberalism, which seeks to present cities as spaces for investment, real estate development, and high-end consumption in classy restaurants, nightclubs, museums, galleries, and more. This is why neoliberal urbanism has been so concerned with segregating and hiding the poor and with criminalizing the non-conforming. Property values and sites of luxury consumption pivot on exiling the poor, on a sort of social cleansing that segregates poor, marginalized, and "deviant" groups. Law and policing have figured decisively in enacting such segregation.

So, new laws would be written, police mobilized, and fines and jail terms imposed to close off alternatives to wage-labor and to remove the "undesired" from bourgeois view. It is instructive in this regard that, for all their talk of "freedom," neoliberals' preferred disciplinary institution has been the prison: it is there that the "undisciplined," particularly young people of color, are to be taught the price of not functioning as obedient cogs in the machinery of capitalist production. In this spirit, a "law and order" crusade has been fashioned, involving draconian policies like three-strikes laws in many U.S. states (under which a third conviction, irrespective of the seriousness of the previous ones, requires harsh jail sentences), joined to tougher conditions for bail and probation and longer sentences. Meanwhile, police and security guards pour into schools with a special mission to hammer on youth of color, as a reminder that discipline and control, not education, are the priorities. So obscene can this get that one predominantly African-American high school in New Orleans had thirty-four security guards compared to twenty-one teachers.[244] Multiple institutions of coercion—from the sweatshop and the locked-down school to the penitentiary—thus intersect in a program designed to impose market discipline by force.[245]

As neoliberals have pursued their disciplinary agenda, law enforcement budgets have soared, while police forces have been militarized, acquiring helicopters, assault weapons, tasers, and more. State spending on prisons has persistently risen, while social welfare programs have been slashed. Notwithstanding falling crime rates, prison building has been a boom-time industry—California has pursued "the largest prison building program in the history of the world" across the neoliberal era—while rates of incarceration have also jumped.[246] Under the guise of a so-called "war on drugs," militarized policing has been imposed on poor and racialized communities across the U.S., as well as countries like Mexico and Colombia. As Ruth Wilson Gilmore has powerfully shown, imprisonment has become the preferred neoliberal form of social control of largely racialized "surplus populations." It is prisons—not schools or even job training programs—that secure the disciplinary ethos of neoliberalism. As a result, while crime rates have fallen, the U.S. has witnessed a 450 percent expansion of its prison population since 1980.[247]

The growth in this prison population during the neoliberal era is staggering. In 1972, the U.S. prison-industrial complex held three hundred thousand inmates; by 2000, the number had hit two million. Today, well over seven million people in the U.S. are in prison, on probation, or on parole.[248] Following in these tracks, the Canadian government has embarked on a $10 billion prison expansion and retrofitting program joined to increased incarceration and longer sentences—despite the fact that crime rates are falling and that government programs that assist the poor are being slashed.[249] All of this is about class discipline. But it is also about racial oppression. Given its constitution in and through colonialism, slavery, and extermination of indigenous peoples, capitalist class formation has been inseparable from the social organization of race and racism. Specific populations—Africans, Asians, the Irish, and the indigenous peoples of the Americas— were subjected to ruthless, even murderous regimes of pillage and brutality, consistently justified by doctrines of racial inferiority. "The discovery of gold and silver in America, the extirpation, enslavement and entombment in mines of the indigenous population of that continent, the beginnings of the conquest and plunder of India, and the conversion of Africa into a preserve for the commercial hunting of black skins, are all things which characterize the dawn of the era of capitalist production," wrote Marx.[250] However, Marx was less clear about the ways in which integral to all these horrors was the construction of systemic racism, a mode of white supremacy, which sustained and reinforced these methods of racialized accumulation.[251] Moreover, as a number of social critics have shown, these violent processes of dispossession are continually re-enacted across the history of capitalism.[252] And because they operate within neocolonial and imperial circuits of global power, these processes continue to ooze racism, even if the latter assumes new forms and is enacted through changing social practices. In fact, America's contemporary "criminal justice" regime is one of the foremost indicators of the enduring presence of systemic racism in the neoliberal era. In the U.S. today, after all, two-thirds of all people incarcerated are Black or Latino. Meanwhile, one in every three African-American men is in prison or under some form of criminal surveillance, such as probation or parole. Similarly, in Canada native men are 25 times more likely to be in a provincial jail than are non-native men; and native women are 131 times more likely to find themselves locked up than their non-native counterparts.[253]

Policing and imprisonment are thus among the most overtly racialized features of late capitalism. But they are just the tip of the iceberg, below which resides a vast web of racially organized social practices. Indeed, the social organization of debt markets, which figure so centrally to the recent crisis of the neoliberal economy, is another key domain of the exploitative practices of racialized capitalism.

"Predatory Inclusion": Race, Debt and Dispossession

Debt, of course, is one of the most ancient forms of economic exploitation. Across millennia, the poor have often needed to borrow from the rich—particularly during times of drought, famine, and war—in order to buy food, seed, livestock, or tools. But woe to those who cannot repay. In one class-based society after another, lenders have had the legal right to exact harsh retribution from delinquent borrowers. In ancient Egypt, Greece, and Rome, failure to repay frequently resulted in debt bondage, a state of outright enslavement, where the debtor could be physically seized and turned over to the lender. Roman landlords often kept private prisons for those unable to repay, and they could legally keep them in chains. Indeed, during some periods Roman law allowed lenders to chop a debtor into pieces and divide up the body parts.[254]

Capitalism transformed debt relations in significant ways. While creditors could seize assets—such as homes, personal belongings and future earnings—the bodies of debtors themselves were generally off limits, though pawnbrokers and loan sharks who might break your legs continue to prey on those turned away by the banks. Most importantly, large institutions like banks became the primary lenders, rather than rich landlords. Large-scale lending by banks came to revolve around lending to businesses to help finance investments. In these cases, banks loan funds that other capitalists will use to exploit labor and produce goods. Banks then receive back a share of capitalist profits as interest payments—which makes bank loans a form of interest-bearing capital.[255] Yet, as capitalist credit systems became more sophisticated, workers were increasingly drawn into their orbit by way of consumer credit and mortgage lending. And during the neoliberal period, workers in the Global North in particular have been inserted more thoroughly into financial circuits than ever before. As the reproduction of working class households in the North have become more dependent on credit cards, mortgages, and bank loans, they have been more deeply integrated into financial markets. The stagnation of working class incomes in the neoliberal period is part of the reason for this. As virtually all the gains of economic expansion went to capital and the rich, and household income stagnated or declined, workers frequently borrowed to make ends meet. At the same time, neoliberal cuts to social programs—from healthcare and education to pensions and social housing—forced workers into markets for these services. Private healthcare and pension plans boomed, and workers often turned to home loans (mortgages) to address housing needs. But alongside home loans, probably nothing better indicates the growing financialization of households than the manic proliferation of credit cards. By the end of 2009, for instance, more than 576 million credit cards were in use in the U.S., representing an average of three and a half per cardholder. On these cards, the average American household held $15,788 in debt—loans that come with a variety of user fees and exorbitant interest rates.[256]

But working class reliance on debt to make ends meet is only one part of the story. For it is not just that workers needed more loans to maintain living standards; as we have seen, banks also needed more borrowers to generate increased profits. In recent decades therefore banks moved aggressively to sell more and larger loans to individuals, frequently at extortionate rates. In fact, many large global banks now have more than half of their loan portfolios devoted to lending to individuals via credit cards, mortgages, and consumer loans.[257] Some commentators have naively observed the rise of "the investor subject," as people ostensibly learn to manage their "assets" by behaving as if they were small businesses.[258] But this is to miss the structural inequalities involved in the relations between individual wage earners and giant financial institutions. For the reality is that in these interactions "the flexible, downsized, mobile and contracted-out worker" faces off against "a specialist in managing money-flows trying to maximize profits."[259] In the process, the stressed-out worker, desperate for additional funds, is subjected to a sort of financial expropriation via high interest rates and service fees.[260] The so-called "investor subject" is thus a financially exploited subject. So lucrative are these stressed-out workers for the banks that they went prowling for as many of them as they could find.

Here, however, efforts to expand lending to individuals collided with enduring histories of racial exclusion, particularly in the United States. Mortgage-borrowing in America has historically observed racial covenants under which white homeowners would collude not to sell to people of color. Laws were even passed protecting the rights of sellers to discriminate without having to show cause.[261] This kind of segregation dovetailed with "red-lining" practices where banks would not lend to individuals and households in areas that had been outlined in red on maps—areas that just happened to be populated principally by African-Americans and Latinos.[262] To make matters worse, the financial services industry has a history of systematic discrimination against women, constructing them as less worthy wage earners and borrowers. Women of color have thus borne the brunt of this ill-treatment, a point to which we shall return.

Determined to increase loans to individual borrowers, American banks soon realized that these gendered and racialized lending practices were limiting profits. As recently as 2002, for instance, fully 20 percent of all U.S. households (half of them white) did not have a bank account. Huge numbers of these individuals were paying lucrative fees—totaling more than $6 billion a year—to storefront services that cash checks or offer payday loans, which advance cash for an average 18 percent cut of workers' paychecks.[263] Recognizing the upsides of expanding their business with such people, banks moved toward forms of predatory inclusion, through which poor people of color in particular are offered financial services they had previously been denied—but on severely extortionate terms. Consequently, while all workers have been subjected to new levels of "financial expropriation" by financial institutions, racial minorities have found themselves incorporated into especially rapacious forms of financialization.

For the least "credit-worthy," according to the gendered and racialized criteria of the financial services industry, predatory incorporation has involved punitive interest rates on credit cards and exorbitant fees for late payments and bounced checks. Indeed, in 2003 financial institutions earned a whopping $22 billion for NSF checks alongside $57 billion in late payment charges.[264] Meanwhile, they also raked it in hand over fist on credit card debt. Not surprisingly, this hit poor people of color especially hard, as individuals from such households rely most on credit cards for "survival spending," like groceries and other necessities.[265] But for sheer financial extortion, little compares to the manipulative use of subprime mortgages among Latino and African-American borrowers.

And here we must remind ourselves that it was the lenders who most wanted these loans—because of the higher fees they earned—and they pushed them aggressively, even on to people who qualified for traditional mortgages. In fact, fully 60 percent of those who received subprime loans actually qualified for less onerous mortgages.[266] These predatory loans went disproportionately to people of color. By 1998, for example, subprime mortgages comprised one-third of all home loans made to African-Americans and a fifth of those made to Latinos. And the numbers just kept rising. By 2005, 70 percent of all subprime loans made in Washington, D.C., went to African-Americans. A year later, African-Americans received 41 percent of all subprime mortgages in New York, while 29 percent went to Latinos. Women of color were especially vulnerable to subprime extortion.[267] Inevitably, as the mortgage rates on these loans kicked higher it became increasingly difficult for the borrowers to make payments, especially as job loss soared, especially among workers of color, reducing people's capacity to pay.

But the original lenders could not have cared less. After all, by the time things went sour these mortgages would have been sold off to an investment bank, repackaged, and sold on as a collateralized debt obligation (CDO). The holders of the mortgage-backed securities thus carried the risk, some of which they in turn could sell off by buying credit-default swaps. But until the day of reckoning arrived, CDOs on subprime mortgages looked hugely attractive. After all, the holders of subprime mortgages would typically pay between $50,000 and $100,000 more than a prime mortgage, all of which went to those who owned sub-prime-based CDOs.[268]

Worse, these mortgages were building up in a black community that was steadily becoming poorer. One of the central features of neoliberalism, after all, has been compression of working class incomes. And racially oppressed working class communities have been hit hardest by this phenomenon. Indeed, despite all the euphoric talk of the great prosperity of the 2000s, the decade was nothing of the sort for African-Americans. Between 2000 and 2007, when the crisis hit, black employment declined by 2.4 percent and black incomes dropped nearly 3 percent. At the same time, subprime loans bled between $71 and $93 billion in wealth from black households between 1998 and 2006. Latino households have been similarly pummeled, their median income contracting up to $3,000 per household between the late 1980s and 1996.[269] The roots of the mortgage meltdown lie here: not in financial markets per se, but in declining employment and incomes in working class communities of color that were now struggling with the extortionate terms of subprime loans. Over-lending in real estate thus intersected with falling incomes for over-leveraged workers and those experiencing job loss, especially workers of color, to create a crisis. And as job loss mounted once recession set in, things went downhill with shocking speed. By 2009, 60 percent of foreclosures were the direct result of job loss. And rising foreclosures drove down housing prices further, leading to yet higher losses on mortgage-based securities, which further weakened the banks. The tidal wave of job loss soon swept prime borrowers into its vortex. So much so that by mid-2010 nearly 40 percent of those behind on their mortgages were highly qualified borrowers.[270] The deep structural issue, in other words, has to do with the dialectics of race and class in a neoliberal capitalism increasingly reliant on debt-fuelled spending. And the damage inflicted by the global slump obeys the same biases: working class people of color suffer the most.

The glaringly racialized effects of the slump also run through the data on job loss and poverty. Astonishingly, four out of every ten African-Americans experienced unemployment during the

Great Recession of 2008–9. Throughout the first half of 2010, official unemployment among blacks was over 16 percent, while among Latinos it hovered around 13 percent. In thirty-five of America's largest cities, official jobless rates for blacks were between 30 and 35 percent—levels equal to the worst days of the Great Depression. Adding in workers who are involuntarily underemployed—working part-time or seasonally because they cannot find full-time work—we arrive at a combined un-employment and under-employment rate for black and Latino workers of 25 percent. Not surprisingly, blacks and Latinos are almost three times more likely to live in poverty as whites. It is shocking enough to realize that half of all U.S. children now depend on food stamps at some point during their childhood; but it is utterly devastating to learn that the figure jumps to 90 percent for black children. Inevitably, differential poverty is reflected in the distribution of wealth: blacks have 10 cents of net worth for every dollar of white net worth, and Latinos have 12 cents of net worth for every dollar of white net worth. Once again, the most grotesque inequalities afflict women of color. Single black women in the U.S. have $100 in net wealth, excluding vehicles, while Latino women have $120—compared to median wealth of $41,500 for single white women. And loss of homes is making all of this worse, as 56 percent of African-Americans who bought homes in 2006 have already been foreclosed upon.[271]

All of this proves the claim that the incorporation of poor people of color into financial markets has been utterly predatory in character. Having suffered ongoing financial expropriation in the form of onerous interest rates and service fees, workers of color in the U.S. are losing homes faster than any other group. Debt, in other words, has become a weapon of dispossession. In this regard, working class people of color in America are experiencing something that has been all too common for peoples of the Global South throughout the neoliberal era.

Debt, Discipline and Dispossession in the Global South
As we have seen, the growth of unregulated international banking in the 1960s, set the context for an explosion of lending to

governments in the Third World. Hundreds of billions of "stateless" dollars circuited through the Eurodollar market, and the banks that held them sought out eager borrowers. These were the early days of financial globalization. In 1960, for instance, only eight U.S. banks had overseas branches, and their assets totaled merely $3.5 billion. By 1978, however, 140 U.S. banks had 750 foreign operations, and these were bringing in half of all profits.[272] International bank lending rose by 25 percent or more per year, much of it to governments in the Third World. In the decade after 1973, Third World debt to global banks quintupled, rising by nearly half a trillion dollars. Then came the Volcker Shock. As interest rates soared, one government after another in the Global South could not meet their payments. Mexico defaulted first, followed within months by Argentina, Poland, Chile, Peru, and Venezuela. Enter the U.S. government and the International Monetary Fund. Through a series of "debt restructurings," the private banks got all their money back as Third World debt was effectively transferred to the IMF, the World Bank, and western governments. Along the way, the western powers also came up with the idea of "debt for equity" swaps, allowing creditors to claim actual assets, i.e. ownership of companies or resources in exchange for the money they were owed. In this way, accumulation by dispossession became explicit policy, and more and more of the enduring wealth of societies in the Global South was simply expropriated by global financial institutions.[273]

Foreign debt has been a phenomenal means of dispossession and expropriation. Perversely, no matter how much countries in the South paid, their total debt just kept growing. Between 1980 and 2002, the developing countries made $4.6 trillion in debt payments. This represents about eight times what they owed at the beginning of this period ($580 billion in 1980). Yet, after making these payments, thanks to the magic of interest, they now owed $2.4 trillion. In other words, twenty-two years on, and more than four and half trillion dollars in debt payments later, they were four times as indebted as when they started in 1980.[274] The human consequences have been staggering. In recent decades, the most impoverished region in the world, sub-Saharan Africa, has paid

out about half a billion dollars *a day* in debt payments, despite a
25 percent decline in per capita incomes between 1987 and 2000,
and heartbreaking rates of infant mortality and epidemic death
rates due to HIV-AIDS, malaria, tuberculosis, and more. Half a
million people on the African subcontinent die of tuberculosis
every year, even though a six-month curative treatment costs a
mere $15.[275] Yet, billions in debt payments keep exiting the region.

One might be forgiven for hoping that the horror story would
stop there. But it does not. This is because, in order to make these
ongoing debt payments, governments in the South have had to
borrow over and over again from the IMF and the World Bank.
And these institutions only lend subject to strict conditions, or
what is known as IMF conditionalities, which do untold damage
to these societies and their peoples.

IMF conditions take the form of the now infamous structural
adjustment programs (SAPs) that have ravaged the Global South.
A typical SAP, whose terms are dictated by IMF officials to the
finance ministry of the adjusted country, contains harshly neoliberal policies like the following: privatization of public assets
(water systems, mines, airlines, electricity companies, and so on);
radical cuts to social service spending and layoffs to thousands
of teachers, nurses, social workers, and the like, all of which
deprives the poor of vital services; removal of subsidies on prices
of essentials (such as rice, grain, and heating oil); opening up the
financial sector to foreign ownership (which typically produces a
financial crisis within a few years); privatization of land (leading
to displacement of peasant farmers by agribusiness, eco-tourism,
and mining and oil companies); and labor market "reforms" that
push down minimum wages, benefits, and pensions, and weaken
unions.[276] The results are entirely predictable: wages fall; the poor
get poorer; employment gets more precarious; multinationals
buy up public assets on the cheap; foreign banks establish control of finance; local and global elites move fortunes out of the
country ("capital flight"); economic growth declines; education
and health standards plummet; infant mortality rates rise; and
the rural poor are pushed off the land. During the 1980s and '90s,
around one hundred nations were structurally adjusted. And vir-

tually everywhere the pattern has been the same. Nevertheless, the IMF, World Bank, and western governments insist economic progress is being made as a result. The facts tell a different story, as the following table indicates.

Table 5.1—Average Annual Growth in Income per Person, 1960–79 and 1980–2005

	1960–79	1980–2005
Latin America	+4%	+0.7%
Sub-Saharan Africa	+1.8%	−0.75%

Source: Data derived from Center for Economic Policy Research, *The Scorecard on Development* (Washington, 2005)

This table clearly demonstrates that neoliberal policies of structural adjustment have been associated with drastically reduced rates of economic growth in the Global South. Latin America has experienced a sharp decline while sub-Saharan Africa has undergone a quarter-century-long contraction. The results in Africa have been catastrophic. In the fifteen years after 1975, per capita spending on healthcare in Africa was chopped in half. Disease rates have skyrocketed, killing children on a massive scale and savagely cutting life expectancy. One million Africans die of malaria every year, 70 percent of them children under five. By 2010 life expectancy had fallen by seventeen years on average in nine African countries: Kenya, South Africa, Mozambique, Zambia, Rwanda, Malawi, Zimbabwe, and Namibia. In seven southern African countries life expectancy has dropped below forty years.[277]

While the data is not so cataclysmic for Latin America, there too we have seen the globalization of poverty across the neoliberal period, with real incomes contracting for the vast majority. Take Mexico, the country that was promised great gains from integration with the Canadian and American economies via the North American Free Trade Agreement (NAFTA). Instead, the minimum wage has fallen by 40 percent; the best-paid workers have suffered an 18 percent cut in income; hundreds of thousands have been forced off the land; and 80 million people now live below the poverty line. Meanwhile, 0.3 percent of the population controls 50 percent of Mexico's wealth.[278]

Lest Mexico be seen as an exception, take the case of Argentina, a country whose standard of living once rivaled those of many nations in the "developed" world. During the lending spree by global banks to Third World governments, the military dictators who ran Argentina were preferred customers. From the dictatorship's start in March 1976, Argentina's foreign debt multiplied roughly twenty times during the next quarter-century, rocketing from $8 billion to $160 billion by 2001. Rather than contributing to "development," as the rhetoric had it, the country's dictators and their big business cronies simply salted this money away in foreign investments and bank accounts. Across the years when this $150 billion ostensibly flowed into Argentina, it was in fact being deposited into private bank accounts in the U.S. Yet, despite the fact that much of it was contracted by military dictators who did not even provide the central bank with records of their borrowing, the people of Argentina have been squeezed and structurally adjusted in order to pay it back. In the two decades after 1970, for instance, wages fell from 40 percent of national income to less than a quarter. Predictably, poverty rates rose catastrophically.[279] A far-reaching program of privatization saw the country's national airline and public mining companies, among many others, sold off for tiny fractions of what they were worth. Estimates suggest that the public treasury took a $60 billion loss as a result of the privatizations of 1990–92. But worse was to come. The sale of the national airline in 1997 (overseen by Wall Street investment bank Merrill Lynch) saw the company's rights over routes, valued at $800 million, sold for less than a tenth of that ($60 million), while its fleet of Boeing 707s went for $1.54—that's right, just over a dollar and a half. Yet, even this was not enough to pay back the debts contracted by the generals and their corporate friends. Next, salaries and pensions were further cut by 30 percent in early 2002. By this point, unemployment had reached 20 percent and half the population was living below the poverty line.[280] This is what it means, as the quote that opens this chapter suggests, when neoliberal bureaucrats in luxury hotel rooms drop economic bombs (SAPs) on people. But this time they miscalculated—for by this point a huge social upheaval was sweeping Argentina, toppling three presidents in a matter of months, a story we pick up in the next chapter.

The sad saga of Third World privatization is a reminder that debt is being used here as a weapon of dispossession. Across Latin America, public oil and mining companies and their huge mineral and oil and gas deposits have been turned over to foreign capitalists, as have electricity and water companies, railroads, airlines, and even hospitals—all as part of generating revenues to repay debts contracted by dictators and antidemocratic politicians. Repeatedly, poor workers, peasants and indigenous peoples in the Global South have been compelled to sacrifice for the borrowing of these despots—by way of job loss, reduced wages, cuts to healthcare, education, and social assistance, and the human suffering that comes with them. And now, as the world slump persists, countries in the Global North too are being structurally adjusted—and their populations hammered in the process. "The IMF is back in business," wrote *Financial Times* columnist Martin Wolf in the early days of the financial crisis.[281] Already, twenty nations, including Latvia, Iceland, Hungary, Pakistan, the Ukraine, and Greece have been subjected to economic discipline by the IMF as a condition of urgent loans since the crisis erupted. Meanwhile other western governments are preemptively structurally adjusting themselves. We have seen in chapter 1 just how savage cuts to pensions, jobs, healthcare, and education have been in Ireland, the United States, Spain, and elsewhere. But more, much more is in store, including the dispossession of public assets. Indeed, in June 2010 Greece announced that it will sell off a railway company, the national post office, two water companies, and more to help pay back debts to world banks.[282]

The use of debt to seize economic assets and resources began in earnest with the Latin American debt crisis of 1982. But it was then extended to the seizure of private assets with the Asian Crisis of 1997, which kick-started a succession of crises from Russia and Brazil (1998–99) to Argentina and Turkey (2000–2002) and culminated in the global financial meltdown of 2008. As each crisis rattled global markets, interest rates on foreign debts rose steeply. This only exacerbated the outflow of wealth from debtor nations.

In fact, between 1998 and 2002 alone, well over half a trillion dollars exited so-called developing nations for banks in the North.[283] If the looting of the national treasury in debtor nations had previously been the norm, during East Asia's crisis foreign multinationals exploited the weakened financial position of private corporations to snap them up on the cheap. Korean firms in steel, autos, construction equipment, and electronics were gobbled up in a vulture-like frenzy involving perhaps "the biggest peacetime transfer of assets from domestic to foreign owners in the past fifty years anywhere in the world."[284] I say "perhaps" because it may very well have been eclipsed by the ferocious dispossession that has transpired in Russia and China.

Russia was the site of the next great regional crisis that rocked global markets. Not that asset expropriation began then; that had started with the 1989 collapse of the ugly Stalinist regimes of Eastern Europe. But while the people sought to use that moment for democratic change, vulture capital from the West seized it for a feeding frenzy, aided and abetted by many of the state bureaucrats who had presided over the years of Stalinist repression. Asset raiding began in earnest with the 1992 introduction of market-oriented "shock therapy" in Russia, aggressively promoted by the IMF, the U.S. government, and a coterie of Harvard economists. Prices were deregulated and factories, mines, and enterprises privatized as rapidly as possible. Fully three-quarters of all large and medium enterprises were auctioned off in less than three years. Gold mines, oil and gas fields, Siberian forests, steel and electrical goods factories, diamond mines, and more were grabbed by a new business elite, which quickly sold them to foreign capitalists, stashing around $150 billion of the proceeds in foreign bank accounts.[285] As assets were raided and money fled, the Russian economy underwent a horrifying collapse. Between 1992 and 1995, the country's gross domestic product plummeted by 42 percent, and incomes dropped in tandem. Virtually overnight, an industrial economy was transformed into a natural resource exporter. By 1998, 40 percent of the population was living on less than $4 per day and life expectancy was plunging. Amazingly, some other Eastern European nations had done even worse. By 2000, for instance, similar processes had left Ukraine's GDP a mere one-third of what it had been ten years earlier.[286]

Then came the crisis of 1998 and the Russian economy dropped like an elevator whose cables have been cut. As lenders fled, the Russian government was compelled to pay an interest rate of 150 percent on loans backed by its government bonds and 50 percent on dollar-backed loans. Then the IMF stepped in with an international lending package that, predictably, left the economy in much worse shape and foreign debts that much higher, thus locking in persistent capital outflows.[287]

The Russian case exhibits "gangster capitalism" in all its ignominy. From a shock and awe program of market reform had emerged a pure and simple system of asset raiding for the benefit of a "new bourgeoisie" that "socked their loot away in secret western bank accounts or squandered it on yachts and villas on the French Riviera."[288] As appalling as this behavior has been, the Russian plunder still does not come close to the extraordinary scale of mass dispossession that has accompanied China's transition to market-style capitalism.

China's turn to the market has also pivoted on an extensive privatization program that provided enormous opportunities for looting. As state enterprises were sold off, the valuable assets of state firms were purchased by insiders—government officials and enterprise managers in particular—who left their debts with the government and the banks. Reasonable estimates suggest that the public sector has been losing assets at a *daily* rate of up to $50 billion.[289] In the process, a new class of Chinese tycoons, frequently linked to capitalists in Hong Kong, has transformed state assets into huge private fortunes. One of the biggest prizes in all of this is land. And, as has been the case since the rise of capitalism, privatization of land—or its enclosure by capital—dispossessed peasants and transformed them into proletarians.

In China's case, land privatization is literally about enclosing the commons. Prior to marketization, agricultural communes owned most rural land.[290] The market reform process broke up this communal land system. Agricultural production was decollectivized, market pricing was introduced, and private ownership of land was promoted.[291] At the same time, rural health care and education systems were gutted, thereby increasing the pressures on peasants to turn to the market to raise cash to pay for formerly public goods. As capitalist market relations took hold in the countryside, an active land market emerged, creating tremendous opportunities for plunder and profit. Commodification of land in turn induced waves of expropriation of rural land by factory owners, urban planners, real estate developers, ruthless speculators, and government officials in league with foreign corporations, all seizing an increasingly valuable asset. Much of this expropriation was technically illegal, but law and the courts have tended to legalize such theft, much as Britain's Parliament did in the case of the rural enclosure movement of the eighteenth-century.[292] Together, land grabbing, forced eviction, and rural impoverishment have displaced hundreds of millions of people in China. Indeed, the Chinese government estimated in 2004 that 114 million people had already exited the countryside, fleeing poverty and expropriation in search of employment as migrant workers in the cities. Some government experts believe the number of displaced, landless workers will hit 300 million by 2020 and eventually reach 500 million.[293]

Dispossession, Enclosure, War, and Displacement

What we are witnessing in China, in other words, is the most gigantic process of "primitive accumulation" in world history. Dispossessed peasants, driven from the land, are being transformed into urban proletarians on an unprecedented scale—literally in the hundreds of millions, massively exceeding the scale of the earliest process of original accumulation in Britain.[294] In the twenty-five years after 1978, China's employed working class tripled, growing from 120 million to 350 million.[295] Huge numbers of these workers—perhaps 150 million at present—are rural migrants, lacking the right to residency and to health care and education in the cities in which they work. And, as we have seen, hundreds of millions more will be on the move in the coming years, as market relations continue to remake the Chinese countryside.

Moreover, displacement is not just a rural phenomenon in China. As the real estate market booms and land prices rise, older working class residents are also being driven out of their homes in urban centers. Between 1990 and 2007, a million and a quarter residents were evicted from plebeian quarters of Beijing to make way for upscale housing, shopping malls, high-end restaurants, and Olympic construction projects.[296] Similar processes of displacement have been engineered in Shanghai, including mass demolitions of traditional housing in preparation for the city's 2010 Expo, in some cases to provide space for the likes of Starbucks and Krispy Kreme donuts.[297] Not surprisingly, dispossession of this sort has sparked protest and pitched battles in a rising stream of clashes over land grabs.

That other ostensible economic success story of our moment, India, has also been the site of significant battles over land and displacement. When talking about the Indian "miracle," it is worth reminding ourselves that, while the country has certainly produced its super rich—forty wealthy Indians were worth a total of over $350 billion in 2007, or nearly $9 billion apiece—more than three-quarters of the population lives on less than $2 per day. The *Global Hunger Index 2008* reports that 200 million Indians suffer from hunger. Notwithstanding all the hype about India's booming economy, the country's ranking in the U.N. Human Development Index has actually fallen—to 134th place today.[298] In this context, land expropriations have sparked major confrontations in states such as Punjab, Jharkhand, Orissa, Maharashtra, and Gujarat, among others. In Orissa, tribal peoples at Kalinganagar have valiantly resisted a bauxite plant, while at Jagatsinghpur protests against land expropriation for a Korean steel company have included kidnappings of company officials. But the most sustained and courageous resistance to displacement in India has come from the hundreds of thousands who are being forced from villages along the banks of the River Narmada and its tributaries. Around fifty million people in India have been dispossessed due to giant dam projects in the last half-century, and a majority of these are *adivasis*, indigenous peoples often referred to as *tribals*. The scale of the Narmada development is overwhelming: thirty major dams and over one hundred medium-sized ones, as well as three thousand minor dams, all part of a project that will displace two hundred thousand people by 2040. Organized under the banner of the Save Narmada Movement (NBA), these peoples, frequently led by women from the affected communities, have for more than twenty years used sit-ins, marches, court challenges, and hunger strikes to stop evictions.[299]

But the most controversial struggles over displacement in India—at least for the Left—have been those in West Bengal, which have pitted the Left Front government, promoting industrial "development" by domestic and foreign capital, against peasants in Singur and Nandigram, who have resisted eviction from lands that hold their farms, schools, temples, and mosques. These struggles have repeatedly erupted in violence, most tragically so in March 2007, when the government sent thousands of police into rural Nandigram, provoking a conflict in which fourteen peasant protestors were killed.[300] These battles highlight the price of "development" under neoliberal capitalism, as even governments of the electoral Left court corporate favor in desperate bids to woo investment. And with a slumping global economy reducing investment projects, governments will feel even more pressure to ignore environmental regulations, repress labor rights, and expropriate land and resources in order to attract capital.

If forced displacement is one part of the story, so is economic dispossession caused by the neoliberal devastation of agriculture in the South. As part of structural adjustment, the IMF and western leaders compelled countries in the South to remove subsidies to farmers and open up markets to mass imports of food from the West. Yet while farmers in the South are denied government support, agribusinesses and in the North receive $300 billion in subsidies every year. These funds, combined with technological advantages, enable them to undersell Third World peasants. The result has been a cataclysmic collapse of agriculture in the South, displacing farmers from the land in the face of rising costs and falling prices for their goods. "Free trade" with Canada and the U.S. has destroyed farming in Mexico and driven hundreds of thousands from the land. Coupled with plant closures and public sector layoffs, peasant dispossession has resulted in half a million Mexicans emigrating to the U.S. each year since NAFTA came into effect. Marketization has had equally devastating effects in India. So desperate have things become that two hundred thousand farmers committed suicide in the decade 1997–2007—two suicides every hour.

After decades of heeding the neoliberal bullies, fewer countries in the world are able to feed their own populations. Since 1990 food production has consistently failed to keep up with world population growth. Of course, less supply has been marvelous news for agribusiness and food merchants, who have enjoyed soaring prices and profits, but not for the more than one billion people on the planet who are undernourished.[301] The intensifying wave of global enclosures will only make all this worse.

Prior to the crisis, governments and giant food companies were scouring the planet for arable land. The most publicized of these land grabs have been in Africa, where twenty million hectares have been bought or leased by state agencies from Saudi Arabia, China, the Gulf states, and South Korea among others. Impoverished Sudan, which has already handed over a million hectares to South Korea and the United Arab Emirates, intends to forfeit fully a fifth of its cultivable land to Arab governments. China meanwhile has become especially active in this area, negotiating scores of deals of its own for African land.[302] But it is not just land that is at issue here—water may be just as big a story. With the world confronting an emerging water crisis, command over land becomes a key means of controlling water. Describing the recent wave of global land deals, the chairman of Nestlé argues, "The purchases weren't about land, but water. For with the land comes the right to the water linked to it." As much as we are witnessing a global land grab at the moment, we are also in the midst, he insists, of "the great water grab."[303]

Although it is African land sales and leases that have captured headlines, they may be exceeded in scale by parallel phenomena in Latin America. Here, food corporations and biofuel firms frequently lead the way, though mining and oil companies also figure prominently. Tens of millions of hectares across the region, much of it communal lands of indigenous peoples, have passed into the hands of foreign multinationals.[304] Indeed, much of the upsurge of indigenous militancy in Latin America in recent years has been a direct response to government efforts to sell off land to resource corporations. In Peru, this has led to military conflicts with the Shuar people over plans to drill for oil in the Amazon; to disputes in Chile with the Mapuche over logging; and to armed confrontations in Ecuador with native peoples resisting mining companies. In the Central American countries of Guatemala and El Salvador, peasants and indigenous peoples have been killed as well, while protesting the actions of Canadian-based mining corporations.[305] Many of these conflicts crucially involve indigenous resistance to the environmental degradation that accompanies such dispossession, as land is converted to soil-depleting industrial farming, rainforests are logged, water systems polluted, land strip-mined, species killed off, and biodiversity reduced. In all these regards, capitalism truly reveals itself as "the enemy of nature," to use Joel Kovel's apt term.[306]

At the same time, we need to realize that many so-called "natural disasters" are seized upon as pretexts for corporations and governments to dispossess people. After Hurricane Mitch killed five thousand and displaced two million in 1998, for instance, the Honduran government repealed legislation prohibiting the sale of indigenous lands. Huge private mansions were then built on territory that had belonged to 150,000 Garifunas, the descendants of African slaves, who have lived on the Atlantic coast for over two hundred years. Governments in Thailand, Sri Lanka, and Indonesia engaged in similar manipulations after the tsunami of 2004, seizing coastal areas for hotel development. Two years later, New Orleans became the scene of widespread displacement of African-Americans as a result of Hurricane Katrina. One hundred billion dollars in government funds may have been allocated for disaster relief, but huge chunks were funneled into the hands of giant firms like Blackwater and Halliburton, which have also raked it in from government contracts in Iraq. Meanwhile, perhaps a third of the residents of New Orleans, the bulk of them African-American, have been displaced throughout the

U.S. Many were evicted by landlords while they were in shelters or homes of friends and relatives elsewhere. At the same time, given the housing shortage created by the destruction, rents rose by almost 50 percent. To make matters worse, the New Orleans City Council used the rebuilding process to attack public housing. In the face of dispossession under "disaster capitalism," communities mobilized to resist.[307] Sensing what was coming, the Community Labor United coalition issued a prescient statement while the city was still underwater: "The people of New Orleans will not go quietly into the night, scattering across this country to become homeless in countless other cities while federal relief funds are funneled into rebuilding casinos, hotels, chemical plants, and the wealthy white districts of New Orleans . . ."[308] As government moneys have been used overwhelmingly for everything but rebuilding working class communities, social justice advocates have raised the right of return as a fundamental demand for the displaced of New Orleans.

Economic coercion and manipulated "disasters" have become key mechanisms of accumulation by dispossession. So has war. Wherever land and water are being seized—along with the timber and mineral, gas, and oil deposits they contain—violence lurks. Across the planet, regional wars and civil wars are flaring over lands and resources, and all of this is likely to get much worse in the context of global slump. In much of Africa, wars are repeatedly fuelled by battles over lands that contain diamonds, copper, oil, and more. Now, conflicts are raging over control of the water resources of the Lake Victoria / Nile River system.[309] Of course, few countries have endured such prolonged histories of civil war as a weapon of dispossession as has Colombia. Across the generations, peasants, indigenous peoples, and Afro-Colombians have been violently evicted from their lands so that capital could exploit minerals, oil fields, and commercial agriculture. In recent years, the Colombian military and right-wing death squads, in collaboration with the U.S. military and its "war on drugs," have dispossessed another two million Colombians.[310] While mainstream commentators view the displacement of millions of Colombians as a side effect of war, it is in fact its central purpose. As Colombian economist Hector Mondragon explains, "There are not only displaced people because there is war, but rather there is war in order that there be displaced people."[311]

Most of these millions, in Colombia and elsewhere are internally displaced. But tens of millions are forced by war, poverty, and landlessness to migrate across borders. After years of civil war and repression, for instance, there are more peoples from El Salvador living in Mexico and the U.S. than in their country of birth. The plight of such migrant workers is one of the urgent political issues of the era of neoliberal dispossession.

Capitalism, Migrant Workers, and the Global Slump

There is nothing very complicated about it. Displace people from their lands; contaminate their water systems; bring in armed thugs, troops, and death squads to enforce evictions and crush resistance—do all this and people will flee if they can. Lacking influence and connections, and concerned for their lives and those of their children, they will often cross borders with only a bag in hand, handing over their earnings to human smugglers who promise safe passage to a new life. Some will perish at sea on overcrowded boats, as have many Haitians; others will die of severe heat or suffocation in trucks or train cars. Even more will be raped, beaten, or robbed en route, and many arrested, thrown into barbaric detention centers—Australia has set up barbed-wire camps in the sweltering outback—and separated from children and loved ones. Incarcerated for years, subjected to beatings by guards, denied medical attention, their hearts and bodies frequently break down. In a six-and-a-half-year period from 2003 to 2010, for instance, 107 migrants died in the custody of U.S. detention centers, while officials often lied about the circumstances.[312]

The criminalization of global migrants is among the most obscene features of the world in which we live. Rather than prosecute mining, energy, and agribusiness firms from the West, many of which carry armed thugs on their payrolls,[313] for stealing lands and destroying ecosystems, governments in the North instead arrest, detain, humiliate, and terrify the millions of people forced from their lands by death squads, troops, civil wars, hunger and poverty. In the U.S., immigration authorities direct a militarized system of border patrol, spending $2 billion per year building walls and posting armed police along the border with Mexico. Every year, hundreds die trying to cross through that militarized zone. Of those who make it across that or another border, hundreds of thousands are apprehended—more than three hundred thousand men, women, and children every year in the United States. Once arrested, these terrified migrants are held in a system of four hundred private detention centers that are not subject to any binding regulations. Immigration detention is big business in America, with private security corporations receiving between $70 and $95 per day for each person they lock up. As with every other capitalist enterprise, it all pivots on minimizing costs (such as food and medical care for detainees) in order to maximize profits. Adhering to this script, Corrections Corporation of America, formerly known as Wackenhut, enjoyed a 29 percent jump in 2007 profits.[314] Meanwhile, detained migrants suffer and die in centers that a former agent for the U.S. State Department describes as "hell-holes." Conditions in these centers, he argues, "can only be described as subhuman—dangerously filthy, and without the most rudimentary sanitary facilities or basic medical care. Those occupying these hell-holes," he continues, "include thousands of legitimate refugees and asylum seekers—who pose no threat to the United States and who have committed no acts of wrong-doing."[315] True—except that, in the Global North, to be a poor refugee or immigrant of color is a crime.

Of course, businesses and government do not actually want to get rid of immigrant labor. As many as fourteen million undocumented laborers may be working in the United States—cleaning hotels and office buildings, cooking in restaurant kitchens, caring for children in the homes of the wealthy, doing the back-breaking work of picking fruits and vegetables in fields and orchards, sewing garments in backstreet sweatshops, doing heavy lifting on construction sites. As one *New York Times* reporter has noted, were all these workers expelled tomorrow, the economic results would be devastating: "thousands of hotels, restaurants, meatpacking plants, landscaping companies, and garment factories would likely close."[316] So, business wants these workers, and government knows it. But deprived of basic civil and human rights, these workers can be paid below minimum wages, worked excessive hours without overtime pay, denied medical and vacation benefits, kept out of unions and generally bullied and intimidated. Always, the threat of arrest and deportation hangs over their heads. Indeed, Immigration and Customs Enforcement harassment, raids, and arrests have been regularly used in the U.S. to break union drives.[317]

While looking at the plight of immigrant and undocumented workers in the United States, it is important not to let other governments off the hook. Italy, for instance, has more than four million undocumented migrant workers, working as nannies and picking fruit for less than $30 a day. In early 2010, thousands of these migrants were apprehended and sent to makeshift detention camps in the midst of a frightening wave of racist violence.[318] In all these contexts, rightless migrants are the ideal neoliberal workers: insecure, bullied, low-paid. In their case once more, state power is mobilized to create the fear essential to market discipline.

Most recently, governments around the world have been rewriting immigration policies in order to create huge pools of legal but precarious immigrants. In so doing, they arrive at something approximating a capitalist utopia for the regulation of labor: temporary migrants on limited work visas who labor for capital but receive neither citizenship nor even an enduring right to stay. This is flexible, precarious labor at its best: brought in when needed, expelled when not. Unlike the undocumented, temporary migrants are registered, processed, documented and tracked, but they remain effectively without rights. By bringing in migrants on temporary work visas, western states construct a subclass of rightless proletarians, workers who, while physically here, are meant to be socially and political absent, i.e. denied basic rights and access to citizenship.

American policy has been moving persistently in this direction since the late 1990s, under pressures from employer groups like the U.S. Chamber of Commerce, the American Hotel and Lodging Association, and the National Retail Federation. Europe too has seen the expansion of so-called "guest worker" programs—as if it is "guests" that are overworked, underpaid, denied healthcare, stuffed into decrepit housing, and evicted at the whim of their "hosts." East Asia is also increasing contract labor programs, with hundreds of thousands of domestic, factory and construction workers from countries like the Philippines now toiling in South Korea, Hong Kong, and Taiwan. Meanwhile, about ten million migrant laborers, many from India, Pakistan, the Philippines, Indonesia, and Eritrea, toil in the Gulf states, where they are denied basic social rights and frequently subjected to long hours, physical abuse, and unpaid wages.

Then there is Canada, a nation whose rulers like to present themselves as caring and compassionate. In recent years, Canadian governments have halved refugee acceptance rates while shifting markedly to a migrant labor system organized through the so-called Temporary Foreign Worker Program (TFWP). This system severely limits the rights and length of stay of migrant workers, keeping them in a state of precariousness with respect to their residency in Canada. While workers brought in under this program pay taxes, they are denied access to basic social services. In 2007, Canada brought in four times more temporary migrant laborers than permanent residents. Then, as the world recession hit, the Canadian government got into the business of conducting American-style armed raids on farms and factories employing undocumented workers. Held on buses and shipped to detention centers, many detainees were deported without ever seeing a lawyer. At the same time, the government was advising employers to lay off temporary migrants before Canadian citizens or permanent residents.[319]

All of this serves to remind us that capitalism remains as racialized as ever, and that one of the principal manifestations of racial capitalism today is the regulation and persecution of migrant laborers. Millions of poor workers of color from the Global South are hounded, arrested, detained, bullied, mercilessly exploited in homes, sweatshops and on farms, denied social services and civil rights, and subjected to racist attacks of the sort that broke out in Italy in early 2010, when African migrants were shot and beaten with metal rods.

And yet, with amazing courage, migrant workers are standing up and fighting back. African migrants in Italy did just that in early 2010, stoning police and smashing shop windows to protest racist assaults. And in France around the same time, thousands of undocumented workers joined strikes and sit-ins at restaurants and building sites, demanding legalization of their status. Hundreds squatted in a Paris building, where they cooked and cleaned in common while enjoying classes in philosophy, immigration law, and the French language provided by retired teachers and political activists.[320] Perhaps the largest and most inspiring mobilizations by migrants and immigrant workers have come in the United States itself where, in 2006, up to a million people reclaimed May Day as a genuine moment of working class internationalism. Marching and demonstrating in the streets, immigrant workers organized by progressive union locals, workers' centers, and social movements reclaimed the streets in a militant and celebratory protest against second-class citizenship. While much immigrant rights organizing shifted to the grassroots level—where groups like the Mississippi Immigrant Rights Alliance helped unionize poultry plants employing new migrants, and overturned discriminatory laws[321]—it burst forth on the national scene again in 2010 in response to legislation in Arizona designed to use racial profiling to target immigrants. As tens of thousands took to the streets on May Day 2010—150,000 in Los Angeles, 65,000 in Milwaukee, 20,000 in Chicago—the spirit of workers' solidarity was in the air. "Todos somos Arizona," chanted the crowds: We are all Arizona. "No somos ilegales," they shouted: We are not illegal.

We shall pick up that story in the next chapter. For it clearly demonstrates that the fight for migrant justice has become a touchstone for any truly transformative politics of the Left. The attacks on migrant workers today show us the real face of neoliberal capitalism in an era of global slump, just as migrant workers struggles for justice show us the possibilities for a genuinely radical form of working class politics. As financialized capitalism accentuates racialized dispossession around the globe, the only authentic politics of working class resistance and social transformation will be those based on unyielding solidarity with the displaced, the racially oppressed and the undocumented. Joined to movements for a living wage, for land and water, for healthcare and education, for gender and indigenous justice, for housing and environmental sustainability, such struggles might engender a Great Resistance that could chart a way out of the displacement, poverty, and insecurity that will otherwise be hallmarks of the decade of austerity.

CHAPTER SIX

Toward a Great Resistance?

"Power lies in unity and hope lies in defiance."
—Striking Chinese workers at KOK International
in a protest letter, June 2010

*"When a people arises, when it develops awareness, when it is
convinced of the rightness of its actions . . . there is nothing that
can stop it. The people sweep aside all obstacles placed in their
path, like a whirlwind cleaning out all the dirt in a country."*
—Rosan Mounien, a leader of the general
strike in Martinique, March 4, 2009

WHILE WORKING CLASS PEOPLE AROUND THE WORLD WERE THROWN
into shock by the scale and ferocity of the Great Recession, some
managed to mount bitter, determined resistance. Within a few
months of the financial meltdown, one government was toppled,
factories were occupied, general strikes declared. This wave of
opposition was courageous and inspiring. It was also inadequate
to the tasks of the moment.

The first government to be brought down was that of Iceland.
As soon as the financial crisis hit, Iceland's banks disintegrated.
Having massively borrowed in foreign currency (mainly euros)
to fund real estate and other speculative manias, the banks created a short-run "boom," which then collapsed as crisis hit and
foreign lenders called in their loans. Within days the economy
was in freefall—jobs disappeared, the currency plunged. In reaction, large crowds, led by angry youth, surrounded the parliament buildings and pelted the prime minister's car with eggs and
rocks in days and nights of rage. In the face of mass discontent,
the government resigned in early January 2009, and a coalition of
the Green Party and the Social Democrats won the ensuing elec-

tion. Despite their verbal attacks on globalization and the banks, the new government did a deal with the International Monetary Fund. Still, the popular anger did not subside. In March 2010, in fact, 93 percent of the people rejected a proposal to repay British and Dutch banks the more than $5 billion they lost in Iceland's bank meltdown.

At the same time that young people were surrounding the parliament buildings in Iceland, small numbers of laid-off workers in the Global North were taking over factories in occupations, on a scale that had not been seen in decades. One of the earliest sit-ins came in Chicago, the city whose labor movement gave birth to May Day as international workers' day more than 120 years earlier. With the U.S. housing industry in freefall in late 2008, workers at Republic Windows and Doors realized they were vulnerable. On December 2, the mostly Latino workforce, along with their black and white sisters and brothers, received termination notices and learned they would not receive severance and sick pay they were owed. That's when the 260 members of the United Electrical Workers union voted to take over their factory, occupying it for a week. With this bold act, the workers of color who led this stirring protest drew upon their experiences in the May Day 2006 mass mobilization of immigrant workers in the U.S. and issued a clarion call to all working people (they also drew upon their successes in getting rid of previous unions that would not fight for workers' rights). Regrettably, the uplifting struggle at Republic did not become the launching pad for a mass movement to save jobs and restart production under workers' control—as similar actions did in Argentina in 2001–2. Instead, after a week, the Republic strikers and their union ended the occupation in return for a better severance package. While these were important gains, they would not prevent the plant from closing.[322] Sadly, the same scenario had prevailed a few weeks earlier, when Irish workers at the Calcast auto parts plant in Derry seized their workplace.

In the months that followed this was too often the pattern. In the spring of 2009, workers at three Visteon auto parts plants in Britain and Ireland also occupied their factories, settling after seven weeks for improved severance pay. The same script was played out at the Aradco auto parts plant in the Canadian city of Windsor in March 2009. Even the incredible seventy-seven-day occupation by metal workers in South Korea, which withstood police attacks and tear gas dropped from helicopters, was constrained by union officials and failed to make a breakthrough.[323] Where workers did win real concessions on jobs, it required more militant methods, such as the "boss-nappings" that rocked France in 2009.

This tactic first emerged when workers at FCI Microconnections in Mante-la-Jolie seized their plant in order to stop layoffs. Seven weeks later, a group of strikers converged on company headquarters in Versailles, where they set up barricades and prevented the chief executive officer and his staff from leaving. In the face of this mobilization, management eventually agreed to keep the factory open until 2014 and to pay the workers for twenty-seven of the thirty-four days they had spent occupying their workplace. In the months that followed, bossnappings occurred at French plants owned by Caterpillar, Goss International, 3M, Sony, and Kleber-Michelin.[324]

These creative and audacious tactics by groups of workers in France, Ireland, Scotland, Canada, and the U.S. are indicative of a powerful spirit of resistance to the recession. In some cases, they have won significant concessions; occasionally they have saved jobs. But they were not able to stop the tidal wave of plant closings and layoffs that threw tens of millions out of work. And they did not manage to spark a mass movement to defend jobs and build workers' control. Indeed, even one-day general strikes, which shut down France on several occasions in the early months of 2009—and enjoyed 75 percent public support according to polls—were not enough. The onslaught against workers and their jobs might get delayed by such actions, but it would not be averted. Indeed, single day actions soon became ritualized events, de-mobilizing their participants. Real victories required much higher levels of radical mass mobilization of the sort that swept Martinique and Guadeloupe in the spring of 2009. We will look at these shortly. But first we need to consider the limits of the main forms of resistance that burst out in 2008–9.

Dispossessing Memory and Resistance

Too often, neoliberalism is seen simply as a set of policies imposed from above. While the neoliberal turn was indeed initiated at the top, it also involved molecular transformations at the most basic levels of everyday life. Senses of self, ways of relating to others, and the organization of communities were all restructured. Essential here were the social and cultural processes that eroded older forms of working class organization, spaces of resistance, and solidarities. Dispossession and displacement, after all, directly impinge on the cultural forms through which classes organize and know themselves. And, as the neoliberal assault broke unions, mothballed factories and mines, relocated investment and jobs, it also destroyed communities that had nurtured enduring working class movements. In some cases, actual towns effectively disappeared: steel towns in the American Midwest; tin mining villages in Bolivia; auto towns in Michigan; and coal mining villages in Thatcher's England.

To be sure, much was deficient about these movements: they were often overwhelmingly white and male, and too often sectional in outlook—though this was least true of Bolivia's tin miners, large numbers of whom were of indigenous descent, and whose union championed many social justice causes.[325] But for all their limitations, they were also sites of memory and resistance. In the union halls, bars, restaurants, and community centers that sprinkled such towns, stories were passed down of the great strikes that had won the union, of the times when workers fought police or troops outside the mine or the factory gates, of the marches of the women demanding bread and roses, of the children who jeered the scabs. In the U.S., for example, old-timers talked of when Mother Jones, Joe Hill, or Emma Goldman had come to town, and of the unsung heroes of local labor wars. In so doing they sustained an oppositional culture and a distinctively working class memory. Across the generations, union songs were sung—"Union Maid," "Solidarity Forever," "Which Side Are You On?"—and in many locales these labor classics were joined by the great anthems of the Civil Rights Movement, like "We Shall Overcome" and "We Shall Not Be Moved."

In all these and hundreds of other ways, cultures of resistance were sustained in and through organized infrastructures of dissent, to use Alan Sears' salient term.[326] But in the great wave of industrial restructuring, geographic relocation and union-busting that consolidated the neoliberal era, much of this was eroded. As plants closed, union halls disappeared, oppositional spaces died out, and people moved on, workers were literally dispossessed of their cultural resources. The sites that sustained memories were obliterated; infrastructures of dissent collapsed. Analyzing the decline of the Great Lakes manufacturing belt in the U.S., Dan La Botz perceptively notes,

> The unions' power had been rooted in the social texture—the neighborhoods, schools, churches, bars, social clubs, and little league teams—of the descendants of the Eastern and Southern European immigrants who had arrived at the opening of the century and of the offspring of the African-Americans who had made the great migration from the plantations of the South.
>
> The unions' power had been rooted in peoples' everyday existence, and that way of life had been based on work; when the work ended, so did the union, so did their community, and so their culture.[327]

All of this meant that, despite a desire to resist, working class movements were ill-prepared for the assaults that would accompany the Great Recession.

Meanwhile, a neoliberal cultural revolution was afoot. This was the heyday of a vigorous new consumerism that invaded social space. Billboards bloomed on every landscape, logos adorned our clothes, ads cropped up in public washrooms. Conspicuous consumption was the new cool, and radicalism was redefined as style—jeans, haircuts and sneakers, cell phones and iPods. Our identities were said to be bound up with our purchases, as if all the complexities of personhood could be reduced to our shopping choices. In social and cultural theory, consumption was now the rage, spawning conferences and journals devoted to the theme. Social engagement, protest marches, and union meetings were declared embarrassingly uncool. Concern for social movements was displaced by obsession with stock market movements. Older collective identities, based on the political struggles of the 1960s and '70s, or the legacies of union organizing, were now boringly passé. A new individualism was vigorously promoted everywhere, finding its most extreme (and absurd) expression in Margaret Thatcher's declaration that "there is no such thing as society." A giddy, postmodern culture was on the march, preoccupied with consumption, style, and fashion. "Delirious New York" emerged as the center of this cultural moment, aspiring to erase "the collective memory of democratic New York."[328] This was the age of the "investor self," described in the previous chapter, the era of people taught to think about their lives in terms of economic balance sheets. And this neoliberal subject, as it has been dubbed, i.e. the human individual reduced to a market actor, was aggressively promoted in parts of the Global South as well.[329]

Of course, no such subject ever actually emerged. These are all trends I am describing, not accomplished states. Not everyone bought the neoliberal zeitgeist. Antipoverty activists, feminists, antiracists, queer organizers, and rank-and-file unionists still fought good fights. And most people, even where they gave their assent to the mantras of the new individualism, continued to care deeply and profoundly about their social, familial, and community connections. But there could be no denying that a cultural shift of real substance had occurred.

There was, however, something so empty and alienating about neoliberal consumer individualism that a counter-reaction was inevitable. A landscape utterly dominated by commodities is a depressing, soulless place. Communities based around shopping malls are barren wastelands, spaces of the living dead mocked in zombie movies such as *Dawn of the Dead*. Moreover, as young people interrogated the seedy underpinnings of the neoliberal age, they discovered the ugly truth about global sweatshops and ecological destruction. Slowly but persistently, political criticism and activism re-emerged. In the mid-1990s, Mexico's Zapatista rebels electrified thousands with their poetic critiques of neoliberalism and the religion of "free trade," and a new generation of activists embraced left-wing writers like Noam Chomsky,

Howard Zinn, and Naomi Klein. This was the moment too when, particularly in Latin America, a series of mass anti-neoliberal upsurges toppled governments and rolled back privatizations, in countries like Bolivia, Ecuador, and Venezuela.[330] Around the world, struggles for land, water, and indigenous rights were converging, giving birth to the World Social Forum and the uplifting slogan, "Another World Is Possible."[331] For a few heady years, it looked like these movements might give birth to a new global Left in short order. Then came the attacks on the World Trade Center in September 2001, and a wave of repression and patriotic nationalism derailed social movements in the North. Street protest retreated, social movements declined. The political and organizational weaknesses of the so-called "anti-globalization movement" were thrown into sharp relief. For all its energy and creativity, the new movements in the North simply lacked the deep roots in working class communities, the political vision and the strategic clarity to be able to sustain themselves when difficult times came.

And here, lessons from the Global South become highly significant. In some areas, new mass working class movements did surge forward—belying all the neoliberal claims about the end of class and the obsolescence of the Left. Bolivia serves as a vital example in this regard.

Bolivia: The Revolt of the New World of Work

In 2000, a mass upsurge in Bolivia overturned water privatization and launched a cycle of revolt that would bring down three presidents and sweep the Movement Toward Socialism (MAS) into office, making its electoral leader, Evo Morales, the country's first indigenous president.[332] I will explore some of the dynamics of these struggles shortly. But, first, we need to appreciate just what a remarkable recovery this was from the crushing defeat of Bolivia's powerful working class movement a mere fifteen years earlier.

The Bolivian working class movement had endured a shattering decomposition as a result of the neoliberal offensive. For more than thirty years (1952–85), the tin miners' union, the

Confederation of Bolivian Workers (COB), had comprised a radical proletarian vanguard that spearheaded a combative class culture. In 1952–53 the miners had taken up arms, rebuffed the army, and effectively seized power. On May Day 1952, forty thousand armed workers marched through the streets of the capital city, which was now under their control. Although the workers' movement then turned power over to radical nationalists who betrayed the cause of labor, the COB remained a hugely influential social force for thirty years. They forced through the nationalization of the tin mines, and they led great struggles of the poor. Then came the privatization law of 1985, which led to more than twenty thousand of the twenty-seven thousand workers in state-owned mines losing their jobs, alongside an equal proportion of all workers in the private mines. The tin miners fought back, but their union was not equal to the challenge. They occupied mines and launched general strikes, only to meet harsh repression. In September 1986 the miners, joined by wives, students, peasants, and teachers, embarked on their March for Life, which was halted by the army. "Without a single shot being fired, the people demobilized . . . The miners gave in to the state and that is when a new era began in Bolivia."[333] The results of this defeat were calamitous. When the dust had cleared, not a single unionized worker was left in the mines. And having defeated the tin miners, employers and the government had carte blanche to downsize, reorganize work, increase hours, cut wages and benefits, and embark on an orgy of privatization. In no time at all, public oil and gas companies, the state airline, the railways, and the long-distance phone company were all auctioned off.[334] The crushing of the tin miners played the same role as the smashing of the air traffic controllers in the U.S. or the defeat of the coal miners' union in Britain. It was the blow that inaugurated a new era of rollbacks for workers. In the aftermath, the percentage of Bolivian workers with a permanent job plummeted from over 70 percent in 1989 to less than 30 percent by 1996.[335] Meanwhile, the average work week soared to fifty-two hours and wages plunged. By 1996 working class incomes were half of what they had been twelve years earlier. Workers were increasingly fragmented as employment became more and more casualized, with half of manufacturing being done in tiny shops of four employees or less. Unions went into a dramatic decline.

Acutely aware of this "new world of work," some far-sighted union militants in Bolivia's second largest city, Cochabamba, realized that major strategic and organizational changes were required. Activists of the Cochabamba Confederation of Factory Workers, the Fabriles, led by machinist Oscar Olivera, understood that along with neoliberalism went "the emergence of a new urban working class," overwhelmingly composed of women and young workers, toiling long hours in small workplaces.[336] In fact, despite the social and political decomposition of the labor movement, in numerical terms the working class had grown considerably during twenty years of neoliberalism in Bolivia: to 3.5 million wage-workers in a population of eight million.[337] Initially, of course, neoliberal restructuring of work meant fragmentation and disarray for workers. But activists from the Fabriles began to agitate and organize on the streets, inviting workers from across the city to come to their union office on the city's main square for support and strategic discussion. Soon, the city's labor movement was connecting with "the invisible world of work" beyond the few large factories that remained. Small grievances were taken up, new connections created. A dynamic social movement unionism from below was emerging, creating new working class alliances in the process. Then came the great battle over water—and this emergent workers' movement was soon spearheading a semi-insurrectionary people's rebellion.

As is so often the case with great popular revolts, things began modestly. In October 1999, peasant activists contacted the union about forming a common front against impending privatization of Cochabamba's water system. The following month saw the formation of the Coalition in Defense of Water and Life, or the Coordinadora, which began to operate out of the Fabriles' office. Meetings and popular assemblies were convened, while two days of road blockades were organized to build the movement. The struggle quickly heated up, drawing wider and wider layers of the population into action: peasants, unionized workers, the unemployed, workers in the informal sector, environmentalists, and professionals. On December 1, the Coordinadora called its first mass demonstration—and organizers were shocked with delight when ten thousand people showed up in a city of six hundred thousand. A vibrant popular movement was clearly taking flight. Then, when the government signed the water privatization contract in January 2000, Cochabambans were hit with 100 percent hikes on their water bills.

At this point, the Coordinadora issued the government an ultimatum: rip up the privatization contract by January 11, or face an escalating campaign of strikes along with road and highway blockades. Several days of mass protests, which were met by teargas-throwing police, brought a growing movement together in the streets. Then, on February 4, the Coordinadora took things to a higher level, calling supporters to "the takeover of Cochabamba." And take over they did. The people seized the city center, only to be attacked by cordons of police. Barricades were thrown up, rocks hurled, the police repulsed. "The entire rest of the town is now in the hands of the people," reported two observers. "A great spirit of solidarity arises, fear conquered, hesitations swept away."[338] The next day, the movement returned to the city center. Again the police attacked. Again they were thrown back. Families filled the streets, joining the barricades, as people brought food, water, and moral support to the popular combatants. The people of Cochabamba were now in open revolt.

Amid the revolt, a radical, participatory democracy was coming to life in the city square, where five times a week mass assemblies of fifty to seventy thousand people planned the next steps in the struggle. In their deliberations, the people set April 4 as the date by which the government had to cancel the water contract. When that day arrived, a general strike was declared and the streets reclaimed. "The people got ready all over the city," recalled Oscar Olivera. "Children, old folks, young men and women—all of them had their faces painted as in war. Young people wore leather gloves to hurl back the gas canisters." On April 8, the government hit back, declaring a state of emergency and arresting Olivera and other leaders of the movement, all of whom were charged with sedition. In the street-fighting that ensued, one hundred people were killed. Still the insurgents did not buckle. Two days later, the uprising of the people reached new heights. Young activists broke the military occupation of the city center, repulsing the troops; highway blockades were extended; the strikes intensified. One hundred thousand people were in a state of semi-insurrection. Realizing that repression has failed to derail the movement, the government retreated, cancelling the water privatization contract.[339]

As Jeffery Webber has brilliantly shown, the victory in Cochabamba ignited a cycle of revolt that continued through 2005, when Evo Morales was elected president. By that time, the capital city, La Paz, and the working class and indigenous neighborhoods of El Alto that ring it on the surrounding hillsides (the *altiplano*), had emerged as the new centers of insurrectionary upheaval. In 2003, following calls for belt-tightening by the IMF, a wave of struggle had converged on the demand to take Bolivia's gas fields under public ownership. The 2003 Gas War was succeeded by the Second Water War in early 2005 and the Second Gas War that spring. Across these struggles, Bolivia saw the highest levels of popular insurgency yet, including a half-million-strong march in the capital, a mass indigenous protest that just about got into the Congress, and repeated use of the mass strike (or *paro cívico*) in El Alto. The results were profound: three presidents toppled, partial victories over gas, oil, and water, and the propulsion of Evo Morales into the presidency. Crucial to these struggles was a deepening alliance between the Federation of United Neighborhoods of El Alto, the Regional Workers Central of El Alto, the Confederation of Original Peoples, the Departmental Workers Central, the Federation of Peasants of La Paz, the Bolivian Workers Central, the Public University of El Alto, teachers unions and many others.[340]

This "rearticulation of left-indigenous forces," to use another salient expression from Webber, involved the emergence of a movement that is both working class and indigenous. Anticolonialism and anticapitalism were bound together in a politics of left-indigenous working class revolt.[341] At the heart of this movement was a dynamic convergence of the militant, democratic traditions of the Bolivian workers' movement, particularly of the tin miners, with the communal traditions of the Aymara and other indigenous peoples. To be sure, these traditions coexist and intersect with those of left-nationalism. And, while such nationalism has an anti-imperialist element, it has also historically been a weapon against radical socialism, as workers and indigenous peoples have been told in its name to subordinate their aspirations to those of the "nation" as a whole—and time and time again this has meant the dominance of bourgeois interests, as during the revolution of 1952–53. As a result, forward movement for the Bolivian struggle today means promoting the socialist dimension of the struggle so that it is not hemmed in by nationalism. And here, many communal indigenous traditions can play an important role.

It is the practice of the neighborhoods of El Alto, where 82 percent of the people identify as indigenous, to organize provision of public services and education through public gatherings and assemblies. So strong are communal practices that many workers in the so-called informal economy participate in collective economic relations. The forty thousand market stalls that dot the highway through El Alto, for instance, are the social property of the community, allocated to households by community organizations.[342] This comprises an experiential basis for new socialist visions that have animated recent upheavals across Bolivia.

The Bolivian uprisings thus comprise a new kind of working class movement—if we understand that term in all its lived complexity, as involving the unity of the diverse groups that are dispossessed of means of production and compelled to live off their own labor.

To begin with, unionized workers in manufacturing play a fundamentally strategic role in this movement. At the same time, the movement also embraces hundreds of thousands of unorganized wage laborers as well as poor petty producers. The latter may not be working class in a formal sense; but they are members of proletarianized communities and participants in radical movements that are articulating anticapitalist demands. This means that they are active members of communities and social movements crucially bound together through working class identities and aspirations. In this decisive sense they are participants in a working class movement. But this term must not be understood in the narrow way familiar to some leftist movements of the past. It is not a question of dictionary definitions but of living social groups. A movement is precisely what the term implies—a rich, complex, dynamic formation, alive with tensions and contradictions, but expressing nonetheless shared experiences and aspirations. In Bolivia (and elsewhere) today, this movement draws together different strata of the urban poor into struggles that express plebeian and working class politics steeped in indigenous identities.

To be sure, this is a changed working class. As Oscar Olivera puts it, in the neoliberal era, "the conditions of class struggle have changed." Reflecting on the April 2000 uprising in Cochabamba, he observes that "Rather than the traditional labor movement, it was the new world of work that came out into the streets: the unemployed, the self-employed, the young, and the women." And he offers a perceptive analysis of this new working class:

> In Cochabamba and the Aymaran *altiplano*, working men and women, young temporary workers, impoverished neighbors, peasants and townspeople and unemployed and employed workers have reclaimed the language of the barricades, of community solidarity, and of the assembly and town meeting, in order to make their voices heard.

And, he continues, they forged sufficient unity in struggle, a unity built through the strengths of their different traditions, to win decisive victories:

> Emerging from the smallest social spaces, previously established neighborhood organizations, newly formed water committees, agrarian unions, and indigenous communities created a powerful network to defend water rights and the traditional practices and uses of water. They took on the state, the police, the army, the bosses, and the politicians. And they won.[343]

Within that popular uprising, a "traditional" section of the working class, the factory workers and their union, played a decisive role. The Fabriles, Olivera notes, "acted as a moral reference point," providing organizational resources and strategic vision. In so doing, they showed themselves "to be capable of reviving the old role played by Bolivia's miners, who led so many popular struggles and were able to lend them greater resonance and strength."[344]

This serves as a reminder that revolutionary memory is never entirely extinguished—despite the efforts of neoliberalism to dispossess workers of the resources of organization, memory, and oppositional culture. Labor organizers such as Olivera, who entered the union movement in 1980, before the great defeat of the tin miners, have served as living bridges between the past and the future, preserving what is most valuable in the courageous struggles of earlier years, while learning from the new forms of organization and resistance that are required in changed circumstances. At the same time, younger women activists, such as Raquel Gutiérrez-Aguilar, have both learned from Olivera and added their own unique experiential knowledge to the movement.[345] In these ways, a new radical synthesis is being created, a concrete and dynamic blending of collective knowledge, practices, forms of organization and cultures of resistance acquired from different sites and periods. Certainly, there are weaknesses to these movements—some of which will be taken up below. But before pursuing that discussion, it is worth examining the case of the Landless Workers Movement (MST) of Bolivia, where similar social dynamics can be observed.

Born in 2000, much later than its Brazilian counterpart, the Bolivian MST is a product of the new cycle of revolt. Indeed, the MST was born in and through a land occupation in February 2000, the very month when the struggle was surging forward in Cochabamba. By 2004, the organization had helped settle one hundred communities of landless people on occupied land, expanding from three thousand to fifty thousand members in the process. Notwithstanding its focus on land, the members of the MST are by no means entirely rural. As one analyst observes,

MST members "do not exclusively identify themselves as campes-inos." Most of them have hybrid rural-urban histories, which include "substantial amounts of time spent living and working in urban settings doing nonagricultural work."[346] Difficulties making ends meet in city or town due to layoffs, casual employ-ment, and low wages often push them to return to the country-side. As a result, the MST cannot accurately be described simply as a peasant movement. Instead, it reflects the complex social con-figuration of people with experience of urban and rural wage-labor, sometimes mixed with farming. Like the movements in Cochabamba and El Alto, and indeed like many mass movements across Latin America, a new dialectic is in play, "a *reshaping of class*" in which wage-labor and peasant farming both figure in the lived histories of individuals. And when we look at house-holds and larger communities, we find that farming, wage-labor, and toil in the "informal" economy overlap and intersect in the processes by which these groups reproduce themselves. Not sur-prisingly then, the social struggles that emerge in such contexts frequently bring together racial, gender, class, urban, and rural experiences, "producing a complex, multidimensional kind of resistance."[347]

To say this is not to glorify these movements. They are encountering numerous difficulties—including, in Bolivia, the demobilizing trap of electoralism joined to a certain left-nation-alism, as many social movements bow before the requests of the Evo Morales government to curb the demands of 2000–2005.[348] The class struggle in Bolivia thus confronts real dangers and con-tradictions. This is why radicals are trying to push forward a new politics of working class resistance appropriate to the neoliberal era—politics that connect with "nontraditional" forms of work, and with the experiences of women and young workers, and that make antiracist demands, like indigenous self-determination, central to their struggles. In so doing, they seek to further the important strides already made in building new organizational capacities able to lead mass insurgencies from below. In all these ways, they point us toward the kinds of politics that will be nec-essary everywhere in the face of the global slump, a politics that will need to be further radicalized if gains are to be secured and extended in the years ahead.

"Stand Up Against Exploitation": Mass Strikes in Guadeloupe and Martinique

The Bolivian struggles we have described preceded the Great Recession. But similar social dynamics were at work in the general strikes in Guadeloupe and Martinique in early 2009, just as the global crisis was nearing its worst point. The initial inspiration for these upheavals may have come from the mass strikes and demonstrations in France, but the struggle in these former slave colonies went to a much higher level.[349]

There are at least two key reasons for this. First, economic conditions are much worse on these Caribbean islands than on the French mainland. Unemployment and poverty rates are twice as high as in metropolitan France, and youth unemployment is at a staggeringly high level, well over 50 percent. To top all this off, the cost of living is punitively high on the islands. Secondly, and arguably most significant, Guadeloupe and Martinique represent textbook cases of racialized, neocolonial capitalism. The local ruling classes are almost entirely white—known as the béké, they are descendants of French slave-owners. Meanwhile, the working class is of African or mixed descent. Patrick Lozès, head of an umbrella group of black organizations in France, summed up the predominant sentiment of working class islanders when he asked, "Is it normal that, 160 years after the abolition of slavery, the descendants of colonists possess 90 percent of Guadeloupe's riches, but represent only one percent of the population?" These intersections of economic hardship and racialized capitalism gave the strike movement a massive popular resonance, similar to the convergence of class and racial struggles in Bolivia.

The battle started on January 20, when a coalition of fifty unions and social movement groups, known as "Stand Up Against Exploitation" (Liyannaj Kont Pwofitasyon, or LKP in the local dialect) initiated a strike whose central demand was a 200 euro ($260 U.S. dollars) per month raise for the lowest-paid workers. Under the leadership of the General Union of Workers of Guadeloupe, strikers shut down banks, schools, and government offices as well as gas stations and hotels. Protestors barricaded the main shipping terminal and closed the airport. Ten days into the strike, sixty thousand people demonstrated through the streets of Pointe-à-Pitre—a mobilization of 15 percent of the island's population. Alarmed by the power of the movement, the French government sent five hundred police who arrived on February 19. But this only further inflamed things, prompting angry youth to occupy the city hall in Sainte-Anne, and others to burn local businesses.

By this point, the strike had spread to the neighboring island of Martinique, where twenty-five thousand people (of a population of four hundred thousand) took to the streets with similar demands. Just days into the strike, tensions were dramatically inflamed when a documentary entitled "The last masters of Martinique" was broadcast by a French TV station. In the course of the show, a French businessman remarked that historians should investigate "the positive aspects of slavery." Days later, thousands joined a march, chanting "Martinique is ours, not theirs."

Not only did this Caribbean strike movement kept growing in militancy, it also spread to the French overseas "department" of Réunion in the Indian Ocean. At the same time, Olivier Besancenot, the popular spokesperson for France's New Anticapitalist Party, proclaimed the island strikes an inspiration "to follow." Sensing that its troubles were escalating, the French government caved in, agreeing on March 4, 2009, to raise salaries for the lowest paid by 200 euros, a 40 percent increase, along with modest improvements of 3–6 percent for better-paid workers. As thirty thousand people marched through the streets of the capital, they learned that the government had also agreed to reduce water rates, hire more teachers, aid farmers and fishers, fund jobs and training for unemployed youth, freeze rents and ban evictions. A week later, the government signed a similar agreement with the strikers in Martinique. The day of the settlement in Guadeloupe, union leader Rosan Mounien summed up the mood of the forty-four-day struggle: "when a people arises, when it develops awareness, when it is convinced of the rightness of its actions . . . there is nothing that can stop it. The people sweep aside all obstacles placed in their path, like a whirlwind cleaning out all the dirt in a country."

However, for all their amazing accomplishments, the workers of Guadeloupe and Martinique did not clean out "all the dirt." With their militancy, creativity and determination, the strikers achieved extraordinary things, proving that one can make major gains in the face of a deep recession. But the basic social relations of racialized capitalism remain intact, even if the ruling class has been shaken. In the accord signed by the strike leaders, they declare their objective of "establishing a new economic order enhancing the status of everyone and promoting new social relationships." That—"a new economic order" based on "new social relationships"—they have yet to achieve.

Oaxaca: From Teachers' Strike to Dual Power in One City

One of the things the inspirational strikes in Guadeloupe and Martinique did not accomplish was to create new institutions of popular, working class power that could begin to take control of social life. Something along those lines did take place, however, in the southern Mexican city of Oaxaca for five months in 2006, when a million people waged one of the great popular uprisings in recent history. This alone makes the Oaxacan struggle of immense importance. So does the overall context in which it arose.[350]

We encounter in the state of Oaxaca, which contains the city of the same name, a striking economic microcosm of neoliberal globalization. One of the poorest states in Mexico, a majority of whose inhabitants are of indigenous descent, it has become a prime target for land and resource dispossession by global capital. Multinational corporations have swooped down on communal lands rich in natural resources, displacing indigenous peoples in the process. This is occurring in a context where over 70 percent of the population lives in extreme poverty, three-quarters have no access to health care, and half have no electricity or running water. With such poverty and displacement comes migration. An estimated 1.5 million Oaxacans reside in the U.S. today, while another quarter-million emigrate each year. These are the grinding circumstances in which the teachers of Local 22 of the National Education Workers Union, with a long history of supporting the left-wing opposition in their union, chose May Day 2006 to launch a battle whose dimensions they could not have imagined.

The teachers of Oaxaca are a strategically located group. Most are of indigenous descent and they work with the children and families of the poor day in and day out. Every year their union organizes a *plantón*, or sit-in, at the city square in the state capital, Oaxaca City. In the spring of 2006 they did the same, establishing their encampment in late May. Because of their unique traditions of struggle, the teachers of Oaxaca did not merely raise demands for better wages and conditions for themselves. To be sure, they demanded well deserved pay hikes. But they also called on the government to provide the children with free schoolbooks, pencils, and supplies. They demanded free school uniforms and insisted that children, many of whom walk to school barefoot, receive one free pair of shoes every year. And they called for doctors' visits to the schools and supplies for medical clinics. In all these ways, they positioned their battle as a campaign against poverty and for social justice.

The teachers' demands resonated widely with poor Oaxacans. On June 2, a crowd of 80,000 demonstrated their support. Five days later, a human wave of 120,000 demonstrators swept through the streets, chanting slogans of solidarity. Then, on June 14, the government struck back. While the teachers, their children and supporters slept, the governor sent in battalions of state police to smash up the sit-in. Deploying helicopters, tear gas and firearms, the police drove the crowd of 20,000 from their encampment. But the stunned teachers regrouped and fought back, growing stronger as thousands of Oaxacans poured out of their homes to join them. After a four-hour battle, the insurgent crowd reclaimed the city center. And, while the street fighters may not have realized it, their heroic resistance of June 14, 2006, would give birth to an extraordinary outpouring of popular power.

Organized through the hundreds of neighborhood barricades erected across the city to curtail police and death squads, and galvanized by general strikes and mass marches of up to eight hundred thousand, working class power was incarnated in the Popular Assembly of the Peoples of Oaxaca (APPO). Formed mere days after the brutal assault on the teachers in a three-day long mass, democratic assembly involving representatives of 365 groups, ranging from unions and indigenous peoples' organizations, to human rights, feminist, and student groups, APPO emerged as an expression of insurgent assembly-style democracy. More than that, it burst forth as a site of dual power—a forum for vibrant popular democracy through which the oppressed of Oaxaca began to manage large parts of everyday social life. For five months, in the words of two analysts, "The APPO ran the city."[351]

In the radical socialist tradition, dual power refers to a situation in which the oppressed create an alternative center of popular power, one based around mass democratic assemblies and/or workers' councils in opposition to the sites of ruling class power—the government, the army, the courts. Situations with two contending centers of power cannot endure; one side or the other must ultimately displace the other, as history has repeatedly shown.[352]

The Paris Commune of 1871 was the first case of an insurgent site of workers' self-government. For more than two months, the workers of Paris ran their city. They replaced the old government and its army, and established deeply participatory, democratic, and egalitarian forms of organization. The Paris Commune, proclaimed Marx, was "essentially a working class government . . . the political form at last discovered under which to work out the economic emancipation of labour."[353] In the early twentieth century, a new institutional form of counter-power was invented—the workers' council, based on delegates elected directly from places of work, often in conjunction with others from working class communities. Council-based insurgencies moved to especially powerful levels in Russia 1917, Barcelona 1936, and Hungary 1956. And elements of dual power have also existed in situations such as Chile 1970–73, notably in the factory-based *cordones*. One of the strengths of upsurges of assembly-style workers' democracy in Latin America today is their deep roots in neighborhoods and their links with communal traditions of indigenous self-governance, as we have seen in both Bolivia and Oaxaca.[354]

The dual power situation in Oaxaca in 2006 has aptly been referred to as "the Oaxaca Commune," in part because, as in Paris in 1871, it represented workers' power in one city. The barricades were a key site of popular power; neighborhood committees effectively used them as spaces of resistance, democratic discussion, and self-organization. The insurgent people also seized key government buildings, in the process paralyzing the traditional institutions of power. Meanwhile, APPO provided a framework for these grassroots neighborhood collectives to converge with unions, student groups, and indigenous and women's organizations. Every morning, people awoke to new stenciled art, woodblock prints, and spray-painted images and slogans across the city. Huge marches brought people together in their tens and hundreds of thousands. But absolutely crucial to the Oaxaca Commune was citizens' radio, where the voices of the oppressed burst forth from the darkness to reclaim the airwaves, rename their circumstances, and coordinate resistance.

In their June 14 assault on the teachers' encampment, government troops also attacked Radio Plantón, the community radio station that had become the voice of the teachers and the popular movement. Following the destruction of Radio Plantón, local university students seized the campus radio station, immediately turning it into a medium of resistance. The student station endured several attacks before it was disabled on August 8. But by then the movement was engaged in a wider campaign to democratize the media. The takeover of radio stations began with the electrifying women's action of August 1, known as the March of Pots and Pans.[355] During the demonstration, the call went out to descend on Channel 9, the state television station. When management would not allow the women to make a broadcast, they seized the station, along with the state radio channel. "You're listening to 96.9, Radio Pots and Pans," declared the rebel broadcaster. When state police destroyed the liberated radio and television equipment three weeks later, the people took over all eleven commercial radio stations in Oaxaca, returning nine of them the next day. Until August 8, they also used the university radio station as a key site of peoples' media, and defended the station against violent attack by federal police using tear gas and live ammunition. These movement-run stations did more than serve as key mechanisms for informing people about the struggle and helping to coordinate their resistance. They functioned as well as a means of autonomous cultural expression and popular education, taking up issues such as the struggle of the Palestinian people for self-determination. Throughout these months, the movement also developed a peoples' police force, the *topiles*, based on indigenous traditions of self-defense. These groups of young men, basically unarmed except for firecrackers and the odd machete, defended seized government offices and radio stations, as well as union offices, while patrolling the streets and apprehending state police and members of death squads.

In seizing the streets, government offices and parts of the media, the working class of Oaxaca developed democratic organs of self-rule, effectively establishing dual power. They maintained momentum through APPO assemblies, mass marches, and a powerful general strike on August 18. But they confronted the same dilemma as had the workers of Paris in 1871: a working class government confined to one city is a very precarious thing.[356]

Then in late October, the government signed an agreement with the teachers, granting many of their demands. Rather than the first step on the road to victory, it was to be a con job. The next day, 4,500 federal police invaded the city, using tanks, helicopters, tear gas and more. Joining with the state police, they beat, murdered, arrested, and tortured. Four activists were killed, one hundred and forty injured, at least one hundred arrested. The teachers' encampment was destroyed, and police occupied the area all through November and into December, as arrests and disappearances mounted. While APPO held an amazing Constituent Assembly of over a thousand delegates of popular organizations on November 11, and then a national assembly in Mexico City six days later, the movement lacked the capacities to galvanize a nation-wide general strike and uprising. APPO continued to do inspiring work in the months that followed, including a mass march on International Women's Day 2007, but it was unable to sustain itself as a forum of mass oppositional education, culture and activism. The Oaxaca Commune had been broken, in part because it could not move beyond the boundaries of a single city. Nevertheless, its spirit lives on—even in cities of the Global North.

Immigrant Workers and the Spirit of Rebellion in the Global North

As we have seen, Oaxaca is a burning microcosm of our age: it is poor, ethno-racially diverse, ravaged by land and resource dispossession, swarming with displaced people, subjected to neoliberal regimes of militarized policing. For all these reasons, Oaxacans are also an extremely mobile population. Already, a million and a half of them reside in the United States. And they are joined by 250,000 more each and every year, making them "one of the most, if not the most, trans-regionalized and trans-nationalized populations in Mexico."[357] As they migrate, Oaxacans carry with them memories of resistance and experiences of popular revolt. These, joined with those of Latinos from other parts of Mexico, from Guatemala, El Salvador, and beyond, then enter the dynamic mix of the immigrant and migrant working class experience in the U.S. and beyond. This helps account for the amazing role of Latino workers in the great May Day 2006 upsurge in American cities. It is no accident that this upsurge came at the same time that the people of Oaxaca were in revolt. Likewise, it is not accidental that Latino workers played a driving role in the factory occupation at Republic Windows and Doors two and a half years later.

Indeed, as Latino immigration has remade cities throughout the U.S., so it is remaking the working class, opening up new and exciting sites of struggle. Major U.S. cities like Los Angeles are now home to a multiracial urban working class that is predominantly black, Latino, and Asian-American.[358] Beginning in the mid-1980s, and running right against the grain of neoliberalism, sections of this urban working class launched rousing organizing drives, such as the Justice for Janitors (J4J) campaign that by

1995 brought 90 percent of Los Angeles building cleaners into unions, compared with a mere 10 percent eight years earlier. J4J did this by breaking with the tepid tactics of business unionism and embracing a mobilizing, grassroots social movement unionism, one that used sit-ins, boycotts, strikes, and multiracial alliances with community organizations to bring real working class power to bear—all of which eventually incurred the wrath of the bureaucrats of their national union.[359] As Mike Davis notes, Justice for Janitors tapped into and stimulated a wave of working class organizing across California led by workers of color, and essentially rebuilt the California labor movement in the process:

> These immigrant based campaigns have become justly celebrated for their creativity in mobilizing and sustaining rank-and-file involvement. With the support of immigrants rights groups, liberationist clergy, Latino/a college students, and other communities of color, they have overwhelmed employers with a tactical repertoire that has included guerrilla theatre and film, public art, a pro-labor masked and caped avenger (Mopman), trade union *foto-novelas* in Spanish, corporate exposés, disruptions of corporate stockholders meetings, mass civil disobedience (from sit-ins in offices to blockages of freeways), pickets in front of bosses' homes or corporate headquarters (even in Japan), community delegations, work-to-rule, union fiestas and marches, and the encirclement of city hall by hundreds of huge trucks, as well as traditional picket-lines and boycotts.[360]

The most perceptive analysts have identified in these organizing practices, and in their vision of democratic grassroots unionism, the beginnings of a strategy for "how the new urban working class can transform America."[361] Radical journalist David Bacon sums it up in the formula, "Blacks Plus Immigrants Plus Unions Equals Power."[362] Of course, the idea of simple addition can be misleading. More than addition, we are talking about a process in which the joining of these forces has a transformative effect, creating something genuinely new, something much greater than the sum of its parts. We are talking, in other words, of a coming together of working class communities that dramatically refashions the organizations in which they work—unions, community groups, and social movements in particular—and in so doing generates new institutions of grassroots power.[363] In the U.S. case, this would mean bringing together the traditions of Oaxaca and Cochabamba with those of Black Power, antiracist feminism, and the mass struggles of the Civil Rights Movement, and then connecting this powerful mixture with the earlier memories of radical U.S. labor, from the Industrial Workers of the World (the "Wobblies") and the sit-down strikes of the 1930s, to the League of Revolutionary Black Workers and the Dodge Revolutionary Union Movement of Detroit in the early 1970s. It would also mean learning from the best antiracist, feminist, working class practices of groups active today, such as the Asian Immigrant Women Advocates in Oakland; *La Mujer Obrera* (The Woman Worker) in El Paso; Black Workers for Justice in North Carolina; the Chinese Staff and Workers Association in New York; Fuerza Unida (*United Force*) in San Antonio; the Bus Riders Union in Los Angeles; the Center for Third World Organizing; People United to Win Employment Rights in San Francisco; and Labor Notes, which brings together rank and file union movements and activists across the U.S.[364] In Canada, the experiences of groups like the Immigrant Workers Centre in Montreal, the Ontario Coalition Against Poverty, the Solidarity Caucus in the British Columbia Federation of Labour, *Justicia* for Migrant Workers, the Communities Solidarity Coalition in Victoria, and No One is Illegal would figure prominently.

Such developments will have to address real contradictions within and among oppressed groups and radical movements, as well as the debilitating and fragmenting legacies of neoliberalism and retreat for the Left. Conscious strategies to build common actions, develop sustained dialogues and joint work, and create a new synthesis of cultures of dissent will be at a premium. We get a glimpse of what practices of building unity in action can look like in the case of the Hotel Workers Rising campaign initiated by progressive locals of UNITE HERE in 2004–5. In response to efforts by employers in the hotel to get rid of African-American workers while hiring more Latinos, UNITE HERE locals in Los

Angeles, Chicago and Boston, among other cities, bargained for both greater protections for Latinos and a commitment to hire more African-Americans. In so doing, they built a form of working class solidarity; not surprisingly, employers resisted this demand more strenuously than any other.[365]

Of course, the self-organization of workers of color will also have to confront the problem of drawing white workers into the struggle. And this can be a complicated and frustrating process given the acceptance of racism, patriotism, and respect for authority frequently found among white working class people. Nevertheless, the experience of white workers is contradictory, for they too suffer from capitalism and they resist many of its effects. Implicated in dominant practices as they often are, white workers are at the same time exploited and alienated by this system. They too are subject to layoffs and foreclosure; they too suffer from economic insecurity and demeaning hierarchies at work. They need to discover that their own compelling interests lie in common struggle—over jobs, working conditions, housing, and so on—at the same time as their racism is challenged by the very radical movements that are defending and supporting them. History shows that white workers can become enthusiastic participants in insurgent multiracial working class movements.[366] But this is not accomplished by trying to find a common ground of "class unity" that ignores or downplays the very real social hierarchies—based on race, gender, sexuality, and ability—that frequently divide workers. It means instead developing a politics of working class solidarity and struggle that both identifies common ground while also challenging many workers' investments in oppressive relations and practices.

One can see today the germs of such a working class convergence—one that could create a new radical labor movement and culture—but for these to grow into sustainable mass movements will require energy, vision, and dedicated organizing. The latter means having a long-term orientation, not a quick-fix one, as we are talking about years of organizing real community- and workplace-based movements in which thousands of people directly and democratically participate and build their own capacities as world-changers. This will also require new radical-left organizations that disavow sectarianism and devote themselves to broad-based anticapitalist and working class organizing along profoundly feminist and antiracist lines. As Mike Davis notes, this entails developing a new Left that creates spaces for nurturing "a cadre of people able to exchange and generalize and coordinate experiences across the struggle so that some kind of genuinely left agenda—which means a pro–working class agenda—becomes possible."[367]

In the Global North, of course, bigger steps in these directions have been taken in places other than the United States, Britain, and Canada. Greece, for instance, which has seen a series of general strikes and mass demonstrations against austerity, has a courageous working class tradition that includes armed struggle in the Civil War of the 1940s and resistance to the military dictatorship of 1967–74. At the same time, its working class movements have suffered from the sectarianism that has often plagued the Left. Recent years, however, have seen a new spirit of non-sectarian collaboration and the birth of the Coalition of the Radical Left (SYRIZA), an alliance of more than ten left-wing groups. The Coalition has played a significant role in building the mass resistance movements in Greece, while also creating a Left front in parliamentary politics, which received nearly 5 percent of the vote and won thirteen seats in the 2007 elections. As the crisis hit in early 2010, and huge cuts to jobs, pensions and public sector wages were decreed, Greek unions launched a series of general strikes—on February 24, March 11, May 5, and May 20—that included huge demonstrations, such as that of May 20 when fifty thousand people poured through the streets of Athens, chanting "Down with the IMF Junta!" and "The struggles of the people will destroy the IMF slaughterhouse!" The mass actions have also shifted public opinion. From a resigned acceptance of the cuts, a majority of Greeks have moved to open opposition.[368]

In learning from the struggles in Greece, it is also urgent that we counter the deceptions of the ruling class. The mainstream media regularly attack the allegedly lazy, over-paid Greek workers who enjoy "rich" benefits while barely showing up to work. The reality—not surprisingly—is dramatically different, as a quick look at the official data provided by Eurostat and the International Labor Organization shows. For instance, Greek people work much longer annual hours than most of their European counterparts: 2,120 hours in 2008 on average compared to 1,430 hours for German workers. The *average* gross monthly wage in Greece is 803 euros (about $1063 US), compared with the *lowest* salary in Ireland of 1,300 euros, or 1,400 in the Netherlands. Meanwhile, the average Greek pension is just over one-quarter of the Belgian and one-fifth the Dutch average. It is rarely understood that public sector workers in Greece have been getting poorer throughout the neoliberal period, having endured salary cuts of 30 percent since 1990. To make matters worse, the cost of living—for everything from breakfast cereal to toothpaste to coffee—is much higher in Greece than most European countries.[369] These are the circumstances in which, in the face of enormous obstacles, Greek workers are mobilizing in the streets and sections of the Left are collaborating to create a larger presence for working class politics.

The radical Left has also charted promising directions in France. Since 1995, French youth, immigrants, workers, and feminists have been in the forefront of worldwide anti-neoliberal resistance, including student upsurges and escalating strike movements that, among other things, forced the government to shelve plans for a lower minimum wage for youth. Similar conflicts see-sawed back and forth over the following years, the government winning some, the opposition in the streets prevailing in others. But neoliberalism was unable to gain cultural and political dominance. Then, in the fall of 2005, the ruling class was rattled by an upsurge of youth of color in the immigrant neighborhoods of France, "the largest revolt the French suburbs had ever known." In response to a police killing of an unarmed youth, young people of color rose up in a three-week long rebellion that swept two hundred towns and destroyed ten thousand vehicles, most of them torched. No sooner had the government used mass arrests to regain control than it introduced a Youth Employment Contract scheme that would have allowed employers to fire workers under twenty-six without giving cause. Again the streets erupted. In the early months of 2006, students occupied three-quarters of the country's universities; high school students joined the protest movement in huge numbers; mass assemblies provided democratic means of coordinating the resistance; and the workers began to move in a wave of solidarity strikes. Once more, the government relented, handing another victory to the millions who took to the streets.[370] Then, when the global crisis broke in 2008–9, workers in France frequently led the way with boss-nappings and other tactics to save jobs, while organizations of the undocumented spearheaded sit-ins and occupations in defense of migrant workers.

As a result of such struggles, a robust oppositional consciousness exists in France, notwithstanding the fact that the number of workers in unions is small. Indeed, the French case demonstrates something that Rosa Luxemburg observed in 1905: the level of active struggle is more important than the degree of formal organization. So, while representing only about 10 percent of all wage laborers, the French unions are "at the same time weak and dynamic," in the words of one activist. Their small implantation in workplaces coexists with high levels of mobilization, "a dynamic union culture" and the involvement and confidence of wide layers of activists.[371] Consequently, despite the organizational weakness of unions, there are hundreds of thousands of class-conscious workers in France alongside large numbers of radical students and social movement activists.

This is the context in which some of the more thoughtful forces of the radical Left seized the moment to create a new broad-based political organization, the New Anticapitalist Party (NPA), launched in early 2009 with nine thousand members drawn from far-left groups, migrant rights organizations (known as the movement of the *sans-papiers*), trade unions, and social movements. Like SYRIZA in Greece, the NPA and its candidates have proved capable of winning about 5 percent of the vote in certain elections.[372] Indeed, provoked in March 2009 to name public figures who will influence the political outcome of the crisis ("Fifty who will frame a way forward"), the *Financial Times* listed the predictable ones: Barack Obama, Wen Jibao, China's prime minister, and German Chancellor Angela Merkel were numbers one through three were. But number thirteen on the list was somewhat less predictable: Olivier Besancenot of the NPA. "The French Trotskyist postman who heads the New Anticapitalist party, France's biggest extreme left group," wrote the journalists, "dreams of using unrest triggered by the recession to overturn the social and political order. Rated in polls as France's most effective opposition politician, he has fought two presidential elections, winning well over 1 million votes in each."[373] More recently, the NPA has come under fire in the mainstream media because one of its candidates in the regional elections, Ilham Moussaid, wears a head scarf, or *hijab*. When challenged over her candidacy for the NPA, Olivier Besancenot proudly replied, "Our party welcomes youth, the unemployed, the precarious, workers of all backgrounds who find their values reflected in the party. Faith is a matter of personal choice that does not create any obstacle to participation in our struggle so long as members sincerely share the secular, feminist, and anticapitalist fundamental principles of our party."[374] While the NPA has a long way to go to generate a real mass breakthrough for radical Left politics in France, it has steadfastly developed a socialist, feminist, antiracist, and working class orientation to the struggles in France. It remains too early to fully assess this new experiment in radical socialist politics. But across the decade of austerity we have entered, these militant, non-sectarian, and democratic ways of organizing offer hope that a genuine new Left might emerge.

Fighting for Reforms, Building Resistance, Changing the World

Every mass movement to change the world begins with struggles to reform society. No movement for radical change begins by demanding revolution as such. Instead, world-transforming struggles emerge when oppressed people take to the streets and shut down places of work to demand a living wage, civil rights, a shorter working day, housing for all, or an end to war. It is in the course of mobilizing—in the process of reclaiming the streets, creating road blockades, occupying workplaces, deliberating in mass assemblies, creating new forms of demŏcratic self-rule—that people gain a sense of their own power, expand their horizons, and begin to imagine that another world is truly possible. Consider, for instance, the popular upheaval in Oaxaca. It began with a mobilization by teachers for better wages, free uniforms, and books for students, and so on. In and of themselves, there is nothing revolutionary about such demands. They are basic reforms. But the *forms of struggle* that the teachers and their allies used were anything but reformist. They did not respect the passive tactics of electoral politics and ordinary collective bargaining. Instead, they seized the city center, built encampments, beat back the police attacks, waged mass demonstrations, occupied radio stations, constructed a people's police force, and created a new mass democratic assembly, APPO, that temporarily dislodged institutions of the ruling class. In the process, they challenged property rights and the legitimacy of government and they asserted mass popular power. In short, the working class of Oaxaca was fighting for reforms by revolutionary means. This is the inherent nature of an insurgent mass upheaval—and it gives these movements a complex, contradictory character.

Two perceptive analysts of the Oaxaca Commune observe that it involved "an ambiguous mix of 'collective bargaining by insurrection,' and a dual power situation in one city."[375] Put differently, it was a mass movement demanding reforms, including the resignation of the state governor, by means of insurrectionary forms of dual power. In this regard, the struggle in Oaxaca fits the analysis of Rosa Luxemburg in her classic piece, *Reform or Revolution*. The difference between those committed to socialist transformation of society and those who confine themselves to piecemeal reform, argued Luxemburg, is not that the latter support reform and the former do not. Both groups, including those dedicated to revolutionary change, are utterly committed to reforms, she insisted. After all, everything that improves the well-being of the poor, the oppressed, and the exploited is to be welcomed. But more significant, the *struggle* for reforms is the rich and indispensable soil without which no genuinely mass democratic movement for change can grow. It is in and through such struggles that people challenge authority, overcome deference, discover new capacities in themselves, build new solidarities, acquire a hitherto unknown self-confidence, and begin to believe that ordinary workers can run society. Consequently, Luxemburg insisted, the issue is not reform or revolution, but reform *and* revolution: "the struggle for reforms is its means; the social revolution its *goal*."[376]

In the battle for reforms, therefore, it is the transformative *process* of mass struggle itself that is crucial. Analyzing a series of insurgent mass movements between 1968 and 1981, Colin Barker remarks that in such struggles,

> New hopes emerge. Previous habits of subordination and deference collapse. A new sense of personal and collective power develops. The "common sense" of class society falters. Historic hierarchies—in workplaces, in the state, in schools and colleges, in families—are threatened and actually begin to tumble . . .
>
> Popular confidence and imagination grow by leaps and bounds. With them practical intelligence also rises; nothing is so mentally numbing as the habit of subordination. Every "festival of the oppressed" involves a sudden release of collective pleasure. Perspectives alter, the horizon of possibility extends.
>
> . . . New languages, symbols, artistic forms are adopted to express the new conditions; the flourishing of posters, symbols, newspapers, leaflets, badges, and jokes bears witness to the profound shifts going on in the consciousness of millions . . .
>
> Previous property rules are challenged. Premises are occupied. Existing uses of places and things are altered. Land is taken over, workplaces seized . . . The workers are in the boardroom, the crowd is in the palace, the confidential files are opened, the workers' commission is inspecting the warehouse. What was closed is open . . .[377]

New Lefts are born out of such episodes. They cannot be conjured into existence; only mass movements create the circumstances in which genuinely radical change begins to feel like a living, breathing possibility, rather than merely the beautiful

dreams of isolated minorities. Without a rebirth of mass struggle, it is impossible to get much beyond the sphere of small radical
groups, some of whom do good work, others of whom are more
intent on squabbling. But when we enter a period of large-scale
resistance, then it becomes urgent that the most serious activists of the Left figure out how to collaborate and strengthen the
oppositional struggles, to help forge new solidarities, to create
democratic forums and assemblies of activists, to increase the
presence of antiracist, feminist, class-struggle politics. Without
such initiatives, there will be an overwhelming tendency for resistance to be squandered, for old bureaucratic structures and rou-
tines to hem in the movement by limiting the scale, creativity,
militancy, and democratic propulsion of the struggle.

In most of the Global North, of course, we are in the early
stages of rebuilding infrastructures of dissent, not usually of
leading mass struggles. But even here, the relationship between
rebuilding at the base and organizing sizable movements is a
complex one. There are times, like the spring 2010 wave of stu-
dent-worker resistance in California or the general strikes and
street demonstrations in Greece, where small forces of the non-
sectarian and anticapitalist Left can play a decisive role in mass
protest. But, the mark of success here is not only the scale and
militancy of the actions that are galvanized. Equally crucial is
the building of viable and sustained movements—spaces of self-
organization, mass mobilization, popular education, and political
development—that develop radical anticapitalist politics and the
infrastructures necessary to nourish them in communities, workplaces, and schools. This will necessarily involve the growth of
workers' centers, solidarity coalitions, radical community groups,
alternative media, union organizing drives, campaigns against
racism and in support of non-status people, the creation of artistic and cultural co-ops, and much more. It will mean building the
democratic spaces and practices that develop organizers who are
in the struggle for the long haul. All of this is essential to overcoming the damage of the neoliberal period—the dispossession
of memory, social fragmentation, and the destruction of solidarities, the political and cultural effects of a long period with-

out sustained mass oppositional politics. Here a complex dialectic will come into play in which a New Left learns from the rich resources of struggle from the past without mimicry—by understanding that real mass movements for revolutionary change are strengthened by remembering the compelling legacies of those who struggled before us while not being confined by their horizons and experiences. While honoring past struggles, revolutionary movements also write a new poetry for the future. And that poetry—joined to the hard-nosed work of organizing—can only develop from the soil of real social struggle, not the concoctions of small groups.

Part of the work of remembering, of overcoming neoliberal amnesia, is to recall those moments in history when the seemingly small-scale local work of grassroots radicals contributed to momentous change. As historians have noted, the year 1934 was one such time in the U.S. That was the year when, despite the Great Depression and a decade and a half of retreat by labor, the hard work of left-wing activists changed politics on a mass scale. A series of key strikes were instrumental here. First was the great longshoremen's revolt in San Francisco that grew into a partial general strike of 130,000 workers from twenty-one unions. Next came the fight of auto parts workers in Toledo, Ohio, supported by the American Workers' Party and the Lucas County Unemployed League—a strike in which, in a single day, up to six thousand union members and their supporters engaged a seven-hour battle with police and the National Guard, three times breaking into their factory. The uprising of Minneapolis labor came next, galvanized by left-wing radicals allied with the dissenting ideas of Leon Trotsky. That strike, spearheaded by a radical local of the Teamsters union, involved the creation of union flying squads, a democratically elected rank and file strike committee, a daily workers' newspaper, and a public strike headquarters that at times housed ten thousand people. At its height between twenty and thirty thousand people cooperated in mass action against police and scabs.[378]

These three strikes broke the pattern of defeat that had prevailed for fifteen years after 1919. They demonstrated that new forms of militant mass struggle could turn back the employers, the police, and the state. They showed the capacities of radical working class activism to make a difference in the here and now. As a result of the long-term presence of organized radicals of the Left in San Francisco, Toledo, and Minneapolis who had done years of patient organizing, a militant working class culture thrived and socialist politics became integral aspects of the daily lives of these working class communities. These activists had not been out for instant results; they had understood that class-struggle politics require sustained commitments. But at the right time, their efforts changed history. After their victories of 1934, things would never be the same. Victory is inspiring and infectious—insurgent labor was on the move. Within a few years a huge working class upheaval, peaking in 1937, would transform the whole political and cultural climate. That was the year the sit-down strike became the order of the day. Labor upheaval swept the country; new unions were born; autoworkers cracked GM through sit-down strikes; children sat down in movie theaters. Like all insurgent moments, the participants were transformed. Black workers led uprisings of textile workers; "a new type of woman was born"—defiant, confident, rebellious—as one commentator noted.[379] And as new working class solidarities emerged, "a veritable revolution of personality" took shape, one analyst observed. Daily life was reshaped as communities forged new bonds of hope and solidarity, developed new practices of cooperation, dreamed of and fought for a better world.[380] But the seeds of this great shift had been sown in the many years of patient, unheralded organizing work that took place during the years of retreat.

These struggles also remind us that unions—particularly when they are transformed by rank-and-file insurgency in the heat of struggle—can still be vital organizations of working class organization and resistance. It is true, especially in the Global North, that trade unions have become deeply bureaucratized practitioners of business unionism. The latter refers to a mode of operation based on a passive, demobilized membership taught to rely on a stable of "experts," from lawyers and professional negotiators to career labor officials; it also refers to a style of union-ism that focuses only on issues of immediate wage and benefit bargaining while effectively discouraging involvement in and sol-idarity with the struggles of oppressed communities around the world. This model systematically undermines the democratic and insurgent capacities that unions have exhibited during periods of working class revolt. That is why determined groups of activists are engaged in the patient work of reclaiming and democratiz-ing unions—which does not simply mean electing better lead-ers, but, rather, radically democratizing the unions as rank and file controlled fighting organizations of workers themselves.[381] And it is why, alongside the reclaiming of some existing unions, periods of labor insurgency usually see new radical and grass-roots labor movements emerge.

It is obvious today that mass protest has re-emerged in the context of the global slump. As I write this chapter, general strikes have been called in Greece, Spain, and Italy. A series of major protests against education cuts—strikes, demonstrations, and sit-ins—has swept California, creating small but important ele-ments of worker-student solidarity in the process.[382] Street-level mobilizations in California have also figured prominently in the renewed upsurge of immigrant workers' protest across the U.S. in response to anti-immigrant legislation in Arizona. As I noted in the last chapter, a May Day 2010 march for immigrant rights in Los Angeles drew 150,000. Meanwhile, a wave of worker pro-test is sweeping parts of China. Launched by migrant workers, the strikes spread from factory to factory, frequently winning substantial improvements in wages for the working poor. In the face of harsh repression, dissident workers in China have dis-played exceptional courage. Twenty year-old Li Xiaojuan, who works on the production line at a Honda components plant in Foshan, has become a public spokeswoman for local workers. In early June 2010 she issued an open letter on behalf of those who negotiated for the strikers. It proclaimed in part, "We must maintain a high degree of unity and not let the representatives of Capital divide us. This factory's profits are the fruits of our bitter toil . . . This struggle is not just about the interests of our

1,800 workers. We also care about the rights and interests of all Chinese workers." And in interviews she has even broached the topic that profoundly worries China's rulers, declaring that "sooner or later we will start to build our own independent union." And striking workers at another sweatshop, KOK International, issued their own simple formula: "Power lies in unity and hope lies in defiance."[383]

It remains the case, however, that the building of a new Left remains in its early stages. Unity and defiance are still rarely joined to mass, democratic anticapitalist organization. In the absence of meaningful revolutionary organization across Mexico linked to movements beyond, even a mighty struggle on the scale of the Oaxaca Commune could not withstand the assault of the Mexican Army. Genuinely world-changing struggles, revolutionary movements that remake society from below, require mass anticapitalist organizations of a sort that simply do not exist today. They remain to be built. And that will be a key project for the next Left.

Yet, that project is on the agenda because the wind of rebellion is blowing from France to Guadeloupe, from Iceland to California, from Greece to Oaxaca. The task will be to do the years of serious, dedicated grassroots organizing to help channel those winds into a Great Resistance that can break through the age of austerity and chart a path to social and economic justice.

Conclusion

"I'm fighting against this economic system that makes
men, women, and entire families suffer. Everyone
realizes this now. This system is starting to explode; it
should no longer exist. It makes the entire world suffer,
it enriches the rich and impoverishes the poor."
—Pierre Piccarreta, fifty-three-year-old French
factory worker and union activist, April 2010

IF WE WANT A SNAPSHOT OF OUR AGE, WE COULD DO WORSE THAN
look at Toronto in late June 2010, when world leaders dined in
luxury behind a security fence while twenty thousand police went
on a rampage, hunting down protestors, beating and arresting
them, and detaining the captured in cages.

The occasion was the annual meetings of the G20, the organization representing the rulers of the world's twenty largest economic powerhouses. As is the custom, the G20 leaders posed for
photo-ops and then retreated behind closed doors, concealing
their deliberations from the public. At the end they issued another
bland communiqué declaring their commitment to "strong, sustainable and balanced growth." All of that may sound entirely
unobjectionable. What was happening in the streets was anything but.

As if G20 leaders were rehearsing their plans to criminalize
resistance to our new age of austerity, protesters were met by
a wave of repression involving teargas and rubber bullets, mass
arrests (over one thousand detained), widespread police brutal-
ity, and violations of civil and human rights, all at a cost of over
$1 billion for "security."[384] Police infiltrated meetings, snatched
community organizers off the streets, donned Darth Vader–type
riot gear, beat peaceful demonstrators, and apprehended people

whose only "crime" was to have dared attend a protest rally. In sharp contrast to vague communiqués, the repression in the streets uncovered the true face of G20 policy. For in order to conduct their war against the poor, our rulers need to use force and intimidation to create a culture of fear.

Seen in this light, it is easier to decode the latent meanings in the G20 statement. In a key passage, for instance, the final declaration states, "advanced economies have committed to fiscal plans that will at least halve deficits by 2013 and stabilize or reduce government debt-to-GDP ratios by 2016."[385] Such insipid rhetoric is meant to lull us to sleep; it is designed to switch off our critical faculties. Instead, our alarm bells should be ringing. For embedded in that statement is the idea that, the banks having been rescued, governments will do nothing to avert the continuing human recession. Instead, they plan to intensify their attacks on social programs and the world working class.

To do this, they need to break the spirit of resistance—one reason for the massive police presence in the streets of Toronto—and to soften up people for the attacks to come by convincing them both of their economic necessity as well as of the futility of opposition.

To this end, they are deploying the neoliberal shock doctrine on a new scale. "Shock doctrine" refers to the idea that our rulers cannot carry through radical neoliberal restructuring without first traumatizing the population. Massive attacks on pensions, healthcare, education, public sector jobs and incomes, and on people's image of the sort of life they ought to expect—none of this can be accomplished without generating a profound sense of social crisis, a panic that life as we know it is now imperiled. Frequently, wars and natural disasters have been strategically manipulated to that end.[386] The shock doctrine, notes Stathis Kouvelakis, involves "creating and staging an 'exceptional' situation, a situation of emergency, in the wake of which, somehow, normal life is disrupted and what seemed until quite recently unimaginable just happens."[387] Across the neoliberal period, such tactics were surgically applied within the Global North. When a harsh right-wing government was elected in the Canadian province of

Ontario in 1995, it set out to drastically restructure education so as to weaken teachers' unions, undermine antiracist and antisexist schooling, and inculcate neoliberal values. To this end, it utilized the shock doctrine—as was revealed when a leaked video recording showed the government's education minister proclaiming the importance of "creating a useful crisis" to accomplish its goals.[388]

Such shock and awe campaigns have been widespread over the past thirty years. But catastrophic reengineering of the whole social order was generally confined to states in the Third World. That is now changing, as nations in the capitalist core are subjected to traumatic restructuring. In very short order, for instance, "millions of Europeans who had been given a foothold in . . . the world of property ownership, secure employment and university education have now been plunged into lives of rented rooms, paltry minimum-wage jobs and dependency on an increasingly feeble state."[389] And now state services are being gutted. Just two years ago it would have seemed unimaginable that Greek pensions might be savaged, that Greeks would be forced in old age to live on *half* of what they had been promised (and had paid for through their lifelong retirement contributions). But the "emergency situation" created by a sovereign debt crisis is designed to create a new normal, one in which the unimaginable is deemed inevitable.

Millions of Greek workers, however, are saying no to this drive toward a new normal; they are refusing dramatically reduced expectations about what life can offer. Through an impressive series of general strikes and street protests, they are challenging their rulers' account of the social crisis; they are disclaiming responsibility for the failures of capitalism. More than this, in the spring of 2010 their strikes and militant street demonstrations broke the pattern of established politics. Hundreds of thousands of strikers and their supporters—students, youth, the unemployed, the retired—reclaimed the streets. Public sector workers clashed with police in confrontations that flared into pitched battles. Mass opposition to the ruling class opened a new political conjuncture, as the *de-politicized politics* of normal bourgeois life were challenged by the radically democratic politics of insurgency from below.[390] Yet, impressive and inspiring as the resistance has been, it is not yet enough. The Greek ruling class is prepared to tack and turn through the stormy seas of mass protest at these levels. Popular success will require that the Left push things to a still higher level of social mobilization, one that generates a crisis of ungovernability. If it does not, there is a risk that the whole of society will slide backward. "If the Left and the organized forces of Greek society are not able to meet the challenge," argues Kouvelakis, "if they appear powerless and fragmented, they will be swept away amid the dislocation of social relations and the rise of despair and, probably, of the most reactionary and regressive tendencies within society."[391]

We do not need to consult the past to see what these "reactionary and regressive tendencies" look like. The recent surge in support for the far-right Freedom Party in the Dutch elections of June 2010 indicates what can happen if the Left fails to build real solidarity and fighting capacities. Exploiting dislocation and despair, the leader of the Freedom Party advocates "less crime, less immigration, less Islam" in a racist triad that carried his party to twenty-four seats in parliament, up from nine just four years earlier.[392] The germs of the same virulent politics lurk in the anti-immigrant laws in Arizona and in government attacks on refugees and immigrants in Canada and elsewhere.[393] They reared their head in the 2009 strike by refinery workers in Britain that commenced with the slogan, "Put British workers first"—before strategic interventions by socialists in the union helped re-channel workers' anger.[394] A prolonged global slump can provide dangerously fertile grounds for nativist and racist sentiments. History serves warning that we cannot underestimate the perils they represent. But it also reminds us that their advance is not inevitable.

New mass working class movements of struggle, solidarity, and intransigent antiracism can redefine the political field, opening up the space for a rupture to the Left. The examples of Cochabamba and Oaxaca show what is possible when working classes rise up in all their diversity, animated by the insurgence of women, youth, indigenous activists, and racialized populations. Partial ruptures already exist in places like Bolivia and

Venezuela, where popular movements are charting an anti-neo-liberal course. But in most contexts today, it will require years of struggle, organizing, and resistance before insurgent mass opposition can redefine the political field.

Periods of enduring crisis and sporadic resistance are complex and dangerous. Desperation, anxiety, and hopelessness preside. The dominant class seems no longer to believe in itself. Rarely does it bother to espouse lofty ideals like freedom and betterment of the human condition. At the beginning of the neoliberal era, by contrast, politicians such as Margaret Thatcher and Ronald Reagan strode forth triumphantly, full of evangelical fervor about the righteousness of their crusade on behalf of markets and liberal individualism. But yesterday's confidence has been replaced by a glum pessimism. Rather than trying to inspire belief in their system, society's rulers seem to have no higher purpose than maintaining the status quo, squeezing profit and privilege out of a decrepit but well protected machinery of power. They know that talk of growth, development and human improvement is idle chit-chat. They understand that their task is to make life worse for the majority. In this climate, our rulers grow increasingly spiteful and unaccountable. They seem indifferent to the public, happy to leave things to PR specialists and spin doctors. *Après moi le déluge* ("After me comes the flood") was the statement attributed to King Louis XV of France as the feudal society of eighteenth-century France fell into a deep funk from which only revolution could relieve it. The aristocracy's days were numbered, and the French king knew it. He expressed the mind-set of a ruling class that realizes it has no vision for the future, a class that has no other principle than to cling to power. In this environment, a general lethargy and cynicism appears to descend on everyone. The same is true of the general mood today. The atmosphere we breathe is one of grinding, mind-numbing domination by faceless bureaucrats in business suits, their declarations parroted by corporate media, and backed up by riot police determined to quell all dissent. Society seems bereft of any uplifting human cause.

The cultural and political moment of mutant neoliberalism is bathed in a similar ambient light. Reduced to harsh neoliberal methods of exploitation and shorn of any ideological claims for freedom and progress, its ethos becomes increasingly morbid. Naked money-grabbing, mercenary politics, and unconcealed use of force in the service of power are the order of the day. Governments seem content to attack the population; the rich live merely to get richer. In all these ways, the decade of austerity becomes one of social and cultural regression.

And yet . . . and yet, there is more to the story of our moment. Below the surface, discontent accumulates. Oppressed people gather in community centers and union halls to organize rallies, strikes, marches, concerts, pickets, and festivals. Underground currents of refusal and resistance flow together, occasionally gathering steam. Anger and imagination converge to carve out liberated zones of activism. A swift outbreak of social protest—student occupations against education cuts, large protests by migrant workers, general strikes in Greece or Guadeloupe, a revolt by racialized youth, a week of street protests against the G20—suddenly splatters hope across a landscape of despair. Crowds jam the streets, the people are on the move, police are pushed back, the thrill of solidarity and the sense of new possibilities electrifies a growing movement. Cries of "This is what democracy looks like!" fill the air; a festival of the oppressed transforms the landscape.

All too often, however, the movement then stalls. The militants lack the organizations and infrastructures necessary to sustain mobilization when the tired bureaucrats retreat. The *ancien régime* regroups; order is restored. Neither side can win an utterly decisive victory. The ruling class tries to hold out in the hope that resistance will exhaust itself (how many one-day general strikes without victory can workers sustain?). In this situation, a sort of *morbid crisis* appears; the old order is corrupt and cynical, the radical opposition too weak and fragile to make a breakthrough. "The crisis," wrote Antonio Gramsci, "consists precisely in the fact that the old is dying and the new cannot be born; in this interregnum a great variety of morbid symptoms appear."[395] These are, as we have noted, times of real danger—moments of anxiety and despair when forces of reaction can seize the agenda. But they are also moments of possibility, when dedicated organizing can produce a series of victories—like those of 1934—that create a sea change in political life.

As we have seen, such dedicated organizing begins on the terrain of concrete struggles for reforms, around basic issues such as housing, jobs, pensions, immigrant rights, environmental justice. But reform struggles need to become the basis for resistance movements, for sustained campaigns and organizations that keep broadening out the movement while deepening its politics. And this is done by drawing out the systemic obstacles capitalism throws up to basic human needs—be it for housing, healthcare, environmental sustainability, or real community. This is how concrete, tangible links are drawn between reform and revolution. Equally crucial is that resistance movements begin to popularize visions of a post-capitalist society, and that they try to give these some small meaning in the here and now by cultivating practices of radical democracy. Neoliberalism in the age of austerity has ceded much of the ground to the Left in these regards. As we have seen, contemporary neoliberalism is largely incapable of summoning up a compelling vision of the future. Equally disabling, it regularly sets itself in opposition to democracy. This opens up vital space for the anticapitalist Left to project its radical imagination and to reclaim democracy—radical, direct democracy in particular—as a core value.

Writing about the development of a New Left in Latin America, one commentator ascribes it to the convergence of four factors: the exhaustion of neoliberalism; the failure of capitalist democracy; the breakdown of allegiances to traditional parties and institutions; the globalization of struggles against neoliberalism.[396] Now, similar conditions are emerging in at least parts of the Global North. The question is whether we too can enter into unyielding processes of rebuilding movements, infrastructures of dissent and oppositional capacities.

A New Left cannot be a mere replica of the old. It must construct a new synthesis of resources from the past joined to emergent elements of the solidarities and forms of struggle that point toward an emancipated future. Analysts have often observed that the Latin American New Left is less monolithic, more diverse, and more intransigently democratic than some of its predecessors. Commitments to radical democracy as both the means and the end of the movement reconnect this Left to the emancipatory impulses of its most subversive histories. This is a Left, for instance, for whom Rosa Luxemburg's injunctions about socialism and democracy resonate loudly. "The struggle for socialism," she wrote, "must be fought out by the masses . . . Socialism will not and cannot be created by decrees; nor can it be established by any government, however socialistic. Socialism must be created by the masses, must be made by every worker. Where the chains of capitalism are forged, there they must be broken." Elsewhere, she elaborated: "The essence of socialist society consists in the fact that the great laboring mass ceases to be a dominated mass, but rather makes the entire political and economic life its own life and gives that life a conscious, free and autonomous direction."[397]

Here, then, we see some elements of the past that can vitalize a socialism for the twenty-first century.[398] This expression itself is crucial, as it embodies the conviction that we are mobilizing past resources to create something new—a vigorous, dynamic, unflagging movement of opposition to capitalism and all its multiple oppressions. The building of such a New Left is a momentous process. It means reawakening the magnificent dream of liberty and equality that has defined the great freedom struggles of the past. It involves drawing out everything that is most vital and radical in the struggles of the present. And it entails finally winning the battle for democracy in its most profound (and ancient) sense—rule of the poor.[399]

There can be little doubt that democracy will be one of the great contested terrains of the period of global slump. As the pain of austerity bites and social protest grows, riot police and jail cells are being deployed as intrinsic parts of the antidemocratic arsenal relied on by our rulers. Indeed, some bourgeois commentators are already blaming democracy for the crisis. "Democracies end in bankruptcy," writes one. He then mobilizes the ancient hostility to democracy as a society in which the oppressed no longer know their place, one in which the downtrodden rebel against their masters. The very idea of democracy now rattles the paranoid imagination of frightened elites, conjuring up images of subaltern masses in revolt. Even worse, frets our bourgeois commentator, democracy is now actually breeding revolution. In response to public spending cuts, he explains,

> Mobs have already taken to the venerable, iconic streets of European states, notably among them Greece, birthplace of Athenian democracy . . .
>
> Already, hundreds of thousands . . . have thronged the streets of Paris and Rome, of Milan and Sarajevo, of Reykjavik and Bucharest (where demonstrators stormed the presidential palace, an insurgent act that invokes the spectre of revolution).[400]

The specter of revolution indeed. Every time tens of thousands mobilize, that specter haunts our rulers' sleep. And so, they stockpile weapons, tear gas, sound cannons, helicopters and more to quell dissent, as they did during the G20 meetings in Toronto, when tear gas and rubber bullets joined with beatings, inhumane detention, and violations of civil rights in a relentless assault on democracy. Still, the ruling class could not break the spirit of resistance, which bravely and defiantly took its protest to the city's police headquarters.[401]

It is the nature of the transformative moment ushered in by the global slump that such protests—and with them the specter of revolution—regularly resurge. Our challenge is to be equal to this moment—to respond by building a genuinely radical *mass* anticapitalist movement for the first time in a very long time. There are no guarantees we will succeed. Nor can there be when we understand the present as history. The future is always open-ended. That is why what we do today, tomorrow, and next year matters. And if we are unequal to the challenge of our times, we might at least leave another generation with greater resources, with historical lessons, tracts and memories from which they might learn—and which might strengthen their struggles. In their own way, they can then pick up where we left off, perhaps with greater courage, dedication and intelligence.

In his brilliant novel, *Birth of Our Power*, Victor Serge meditated on the complex relationship between defeats and victories for revolutionary movements. Having been released from prison, where he had spent five years for his anarchist convictions, Serge participated in a failed uprising in Barcelona in 1917, then headed to Russia, where a workers and peasants uprising had toppled the Czar and brought a coalition of the Left to power. In his novel, a group of worker radicals engages in a spirited discussion about what had transpired. The narrator offers his explanation of events:

> It takes time, years, thousands of people, thousands of years in prison . . . betrayals, provocations, fresh start after fresh start until, in the end, an old Empire, eaten away by termites, suddenly collapses because some workers' wives have begun to shout "Bread!" in front of the bakeries, because the soldiers fraternize with the mob, because . . . I don't have to teach them, they understand these things perfectly. But someone wants the incredible truth repeated: that it has really happened. Someone demands, his hand outstretched:
> "Well, and the Czar? . . ."
> "No more Czars" . . .
> "The army?"
> "With the people."
> "The police?"
> "No more police."
> "The prisons?"
> "Burned."
> "The power?"
> "Us."[402]

Of course, the democratic working class power born in Russia's revolution did not survive. Foreign invasion, civil war, famine, and the emergence of a new bureaucracy crushed those dreams. Serge himself was arrested by Stalin's secret police, imprisoned, and driven into exile.[403] He then threw his heart and soul into support for the insurgent struggle against fascism in Spain, only to witness the tragic defeat of the workers' revolution in Barcelona in 1936–37. Despite all this, he recognized that his generation of uncompromising fighters for liberation had accomplished something that could never be extinguished. They had kept alive the flame of freedom so that its torch might be taken up by other hands. Reflecting on how working class movements fight to seize cities—he was thinking of Barcelona, but it could equally be Paris in 1871, or Oaxaca in 2006—he wrote,

> Tomorrow is full of greatness. We will not have brought this victory to ripeness in vain. This city will be taken, if not by our hands, at least by others like ours, only stronger ... If we are beaten, others, infinitely different from us, infinitely like us, will walk, on a similar evening in ten years, in twenty years (how long is really without importance) down this *rambla*, meditating on the same victory. Perhaps they will think about our blood ... But they will take the city.[404]

As we confront a decade of slump and austerity, we need the reminder that it can take "fresh start after fresh start until, in the end, an old Empire, eaten away by termites, suddenly collapses." It is true that the global Left is dramatically weakened by the defeats of the neoliberal period. The obstacles before us are enormous. But the implications of failing to build forces of resistance and transformation are equally momentous. For, it is also true that crisis-prone capitalism promises immense suffering for the mass of humankind—dispossession, war, exploitation, racism, hunger, and the pain of alienation that diminishes the human spirit. This is what makes the cause of anticapitalism and human freedom so compelling, whatever the odds. And it is what keeps hope alive amid the day-to-day work of organizing, resisting, agitating and protesting.

Reflecting on the years of work that prepared the victory against water privatization in Cochabamba, Oscar Olivera notes:

> Only this patient work—ant-like, honest, clear, and committed—could have resulted, years later, in the only workers', peasants' and popular organization that has proven itself capable of throwing out a foreign corporation, defeating the state, and, for one week, replacing the state with assembly-style self-government.

When we do such work, he continues, when we "find with each person in each neighborhood, in each school, in each market square, in each factory and university, those things that unite us . . . then we can win many victories."[405] And that is when another world becomes truly possible.

Glossary

Accumulation by dispossession: A term coined by David Harvey to describe how powerful groups or corporations accumulate wealth by seizing assets—particularly land and the natural resources to which it provides access—from others. This process frequently involves the forcible displacement of people from the lands on which they have lived. The result is that people are dispossessed of what they once owned, either individually or communally. See also: *primitive accumulation*.

Capital: In everyday language and mainstream economics, this refers to the assets accumulated by banks and nonfinancial corporations in order to make profits. Factories, offices, mines, agribusinesses, investment funds, and so on are business assets of this sort, and are thus frequently described as "capital." Karl Marx's great innovation was to insist that capital is fundamentally a social relation between owners of such assets ("capitalists") and wage-earners who are dispossessed of means of producing for themselves. See also: *primitive accumulation*.

Deleveraging: The process by which individuals, banks, corporations and / or governments reduce their debt loads (or "leverage").

Financialization: The multiple processes through which relations among people become ever more embedded in financial transactions, in buying and selling. The result is greater dependence on markets and money for everything from food and water to housing, health care, education and pensions. In some usages, the term also refers to both increasing reliance of the capitalist economy on credit and to growth in the share of wealth and profits going to banks and other financial (as opposed to industrial) institutions.

Globalization: This term typically refers to the international spread of manufacturing corporations and banks since the 1960s, often promoted by the World Bank and International Monetary

Fund. For this reason, it is most accurately described as *capitalist globalization*. It is also associated with neoliberalism (see next entry below) because the latter advocates the global spread of capitalist markets. In response, social justice movements have often called for the *globalization of resistance*.

Neoliberalism: The policies, practices and ideas associated with the sharp turn to market regulation of social life since the 1970s. Because this glorification of the market was first preached by the liberalism of the eighteenth- and nineteenth-centuries, the recent version is commonly referred to as a new or *neo*liberalism. Neoliberalism preaches hostility to socialism, trade unions, and social welfare programs, all of which are alleged to "interfere" with the market. Economists like Friedrich Hayek and Milton Friedman are often associated with this doctrine, as are politicians such as former British Prime Minister Margaret Thatcher and former U.S. president Ronald Reagan. The effects of neoliberalism have included increased social inequality, indebtedness for much of the Global South, and heightened policing and militarism.

Over-accumulation: The process by which capitalist enterprises accumulate more productive capacity—factories, machines, offices, mines, shopping malls, buildings, and so on—than they can profitably utilize. This is caused by intense competition to boost the productiveness of their companies by investing in new plants and technologies, which results in *over-capacity*.

Primitive accumulation: A term that Karl Marx used (probably better translated as *original* or *primary* accumulation) to indicate the processes of dispossession without which a capitalist economy could never get going. In Marx's analysis, capitalism requires rendering millions propertyless, while enabling a minority to accumulate great fortunes. The displacement of peasants from the land looms large in Marx's account, as do colonialism, the expropriation of indigenous lands, New World slavery, and the slave trade.

Sovereign debt crisis: A crisis triggered by government's taking on more debt (typically by selling bonds) than investors believe they are capable of repaying.

Notes

1   Carmen M. Reinhart and Kenneth S. Rogoff, *This Time is Different: Eight Centuries of Financial Folly* (Princeton: Princeton University Press, 2009), 208.

2   Georg Lukács, *History and Class Consciousness*, trans. Rodney Livingstone (London: Merlin Press, 1971), 204, my emphasis. Lukács's statement concerning the present "as an historical problem," appears on p. 157. Paul Sweezy reformulated Lukács's insight to create the memorable title for his volume of essays, The Present as History (New York: Monthly Review Press, 1953).

3   "The Future of Capitalism," *Financial Times*, March 8, 2009.

4   The Bank of England tagged the rescue cost for the financial system in the U.S., United Kingdom, and Eurozone at about $14 trillion (Bank of England, *Financial Stability Report*, October 24, 2009). But even that figure underestimates the full scale of the bailout, which has been more accurately placed at nearly $12 trillion for the U.S. alone once all forms of financial sector support are tallied, including the rescue of the auto sector (Mark Pittman and Bob Ivry, "Financial Rescue Approaches GDP as U.S. Pledges $12.8 Trillion," Bloomberg.com, March 31, 2009). I have then factored in global fiscal stimulus plans—of nearly $1 trillion in the U.S., almost $600 billion in China, over $200 billion in Japan, alongside nearly $500 billion between Russia, France, Canada, Australia, South Africa, Italy, Britain and Argentina (Tina Cowan, "Fiscal Stimulus," Globe and Mail, April 2, 2009; and Reuters, "Keeping the Stimulus Tap Open," Globe and Mail, December 9, 2009), and then added in the $1 trillion emergency fund created by the European Union in April/May 2010 to halt the spread of the Greek crisis to other parts of Europe. This combined global anti-crisis intervention appears to be in excess of $20 trillion, an amount equal to almost one and a half times U.S. GDP. I recognize that not all of these funds will necessarily be spent in the end, and small amounts have been repaid. Nonetheless, this figure does give us some sense of the extraordinary scale of the intervention.

5   Stephen G. Cecchetti, M. S. Mohanty, and Fabrizio Zampolli, "The Future of Public Debt: Prospects and Implications," *BIS Working Paper 300* (Basel: Bank for International Settlements, March 2010).

6   Nicole Bullock, "Investors Fear Rising Risk of US Regional Defaults," *Financial Times*, July 5, 2010.

7   *Global Economic Prospects 2010: Crisis, Finance and Growth* (Washington, D.C.: World Bank, 2010).

8   Philip Beresford, "The Sunday Times Rich List 2010: Rising from the Rubble," *The Sunday Times*, April 25, 2010.

9   This astute observation was made by Los Angeles socialist and teacher-activist Sarah Knopp, in discussion during my presentation, "The Mutating Crisis of Global Capitalism" at the Socialism 2010 conference in Chicago, June 20, 2010.

10   William Shakespeare, *Coriolanus*, Act 1, Scene 1, lines 20–22. I have dis-

cussed this play in David McNally, *Monsters of the Market: Zombies, Vampires and Global Capitalism* (Leiden: Brill, forthcoming), chap. 1.

11 Alan Beattie, "Wealthy Nations Urged to Make Rapid Cuts," *Financial Times*, June 10, 2010; Bob Davis, Sebastian Moffett, Alkman Granitsas, and Nick Skrekas, "Greek Resistance a Challenge to IMF and Allies" *Globe and Mail/Wall Street Journal*, May 31, 2010; and Doug Sanders, "Britain Unveils Harshest Budget in a Generation," *Globe and Mail*, June 23, 2010.

12 Paul Krugman, "The Third Depression," *New York Times*, June 27, 2010.

13 Charles Roxburgh and others, *Debt and Deleveraging: The Global Credit Bubble and its Economic Consequences* (Washington: McKinsey Global Institute, January 2010). A similar argument, with copious evidence, is made by Reinhart and Rogoff, *This Time Is Different*, 224–33.

14 See Bloomberg, "Japan Faces 'Debt Curse' Till 2084, IMD Report Warns," *Globe and Mail*, June 5, 2010.

15 Mark MacKinnon, "The Garlic Barometer: Inflation Threatens to Slow China's Racing Economy," *Globe and Mail*, May 11, 2010.

16 Alison Smale, "Leaders in Davos Admit Drop in Trust," *New York Times*, January 30, 2010. See also Carolynne Wheeler, "China Roars Back," *Globe and Mail*, October 23, 2009.

17 See Andy Hoffman, "A Shiny New City Fuels Talk of a Bubble," *Globe and Mail*, February 23, 2010; and "China to Triple Size of Subway System," *Bloomberg News*, May 14, 2010. On the concept of over-accumulation see the glossary and the explanation in chap. 3.

18 Tavia Grant, "China's Red-Hot Risks," *Globe and Mail*, January 8, 2010.

19 Geoff Dyer, "The Soap Opera of China's Housing Boom," *Financial Times*, January 6, 2010; and Andy Hoffman, "China's Regulators Apply Brakes to Bank Lending," *Globe and Mail*, January 21, 2010.

20 Brian Milner, "China Move Forces Banks to Curb Lending," *Globe and Mail*, January 13, 2010; and Andy Hoffman, "China Tightens Loose Lending," *Globe and Mail*, February 13, 2010.

21 Jonathan Bell, "China at Risk of a Home-Grown Financial Crisis," *Financial Times*, February 22, 2010.

22 Martin Mittelstaedt, "Falling Money Supply Creates Downturn Fears," *Globe and Mail*, April 16, 2010; Gretchen Morgenstern, "Ignoring the Elephant in the Bailout," *New York Times*, May 9, 2010; Martin Wolf, "Fear of the Markets Must Not Blind Us to Deflation's Dangers," *Financial Times*, June 9, 2010; see also economist Carl Weinberg's observations in Kevin Carmichael, "G20 Plan's Dilemma: Boosting Growth With Less Spending," *Globe and Mail*, June 29, 2010.

23 As Fredric Jameson points out, the term "late capitalism" seems to originate in the writings of Theodor Adorno and Max Horkheimer around the period of the Second World War and later came into widespread usage among the German Left. The expression was popularized with the appearance of Ernest Mandel's *Late Capitalism* (London: New Left Books, 1975), originally published in German in 1972. Mandel used the term to indicate the "monopoly capitalism" of the "imperialist epoch" as analyzed by Lenin (*Late Capitalism*, p. 10). I do not use it in this sense. I follow Jameson in deploying it in terms of the financialized capitalism of

the neoliberal period, though I differ from Jameson's view that the bulk of world manufacturing has relocated to the Third World. See Jameson, *Postmodernism; or, The Cultural Logic of Late Capitalism* (London: Verso Books, 1991), xvii–xxi.

24 Karl Marx, Thesis Eleven of '"Theses on Feuerbach." Available at http://www.marxists.org/archive/marx/works/1845/theses/theses.htm

25 Henry M. Paulson, Jr., *On the Brink: Inside the Race to Stop the Collapse of the Global Financial System* (New York: Business Plus, 2010), 215.

26 Alan Greenspan, "Testimony to the House Committee on Oversight and Government Reform," October 23, 2008. Available at http://oversight/hoU.S.e.gov/documents/20081023100438.pdf.

27 Greg Farrell, "Merrill Chief Sees Severe Global Slowdown," *Financial Times*, November 11, 2008; and "Doom and Gloom Rule on Wall Street," *Globe and Mail*, November 13, 2008.

28 Bloomberg, "Geithner Recounts AIG Rescue in Testimony to U.S. House (Text)," January 27, 2010. Available at http://www.businessweek.com/news/2010-01-27/geithner-recounts-aig-rescue-in-testimony-to-u-s-house-text-.html.

29 Tara Perkins, "Weak Growth Delays Attack on Deficit," *Globe and Mail*, November 21, 2009.

30 See Barry Eichengreen and Kevin H. O'Rourke, "A Tale of Two Depressions," *Vox*, June 4, 2009 and updated March 8, 2010. Available at http://www.voxeu.org/index.php?q=taxonomy/term/1619.

31 Throughout this work, I use the term "ruling class" in both the singular and the plural. This is because capitalism both pushes capitalists together—in their opposition to the workers of the world—and pulls them apart, in their competition for markets and profits. Capitalists are thus "hostile brothers," as Marx put it in *Capital*, vol. 3. They struggle against one another—and this is the sense in which they are a competing set of ruling class*es*—and they join together to defend their common interests against global labor, thus forming a single world ruling class. Marx's concept of the ruling class includes both of these tendencies, which is why it also involves the necessity of a bourgeois state to mediate the antagonisms between capitalists and forge class unity. And coordination among dominant states—via institutions like the G8, G20, World Bank, and International Monetary Fund—is designed to produce unified global capitalist policy. At different points in this text I will use the term "ruling class" in a way that reflects which feature—its unity or its divisions—dominates in a particular context. For Marx's use of the term "hostile brothers," see *Capital*, vol. 3, chap. 15, available at http://www.marxists.org/archive/marx/works/1894-c3/ch15.htm.

32 See, "The Future of Capitalism," *Financial Times*, March 8, 2009, and Gillian Tett, "Lost Through Destructive Creation," *Financial Times*, March 9, 2009.

33 Certainly this was true for me, having been more widely interviewed on television, radio, and in newspapers than ever before. And it was even more the case for my York University colleague, Leo Panitch.

34 Kate Connolly, "Booklovers Turn to Karl Marx as Financial Crisis Bites in

Germany," *Guardian*, October 15, 2008; and Leo Lewis, "Karl Marx Goes Manga in a Kapital Comic Strip," *Times of London*, November 18, 2008.

35 Douglas Clement, "Interview with Eugene Fama," *The Region*, Federal Reserve Bank of Minneapolis, November 2, 2007.

36 Justin Fox, *The Myth of the Rational Market: A History of Risk, Reward and Delusion on Wall Street* (New York: Harper Collins, 2009).

37 Rich Miller and Josh Zumbrun, "Greenspan Takes Issue with Yellen on Fed's Role in House Bubble," *Bloomberg.com.*, March 27, 2010.

38 Sigmund Freud, "Five Lectures on Psycho-Analysis" in *Two Short Accounts of Psycho-Analysis* (Harmondsworth: Penguin Books, 1991).

39 Alan Greenspan, "The Crisis," Brookings Papers on Economic Activity, 3. Available at http://www.brookings.edu/~/media/Files/Programs/ES/BPEA/2010_spring_bpea_papers/spring2010_greenspan.pdf.

40 Ben S. Bernanke, "The economic outlook," Testimony before the Joint Economic Committee, U.S. Congress, March 28, 2007. Available at http://www.federalreserve.gov/newsevents/testimony/bernanke20070328a.htm; and International Monetary Fund, *World Economic Outlook 2007* (Washington: IMF, 2007), 162.

41 Lawrence G. McDonald, *A Colossal Failure of Common Sense: The Inside Story of the Collapse of Lehman Brothers* (New York: Crown Business, 2009), 1.

42 Francesco Guerrera and Nicole Bullock, "Struggle to Unearth Quake's Epicentre," *Financial Times*, July 31, 2008.

43 Michael Lewis, *The Big Short: Inside the Doomsday Machine* (New York: Norton, 2010), 262.

44 Obama advisor David Axelrod, speaking to CCN, as quoted by Brent Kendall, "White House Aides Out in Force Pushing for Bernanke Approval," *Wall Street Journal*, January 25, 2010.

45 Paulson, *On the Brink,* 106.

46 As reported by Senator Chris Dodd on PBS, "Frontline: Inside the Meltdown," February 17, 2009.

47 Greenspan, "The Crisis," 18.

48 The IFI report refers to "two parliaments of pain," which is the equivalent of a decade. See Steve Schifferes, "UK Economy Faces Decade of Pain," BBC news, April 23, 2010. Available online at http://news.bbc.co.uk/2/hi/business/8015063.stm.

49 Abby Goodnough, "States Turning to Last resorts in Budget Cuts," *New York Times*, June 22, 2009; Barrie McKenna, "Think Greece is a Drag on Europe? California's Sorry State a Bigger Threat to U.S.," *Globe and Mail*, February 16, 2010; Bob Herbert, "A Ruinous Meltdown," *New York Times*, March 20, 2010; and Nicholas Johnson, Phil Oliff, and Erica Williams, *An Update on State Budget Cuts: Governors Proposing New Round of Cuts for 2011; At Least 45 States Have Already Imposed Cuts That Hurt Vulnerable Residents*, Center on Budget and Policy Priorities, March 8, 2010. Available at http://www.cbpp.org/cms/index.cfm?fa=view&id=1214.

50 Jason DeParle and Robert Gebeloff, "Food Stamp Use Soars across U.S., and Stigma Fades," *New York Times*, November 29, 2009; and Agence France-Presse, "Half of U.S. Kids Depend on Food Stamps During Childhood," November 2, 2009.

51 Eric Eckholm, "More Homeless Pupils, More Strained Schools," *New York Times*, September 6, 2009. I explain the real unemployment rate in chapter 5.

52 See KPMG, "Tough Choices Ahead: The Future of the Public Sector," February 8, 2010. Available at http://www.kpmg.com/Global/en/IssuesAndInsights/ArticlesPublications/Pages/Tough-Choices-Ahead.aspx.

53 On British Columbia see Peter McMartin, "After the Pricey 2010 Party, the Poor Take it in the Teeth," *Vancouver Sun*, April 3, 2010. On the Ontario case, see the superb ongoing coverage by the Ontario Coalition Against Poverty, available at http://www.ocap.ca/.

54 Neal Lipschutz, "Summers: 'Statistical Recovery and Human Recession,'" *Wall Street Journal Blogs*, January 30, 2010. Available at http://blogs.wsj.com/davos/2010/01/30/summers-statistical-recovery-and-human-recession/.

55 Philip Beresford, "The Sunday Times Rich List 2010: Rising from the Rubble, *The Sunday Times*, April 25, 2010.

56 Helena Smith, "Greece's Spending Cuts are Making Debt Crisis Worse, Says National Bank," *Guardian,* March 22, 2010.

57 Steven Rattner, "Volcker Asserts U.S. Must Trim Living Standards," *New York Times*, October 18, 1979.

58 In the case of Canada, it was then–prime minister Pierre Trudeau who launched the war against expectations with his 1976 introduction of wage controls.

59 I explain over-accumulation and declining profitability in the next chapter.

60 I call the neoliberal period a more virulent form of capitalism, not because it is the job of the Left to advocate for better variants of the system (in which exploitation and oppression are inherent), but to register the fact that during some periods capitalism incorporates greater concessions to the working class—stronger union rights, better social services—as a result of histories of mass struggle.

61 Makoto Itoh regularly refers to the period since 1973 as a "great depression." See for example, Itoh, *The World Economic Crisis and Japanese Capitalism* (London: Macmillan, 1990), 4, 5. He reiterated this position in his lecture at the 2007 Historical Materialism conference in London. John Bellamy Foster and Fred Magdoff assert in *The Great Financial Crisis: Causes and Consequences* (New York: Monthly Review Press, 2009), 15, that "slow-down or stagnation has now persisted for four decades, and has only gotten worse over time." While the late Chris Harman rightly came to reject his earlier position—expressed in *Explaining the Crisis: A Marxist Re-Appraisal* (London: Bookmarks, 1984)—that we are living in an age of "permanent crisis" of capitalism, he continued to argue that capitalism since 1973 has exhibited "an overall tendency to stagnation," as he put it in "The Rate of Profit and the World Today," *International Socialism Journal*, 115 (2007). Harman's last book, *Zombie Capitalism: Global Crisis and the Relevance of Marx* (London: Bookmarks, 2009), provided his most nuanced analysis, even if his standard of comparison continued to be the Great Boom (see e.g. the argument and the data series he uses in chap. 8, and his claim, p. 232, that while there was "a certain recovery of profit rates"

across the neoliberal period it was "not sufficient to return the system to the long term dynamics of the long boom."). But the most well-known argument in this area is that of Robert Brenner, who has deployed the term "long downturn" to describe the state of the world economy since 1973. Brenner is attentive to *some* of the dynamics of change within the world economy throughout this period, but he too tends to see the system as mired in a protracted slowdown that comprises an era of "crisis." See, for instance, Brenner, *The Boom and the Bubble: The US in the World Economy* (London: Verso, 2002) and *The Economics of Global Turbulence: The Advanced Capitalist Economies from Long Boom to Long Downturn, 1945–2005* (London: Verso 2006). A very important response to Brenner, one that raises the critical questions of credit and international finance, as well as the problem of his commitment to rational choice theory, is offered by Ben Fine, Costas Lapavitsas, and Dimitris Milonakis, "Addressing the World Economy: Two Steps Back," *Capital and Class* 67 (1999): 47–90. More recently, in a book that appeared just as I was finishing this text, Alex Callinicos has tried to defend Harman and Brenner against the criticisms I mounted in my article, "From Financial Crisis to World Slump: Accumulation, Financialisation and the Global Slowdown," *Historical Materialism* 17, no. 2 (2009): 35–83 (see Callinicos, *Bonfire of Illusions: The Twin Crises of the Liberal World* (London: Polity, 2010), 58–59 and 152–54). He suggests, as I acknowledged in "From Financial Crisis," that Brenner grasps aspects of the restructuring of capital that occurred across the neoliberal period, and he argues that Chris Harman does so, as well, in *Zombie Capitalism*, a work that appeared after my article. Although Callinicos accuses me of being "thoroughly unfair" (p. 153) to those I am criticizing, he fails to address what is clearly the central question in dispute: not whether writers like Brenner and Harman acknowledge *some* economic restructuring (we both agree that they do), but whether the period 1982–2007 can best be characterized as a "crisis" or "long downturn," as they insist. In fact, in his latest work Callinicos continues to describe this period as one of "a long term crisis of overaccumulation and profitability" (p. 50). That is the claim, however nuanced, that I reject. And it is not "unfair" to ascribe it to Brenner, Harman, or Callinicos, as the latter's text makes abundantly clear. Reading Callinicos's summary I get the distinct impression that an ongoing series of *ad hoc* adjustments to an essentially fixed position are being made in light of the compelling weight of empirical evidence but that a sustained questioning of the pre-established paradigm—the "long crisis" or "long downturn"—is being ruled out of court. As should be clear, I find that paradigm to be both empirically misleading and theoretically untenable.

62 Jeffrey A. Frieden, *Global Capitalism: Its Fall and Rise in the Twentieth Century* (New York: W. W. Norton, 2006), 281.

63 This is a slightly misleading statement, since Mexico is often included as part of North America. Because I place Mexico more appropriately in the Global South, when I use the term "North America," I intend Canada and the United States.

64 For four decades, from the 1960s through the 1990s, South Korea aver-

aged rates of capital accumulation above 10 percent, virtually unprecedented until China's more recent arrival on the scene.

65　By "core capitalist countries" I refer to those capitalist nation-states that have dominated the global economy since the 1950s.

66　Philip Armstrong, Andrew Glyn, and John Harrison, *Capitalism Since World War II* (London: Fontana, 1984), 168, 174–75.

67　Fig. 2.1 is reproduced from Simon Mohun, "Distributive Shares in the US Economy, 1964–2001," *Cambridge Journal of Economics* 30, no. 3 (2006): 348. Essentially the same results—though not the same conclusions—are produced by, among others, Brenner, *Economics of Global Turbulence*, 7; Fred Moseley, "The Rate of Profit and the Future of Capitalism," *Review of Radical Political Economics* 28, no. 4 (December 1997): 23–41); Minqi Li, *The Rise of China and the Demise of the Capitalist World Economy* (New York: Monthly Review Press, 2008), 75; Gérard Duménil and Dominique Lévy, *Capital Resurgent: Roots of the Neoliberal Revolution* (Cambridge, MA: Harvard University Press, 2004), 24; and Armstrong, Glyn, and Harrison, *Capitalism Since World War II*, 255–56.

68　Armstrong, Glyn, and Harrison, *Capitalism Since World War II*, 168.

69　The physical ratio of machines per worker is what Marx calls "the technical composition of capital." Equally crucial is what he calls "the organic composition," which is the value (as opposed to physical) ratio of machines to workers, as it mirrors changes in the technical composition. These distinctions have confounded many commentators. An excellent discussion of this issue can be found in Alfredo Saad-Filho, *The Value of Marx: Political Economy for Contemporary Capitalism* (London: Routledge, 2002), chap. 6.

70　Of course, as I show in the next chapter, not everything is equal, so the decline in the rate of profit is a more complicated and less direct business than my sketch suggests. On this point see my article "Economic Crisis" in *The Marx Revival*, ed. Marcello Musto (New York: Palgrave Macmillan, forthcoming). Nevertheless, it is clear that during the postwar boom just such a decline did occur.

71　Armstrong, Glyn, and Harrison, *Capitalism Since World War II*, 184, 186; and Frieden, *Global Capitalism*, 280, 347.

72　As I point out in chapter 3, two trends interact in crises of profitability: the displacement of labor by machines *and* the destruction of values embodied in older and less efficient means of production.

73　As quoted by Robert J. Gordon, "Introduction: Continuity and Change in Theory, Behavior, and Methodology," in *The American Business Cycle: Continuity and Change*, ed. Robert J. Gordon (Chicago: University of Chicago Press, 1986), 2.

74　I say "in this context," because, *contra* the monetarists, not every increase in the money supply pushes up prices, as events since 2008 have proved. But in the 1970s, amidst the inflationary dynamics of a falling U.S. dollar and wage struggles by unions, expanded money supplies tended to be inflationary. The Quantity Theory of Money, according to which price levels are determined by the money supply, is both reductionist and fallacious. Rather than a general law, however, there are circumstances in which monetary expansion will tend to have inflationary results.

75 According to Georg Koopman, Klaus Matthies, and Beate Reszat, rising oil prices may have been responsible for one-quarter of the inflationary rise at the time. See their book, *Oil and the International Economy* (Hamburg: Hamburg Institute of Economic Research, 1984). Yet, even here we must be cautious, as issues of causation are crucial. On this point see Stephan Schulmeister, "Globalization Without Global Money: The Double Role of the Dollar as National Currency and World Currency," *Journal of Post Keynesian Economics* 22, no. 3 (Spring 2000): 369–74.

76 This paragraph draws on Frieden, *Global Capitalism*, 364–69, and Armstrong, Glyn, and Harrison, *Capitalism Since World War II*, 300–307. I reiterate here that I do not hold that an increase in the money supply necessarily generates inflation—everything here depends on wider economic dynamics. But in the conditions of the 1970s, monetary growth did fuel inflation. For extended treatments of the dynamics of this period see Paul Mattick, *Economics, Politics, and the Age of Inflation* (London: Merlin Press, 1978); and Ernest Mandel, *The Second Slump* (London: New Left Books, 1978).

77 I say this with respect to the mainstream Keynesianism that held intellectual sway during this period, represented most publically by Paul Samuelson. There are some critical currents in post-Keynesian economics that have more to commend them, though most of their insights are to be found in critical Marxian political economy. For an interesting assessment of the limits of neo-Keynesianism and post-Keynesianism, see Ben Fine and Dimitris Milonakis, *From Economics Imperialism to Freakonomics: The Shifting Boundaries Between Economics and Other Social Sciences* (London: Routledge, 2009).

78 Monetarism essentially refers to the doctrine that economic disturbances derive from "unnatural" changes in the supply of money. While it has certain predecessors in right-wing economists like Friedrich Hayek, its main intellectual champion was the University of Chicago economist Milton Friedman. Although it is not essential to their (simplistic) core theory, monetarists tend to be doctrinaire free-marketers, deeply suspicious of government intervention—except when it is used to bail out banks. I discuss the work of Hayek in my book, *Against the Market: Political Economy, Market Socialism and the Marxist Critique* (London: Verso, 1993). For brief introductions to neoliberal thought, see Toussaint, chap. 14; and David Harvey, *A Brief History of Neoliberalism* (Oxford: Oxford University Press, 2005), 19–22. Harvey discusses Chile's neoliberal experiment on pp. 8–10.

79 On Volcker's purely pragmatic, not theoretical, adoption of monetarist targets, and his subsequent move away from them, see William Greider, *Secrets of the Temple: How the Federal Reserve Runs the Country* (New York: Simon and Schuster, 1987), 105–7, 543–44.

80 See Naomi Klein, *The Shock Doctrine: The Rise of Disaster Capitalism* (Toronto: Knopf, 2007), 87–101; and Eric Toussaint, *Your Money or Your Life: The Tyranny of Global Finance*, updated edition (Chicago: Haymarket Books, 2004), 263–64.

81 Greider's narrative, especially chap. 6, is fascinating in this regard.

82 Paul Volcker as summarized in "Summary of Discussion" in *American*

Economic Policy in the 1980s, Martin Feldstein, ed. (Chicago: University of Chicago Press, 1994), 162.

83 George Cloutier, Profits Aren't Everything, They're the Only Thing (New York: HarperBusiness, 2009). Cloutier is the chief executive officer of American Management Services.

84 Doug Henwood, After the New Economy (New York: The New Press, 203), 210.

85 As David Kotz points out, the expansionary wave of neoliberalism comprised three discrete expansions—1982–90, 1991–2000, and 2001–7—interrupted by recessions. See Kotz, "The Financial and Economic Crisis of 2008: A Systemic Crisis of Neoliberal Capitalism," Review of Radical Political Economics 41, no. 3 (2009): 308–9.

86 See note 4 above.

87 Brenner, Economics of Global Turbulence, xxii. I frequently take issue with aspects of Brenner's analysis here because he offers the richest and most nuanced case for the "long downturn" thesis.

88 "To analyse the parts and aggregate to the whole is 'vulgar,'" observes John Weeks. See his article, "Surfing the Troubled Waters of 'Global Turbulence': A Comment," Historical Materialism 5 (1999): 213. This does not mean that it is illegitimate to break wholes into parts for analytical purposes. It simply means that the whole cannot be understood by starting with the parts, assuming we can have knowledge of them in isolation, and then imagining that we can arrive at the whole by adding them together. Instead, the parts are powerfully determined by the whole in which they inhere and cannot be understood outside it. Just as one cannot adequately comprehend a human organ in isolation from the organism in which it operates, the same is true for the component parts of the global capitalist economy. How each part behaves has to do with the interrelations among all the parts, interrelations that have a systemic character. Just as the human lungs are part of a system, and only make sense in relationship to the heart, the respiratory process, and so on, the same is true for a single economy. How it acts has to do with the system of which it is a part. This is what it means when dialectical theory insists on the need to understand the "internal relations" among entities and phenomena. On this issue, see Bertell Ollman, Alienation (Oxford: Oxford University Press, 1970).

89 "It is only foreign trade, the development of the market to a world market, which causes money to develop into world money and abstract labour into social labour," argued Marx, Theories of Surplus Value, Part III (Moscow: Progress Publishers, 1969) 253.

90 "The tendency to create the world market is directly given in the concept of capital itself," Karl Marx, The Grundrisse, trans. Martin Nicolaus (Harmondsworth: Penguin Books, 1973), 408.

91 Profits are not the only form of surplus value—much of capitalist rent and bank profit derives from surplus value, too.

92 The classic case throughout the 1990s was Japanese capital. As Japanese-based multinationals invested feverishly throughout the rest of East Asia in an aggressive campaign to boost their profitability, they contributed to

a domestic slowdown in capital formation at the very time "the national economy" desperately needed private (as well as public) stimulus.

93 This approach is taken by Callinicos, *Bonfire of Illusions*, 59–60.

94 I refer to it as "classic" largely because it conformed to the overall pattern described by Marx.

95 Brenner's notion of "global turbulence" since 1973 thus has decided merits, and accords with much of his own empirical description more cogently, in my view, than does his concept of a "long downturn." Callinicos, on p.153 of *Bonfire of Illusions*, seems to suggest that because Brenner's narrative integrates some of the former, therefore my criticisms of his theoretical and empirical invocation of a long downturn are misplaced. I disagree. Brenner is too scrupulous not to acknowledge those parts of the global restructuring that come to his attention—though, notably, China barely does. However, his commitment to the idea that fixed capital was not widely renovated and his disinclination to attend to new centers of accumulation mean that his partial insights sit uncomfortably with the structure and trajectory of his overall argument.

96 Brenner frequently tends in both *Boom and Bubble* and *Economics of Global Turbulence* to see credit creation as the basis of whatever dynamism capitalism had after 1974, seeing there the basis for sustaining effective demand. As Karl Beitel thus notes of Brenner, "his post-1998 contributions veer toward a left-Keynesian position." See Beitel, "The Rate of Profit and the Problem of Stagnant Investment: A Structural Analysis of Barriers to Accumulation and the Spectre of Protracted Crisis," *Historical Materialism* 17, no. 4 (2010): 73. Beitel's article represents a most important contribution. With respect to the question of lower rates of investment in the core (particularly the United States) in the neoliberal period, I believe that Beitel points (pp. 76–78, 83–84) to one crucial part of the story: falling prices for capital goods brought on by big increases in labor productivity, which allowed new investment to be accomplished at less cost (and then appear statistically as less real investment in technical terms). I would add that the turn of multinational corporations in the Global North to foreign investment, in Mexico, parts of Central and South America, Eastern Europe, and East Asia in particular, produced less robust rates of investment in the North than was the case globally.

97 For an excellent overview of the Canadian case see Leo Panitch and Donald Swartz, *From Coercion to Consent: The Assault on Trade Union Freedoms*, 3rd ed. (Aurora: Garamond Press, 2003).

98 See Kim Moody, *Workers in a Lean World* (London: Verso, 1997), 183.

99 James Petras and Henry Veltmeyer, *Globalization Unmasked: Imperialism in the 21st Century* (Halifax: Fernwood Publishing, 2001), 85–86.

100 *El Financiero*, May 31, 2007.

101 Data for the U.S. from Thomas Picketty and Emmanuel Saez, *Income Inequality in the United States, 1913–98*, including updates through 2006 available at http://elsa.berkeley.edu/saez/. The OECD data can be found in Organization for Economic Cooperation and Development, *Growing Unequal? Income Distribution and Poverty in OECD Countries* (Paris: OECD, 2008).

102 David Cay Johnston, "Corporate Wealth Share Rises for Top-Income Americans," *New York Times*, January 29, 2006.

103 Boston Consulting Group, *Tapping Human Assets to Sustain Growth: Global Wealth 2007* (Boston: Boston Consulting Group, 2007).

104 See David McNally, *Another World Is Possible: Globalization and Anti-Capitalism* (Winnipeg and London: Arbeiter Ring Publishing and Merlin Press, 2006), 130.

105 Brenner's account often *describes* key parts of the restructuring that has taken place over the neoliberal period. But his analysis regularly flounders on his insistence that government stimulation and debt build-ups "cut short the process of destruction unleashed by the recession" (*Economics of Global Turbulence*, 158), inhibiting the restructuring necessary to restore profitability.

106 Eric Hobsbawm, *The Age of Extremes: The Short Twentieth Century, 1914–91* (London: Abacus, 1994), 304.

107 Wally Seccombe and D. W. Livingstone, *"Down to Earth People": Beyond Class Reductionism and Postmodernism* (Aurora: Garamond Press, 2000), 13–15.

108 Data on the steel industry is drawn from Roger S. Ahlbrandt, Richard J. Fruehan and Frank Giarratani, *The Renaissance of American Steel* (Oxford: Oxford University Press, 1996); William T. Hogan, *Steel in the 21st Century* (Lexington: Lexington Books, 1994); Anthony P. D'Costa, *The Global Restructuring of the Steel Industry* (London: Routledge, 1999); Ben Fine, Aristeidis Petropoulos and Hajime Sato, "Beyond Brenner's Investment Overhang Hypothesis: The Case of the Steel Industry," *New Political Economy* 10, no. 1 (March 2005): 43–64; Don Goldstein, "Weirton Revisited: Finance, the Working Class, and Rustbelt Restructuring," *Review of Radical Political Economics* 41, no. 3 (Summer 2009): 352–57; and Frieden, *Global Capitalism*, 418.

109 Moody, *Workers in a Lean World*, 86.

110 Simon Mohun, "Aggregate Capital Productivity in the US Economy, 1964–2001" *Cambridge Journal of Economics* 33, no. 5 (September 2009): 1023–46. See also Mohun, "Distributive Shares in the US Economy, 1964–2001," *Cambridge Journal of Economics* 30, no. 3 (2006): figs 357–58, figs 4 and 5. Michel Husson estimates that increases in the rate of exploitation have figured even more decisively in restoring profit rates in Europe than in the U.S. See Husson, "Riding the Long Wave," *Historical Materialism* 5 (1999): 86.

111 See David Kotz, "The Financial and Economic Crisis of 2008: A Systemic Crisis of Neoliberal Capitalism," *Review of Radical Political Economics* 41, no. 3 (Summer 2009): 309.

112 Data from U.S. Bureau of Labor Statistics 2008. The calculations with respect to manufacturing are provided by Henwood, *After the New Economy* 46.

113 Minqi Li shows a rising profit trend in the U.S. from 2001–5, which must, as I have noted, be treated with some caution. See his *The Rise of China and the Demise of the Capitalist World Economy* (New York: Monthly Review Press, 2008), 75, fig. 3.2.

114 Frieden, *Global Capitalism*, 371.

115 It is important to underline that much of the world was left out of these

processes of capitalist globalization. Most of sub-Saharan Africa, much of Latin America and the Middle East, and parts of South Asia saw very little increase in fixed capital flows.

116 Martin Hart-Landsberg and Paul Burkett, *China and Socialism: Market Reforms and Class Struggle* (New York: Monthly Review Press, 2005), 106–7.

117 James Brooke, "Hot Growth in China Brings Chill to Japan," *New York Times*, November 22, 2001, as quoted by Hart-Landsberg and Burkett, *China and Socialism,* 107.

118 Data on Japanese and German FDI come from OECD, *Economic Survey of Japan* and *Economic Survey of Germany*, various years.

119 As I discuss in chap. 5, "primitive accumulation" is the awkward translation of the term Marx uses to describe the originating processes—centrally including dispossession of peasants from their lands—that give birth to ongoing capitalist accumulation. See Marx, *Capital*, vol. 1, trans. Ben Fowkes (Harmondsworth: Penguin Books, 1976), part 8. In *The New Imperialism* (Oxford: Oxford University Press, 2005), David Harvey undertakes to expand this concept, dubbing it "accumulation by dispossession." I also discuss the strengths and weaknesses of Harvey's concept in chap. 5.

120 International Monetary Fund, *World Economic Outlook 2007* (Washington: IMF, 2007); IMF, "Globalization of Labor," *Finance and Development* 44, no. 2 (Washington: IMF, 2007): 20–21; and World Bank, *World Development Indicators* (Washington: World Bank, 2004). The "export-weighted" measure of the industrial working class is constructed by weighing a country's labor force in relation to its ratio of exports to GDP. This, of course, tends to underestimate the size of working classes overall, but it does provide a useful index of the relative growth of the world working class.

121 See Mike Davis, *Planet of Slums* (London: Verso Books, 2006).

122 J. Yardley, "In a Tidal Wave, China's Masses Pour from City to Farm," *New York Times,* September 12, 2004.

123 On the key role of migrant workers in China's boom, see Hart-Landsberg and Burkett, *China and Socialism,* 45; Harvey, *Brief History,* 126–28; and Martin Hart-Landsberg, "China, Capitalist Accumulation, and the World Crisis," *Marxism* 21 (2010): 278–79. See also Au Loong-yu, "China's Disposable Labor," *Against the Current* 140 (May/June 2009): 9–10; and Tom Mitchell, "Chinese Migrant Workers Face High Hurdles," *Financial Times*, April 15, 2010.

124 Andrew Glyn, *Capitalism Unleashed: Finance, Globalization and Welfare* (Oxford: Oxford University Press, 2006), 88; and Denise Yam and Andy Xie, "Any Hope for Export Pricing Power?" *The Morgan Stanley Global Economic Forum*, October 16, 2002. Available at http://www.morganstanley.com/GEFdatya/digests/latest-digerst.html. OECD refers to the Organization for Economic Cooperation and Development.

125 The annual *World Investment Report* from the United Nations Conference on Trade and Development provides the relevant data.

126 Frieden, *Global Capitalism,* 418.

127 Brenner, *Economics of Global Turbulence,* 300.

128 Peter Marsh, "Global Supply Chain: Marvel of the World Brings Both Benefit and Risk," *Financial Times,* June 11, 2010.

129 This paragraph draws on Hart-Landsberg and Burkett, *China and Socialism*; Li, *Rise of China*; Chen Zhilong, "Two Decades of Utilising FDI in China: Stages, Structure and Impact," *China Report* 38, no. 2 (2002): 471–80; Yakov M. Berger, "FDI in China: Contributions to Modernisation and Solutions to Major Social Problems," *China Report* 38, no. 2 (2002): 481-9; and Harvey, *Brief History*, chap. 5.

130 Nicholas R. Lardy, "China: Rebalancing Economic Growth" in *The China Balance Sheet and Beyond* (Washington, D.C.: Center for Strategic and International Studies and the Peterson Institute for International Economics, 2007), 2. See also Li, *Rise of China*, 87.

131 Nicholas Lardy, "The Economic Future of China," Speech to the Asia Society (April 29, 2002) 3. Available at www.asiasociety.org/speeches/lardy/html.

132 Keith Bradsher, "As China Surges, It Draws High-Tech Researchers from America," *New York Times*, March 18, 2010.

133 See Marsh, "Global Supply Chain," *Financial Times*, June 11, 2010. As these figures suggest, China has also taken some share of world manufacturing from other parts of the Global South, such as Mexico.

134 Of course, manufacturing workers in the G-7 countries are generally more productive than in China, largely because of the more technologically sophisticated industries in which they work. It is estimated, for instance, that U.S. manufacturing workers are two and a half times more productive, largely for technological reasons, than their Chinese counterparts. Nevertheless, there can be no denying the crucial spatial reorganization of global manufacturing or the dramatic industrial expansion in China.

135 Lardy, "Economic Future," 1.

136 "A Workers' Manifesto for China," *The Economist*, October 11, 2007.

137 This paragraph draws on Li, *Rise of China*, 89–90; Hart-Landsberg and Burkett, *China and Socialism*, 70–71; Harvey, *Brief History*, 147; Hart-Landsberg, "China, Capitalist Accumulation, and the World Crisis." 279-80; and Zhong Wu, "China's 'Most Wanted' Millionaires," *Asia Times Online*, September 19, 2007.

138 See the important discussions in Hart-Landsberg and Burkett, *China and Socialism*, 79–85, and Hart-Landsberg, "China, Capitalist Accumulation, and the World Crisis," 281, 291.

139 Peter Engardio and Dexter Roberts, "Special Report: The China Price," *Business Week*, December 6, 2004.

140 Graham Turner, *The Credit Crunch: Housing Bubbles, Globalisation and Worldwide Economic Crisis* (London: Pluto Press, 2008), 21–22; and Raphael Kaplinsky, *Globalization, Poverty and Inequality* (Cambridge, UK: Polity Press, 2005), 181–86.

141 This does not involve a simple cause-and-effect relationship one way or the other; the two processes are interconnected and mutually determining.

142 John Eatwell and Lance Taylor, *Global Finance at Risk* (New York: New Press, 2000), 162: McNally, "Globalization on Trial: Crisis and Class Struggle in East Asia," *Monthly Review* 50, no. 4 (September 1998): 4.

143 McNally, "Globalization on Trial," 2–4.

144 World Bank, *East Asia: The Road to Recovery* (Washington: World Bank, 1998), chap. 2.

145 P. Phongpaijit and C. Baker, *Thailand Economy and Politics* (Kuala Lumpur: Oxford University Press, 1995), 155.

146 Joan Robinson, *Economic Heresies* (Basingstoke: Macmillian, 1971), 143.

147 Charles P. Kindelberger, *The World in Depression 1929–1939* (London: Allen Lane, 1973), 20. Some commentators trace the earliest capitalist cycles to the 1790s. See, for example, Wesley Mitchell, *What Happens During Business Cycles* (New York: National Bureau of Economic Research, 1951).

148 Probably the most important theorists of capitalist crises are Karl Marx, Joseph Schumpeter, and John Maynard Keynes. Working along broadly Keynesian lines, Hyman Minsky advanced a more developed account of financial crises. As will become clear later in this chapter, I consider Marx's theory of capitalism and its crises to be far and away the most profound.

149 Hyman Minsky, *Can "It" Happen Again? Essays on Instability and Finance* (Armonk, NY: M. E. Sharpe, 1982).

150 Lester Chandler, *America's Greatest Depression, 1929–1941* (New York: Harper and Row, 1970); and Kindelberger, *World in Depression*, chap. 4.

151 David Rosenberg, "Real Test for Markets is Still to Come," *Globe and Mail*, February 23, 2010.

152 Hansen as quoted by Robert Skidelsky, *John Maynard Keynes*, vol. 2 (London: Macmillan, 1994), 341; and Fisher quoted by John Kenneth Galbraith, *The Great Crash, 1929* (Boston: Houghton Mifflin, 1961), 99.

153 Frieden, *Global Capitalism*, 159.

154 Michael A. Bernstein, *The Great Depression* (Cambridge: Cambridge University Press, 1987), 187.

155 The preceding paragraph draws on Robert J. Gordon, "The 1920s and the 1990s in Mutual Reflection," paper presented to Economic History Conference, "Understanding the 1990s: The Long-Term Perspective," Duke University, March 26–27, 2004; Galbraith, *Great Crash*, chap. 2; Hobsbawm, *Age of Extremes*, chap. 3; Chris Harman, *Zombie Capitalism: Global Crisis and the Relevance of Marx* (London: Bookmarks, 2009), chap. 6; and Kindelberger, *World in Depression*.

156 Galbraith, *Great Crash*, 16.

157 Gordon, 10. For an over-investment account of the Great Depression, see James P. Devine, "Underconsumption, Over-Investment and the Origins of the Great Depression, *Review of Radical Political Economics* 15, no. 1 (1983): 1–27. While I have some differences with Devine's analysis, it insightfully explores a number of issues having to do with over-investment in the 1920s.

158 Frieden, *Global Capitalism*, 161.

159 Harman, in *Zombie Capitalism*, 151–52, argues for a long wave of declining profitability in the U.S., Germany and Britain prior to 1929. There may be something to this, but the actual timing and dynamics of the Great Slump are tied to the cycle of over-accumulation and declining profitability that was manifest by 1927–28. I survey the theoretical basis for this claim later in this chapter.

160 Howard Sherman, *The Business Cycle* (Princeton: Princeton University Press, 1991), 110.

161 John Maynard Keynes, *The General Theory of Employment, Interest, and Money* (New York: Harcourt, Brace and World, 1964), especially chaps 4, 5, 13, and 15. For an instructive comparison of Keynes and Marx, see Paul Mattick, *Marx and Keynes: The Limits of the Mixed Economy* (Boston: Porter Sargent, 1969).

162 If not utterly landless, millions were at least land-poor, possessing small tracts of land that could not fully support them or their families.

163 On Robin Hood, see Rodney H. Hilton, "The Origins of Robin Hood" in R. H. Hilton, ed. *Peasants, Knights and Heretics: Studies in Medieval English Social History* (Cambridge: Cambridge University Press, 1976), 221–35. On rebel pirates see Colin Woodward, *The Republic of Pirates* (Orlando: Harcourt Books, 2007); Marcus Rediker, *Between the Devil and the Deep Blue Sea* (Cambridge: Cambridge University Press, 1987), chap. 6; and Peter Linebaugh and Marcus Rediker, *The Many-Headed Hydra: Sailors, Slaves, Commoners, and the Hidden History of the Revolutionary Atlantic* (Boston: Beacon Press, 2000), chap. 5.

164 See my books, *Against the Market: Political Economy, Market Socialism and the Marxist Critique* (London: Verso, 1993), chap. 1; and *Another World Is Possible: Globalization and Anti-Capitalism*, 2nd ed. (Winnipeg and London: Arbeiter Ring Publishing and Merlin Press, 2006), 89–96.

165 This concept has been developed most clearly by Ellen Meiksins Wood, *The Origins of Capitalism: A Longer View* (London: Verso, 2002).

166 See Eric Williams, *Capitalism and Slavery* (London: Andre Deutsch, 1964; David Brion Davis, *The Problem of Slavery in the Age of Revolution, 1770-1823* (Ithaca: Cornell University Press, 1975); Robin Blackburn, *The Making of New World Slavery* (London: Verso, 1997); Eduardo Galeano, *The Open Veins of Latin America* (New York: Monthly Review Press, 1997); and McNally, *Another World*, chap. 4.

167 See, for example, Kevin Bales, *Disposable People: New Slavery in the Global Economy* (Berkeley: University of California Press, 2004) and Kevin Bales and Ron Sodalter, *The Slave Next Door: Human Trafficking and Slavery in America Today* (Berkeley: University of California Press, 2009). Geneviève LeBaron's forthcoming dissertation in Political Science at York University develops a powerful historical materialist deepening of the work of such authors.

168 As quoted in David Bensman and Roberta Lynch, *Rusted Dreams: Hard Times in a Steel Community* (Berkeley: University of California Press, 1988).

169 See Karl Marx, *Capital*, vol. 1, trans. Ben Fowkes (Harmondsworth: Penguin Books, 1976), chap. 1.

170 Kevin O'Leary on CBC Radio One, February 16, 2009.

171 Of course, public authority can intervene to make it relevant, by imposing fines and special taxes. But this involves the imposition of a non-market logic on market processes.

172 As quoted in Doug Sanders, "What Does Oil Have to Do with the Price of Bread? A Lot," *Globe and Mail*, October 25, 2008.

173 "Food Crisis: The Facts," *New Internationalist*, December 2008.

174 This and following formulas come from Marx, *Capital*, vol. 1, chap. 4.

175 Marx shows in Chapter 6 of *Capital*, volume 1 why labor is the source of

the extra value created in the circuit M-C-M', i.e. of the *surplus value* that represents the difference between M and M'. In the sphere of production, where human laboring abilities are "consumed" by capital, living labor adds a value to commodities that is systematically greater than the wages spent on it. It follows that capitalism is a system of accumulation via the exploitation of labor. While this claim is controversial in mainstream circles, I believe it to be a fundamental radical insight into the workings of the system.

176 Of course, things are not always so simple. In an inflationary environment, where most prices regularly rise, a firm can gain market share by increasing prices more slowly than its rivals. Its relative prices would thus be declining (that is, its prices relative to the Consumer Price Index), even if they are increasing in nominal terms.

177 Marx, *Capital*, vol.1, 742, and *Capital*, vol. 3, trans. David Fernbach (Harmondsworth: Penguin Books, 1981), 589.

178 Marx, *Capital*, vol. 1, 742.

179 Roland Leuschel, then head of the investment strategy division of Banque Bruxelles Lambert, in *Le Monde*, April 5, 1995, as quoted by Eric Toussaint, *Your Money or Your Life*, updated edition (Chicago: Haymarket Books, 2005), 86.

180 John Steinbeck, *The Grapes of Wrath* (Harmondsworth: Penguin Books, 1976), 33.

181 It is beyond the scope of this work to fully explore Marx's claim that *in capitalist society* labor is the source of all new value. For important discussions of this question, see Ben Fine and Alfredo Saad-Filho, *Marx's 'Capital,'* 4th ed. (London: Pluto Press, 2004), chap. 2; and, at a somewhat more demanding level of exposition, Alfredo Saad-Filho, *The Value of Marx: Political Economy for Contemporary Capitalism* (London: Routledge, 2002), chap. 2.

182 In Marx's terms, the organic composition of capital rises. I discuss these issues—and the dynamics of falling profitability, which are somewhat more complex than I have here outlined, in McNally, "Economic Crisis" in *The Marx Revival*, ed. Marcello Musto (New York: Palgrave Macmillan, forthcoming 2011).

183 See Paul Mattick, Jr., "Profits, the Business Cycle and the Current Crisis" in *The Economic Crisis Reader*, ed. Gerald Friedman, Fred Moseley and Chris Sturr (Boston: Dollars and Sense, 2009), 54.

184 As Guglielmo Carchedi puts it, "ultimately crises are the consequence of *labour-reducing but productivity*-increasing technological innovations." See his article, "From Okishio to Marx through dialectics," *Capital and Class* 99 (Autumn 2009), 61. As I have pointed out elsewhere (McNally, "Economic Crisis"), the actual process is more complex, with a variety of counter-tendencies. But this explanation does justice to a key part of the dynamics at work.

185 In fact, as Marx argues in *Capital*, vol. 3, the most efficient firms will actually appropriate some of the surplus labor performed by workers employed by less efficient firms. Capitalist competition, in other words, redirects profit from less to more efficient units of capital. Effective mech-

anization can thus *raise* profits for the cutting-edge companies while tending to lower the rate of profit system-wide. See Marx, *Capital,* vol. 3, trans. David Fernbach (Harmondsworth: Penguin Books, 1981), chap. 10.

186 These dynamics make the tendency for the rate of profit to decline a much more volatile and complex cyclical process than many commentators have portrayed it. Moreover, the wiping out of less efficient technologies will tend to lower what Marx calls the organic composition of capital (something like the capital/labor ratio) and therefore begin to restore profitability. For analyses in this spirit see Ben Fine and Laurence Harris, *Rereading Capital* (London: Lawrence and Wishart, 1979); David Harvey, *The Limits to Capital* (Chicago: University of Chicago Press, 1985); and John Weeks, *Capital and Exploitation* (Princeton: Princeton University Press, 1985).

187 Note again that these trends are internally connected, i.e. they are really different aspects of a unitary phenomenon.

188 I am here summarizing Marx's argument in *Capital,* vol. 3, chap. 25, 29 and 30.

189 It is true that there is a speculative element to all capitalist investment insofar as it inevitably rests on estimates of future states. But these estimates are typically done on the basis of cost assessments and future profit projections based on existing prices, wages, rates of interest, rent and so on. Investment becomes purely speculative when these costs become irrelevant and all that matters is expectations as to the ongoing rise in prices for paper assets like stocks and bonds.

190 Loren Fox, *Enron: The Rise and Fall* (Hoboken, NJ: John Wiley and Sons, 2003), chaps. 10–12.

191 Marx, *Capital,* vol. 3, 621.

192 Ibid., 362.

193 Ibid., 362–63.

194 E. A. Preobrazhensky, *The Decline of Capitalism* (New York: M. E. Sharpe, 1985), 33.

195 Armstrong, Glyn, and Harrison, *Capitalism Since World War II,* 26.

196 John Eatwell and Lance Taylor, *Global Finance at Risk: The Case for International Regulation* (New York: The New Press, 2000), 1.

197 Marx, *Capital,* vol. 3, 621.

198 Martin Wolf, "Why Paulson's Plan Was Not a True Solution to the Crisis," *Financial Times,* September 24, 2008; Kevin Phillips, "The Destructive Rise of Big Finance," *Huffington Post,* April 4, 2008; and Robert Guttman and Dominique Plihon, "Consumer Debt and Financial Fragility," *International Review of Applied Economics* 24, no. 3 (May 2010): 269–71. Available at http://www.peri.umass.edu/fileadmin/pdf/conference_papers/SAFER/Guttmann_Plihon_Consumer.pdf, see p.2.

199 Excerpts from Jeffrey Skilling's speech at the Arthur Andersen Oil and Gas Symposium, December 6, 1995, as quoted by Loren Fox, *Enron: The Rise and Fall* (Hoboken: John Wiley and Sons, 2003), 76. See also Frank Partnoy, *Infectious Greed* (New York: Henry Holt, 2003), 258 .

200 Jean Baudrillard, *Symbolic Exchange and Death* (London: Sage, 1993) 8, as quoted by McNally, *Bodies of Meaning: Studies on Language, Labor and Liberation* (Albany: State University of New York Press, 2001), 62–64.

201 The idea of a "financial coup" is advanced by Gérard Duménil and Dominique Lévy, *Capital Resurgent: Roots of the Neoliberal Revolution* (Cambridge, MA: Harvard University Press, 2004), 79. Works that focus, often in insightful ways, on deregulation, but without a sense of the broader structural transformations in late capitalism that drove policy changes include Nomi Prins, *Other People's Money: The Corporate Mugging of America* (New York: The New Press, 2004); Dean Baker, *Plunder and Blunder: The Rise and Fall of the Bubble Economy* (Sausalito: PoliPoint Press, 2008); and Robin Blackburn, "The Subprime Crisis," *New Left Review* 50 (March–April 2008): 63–106.

202 See Barry Eichengreen, *Globalizing Capital: A History of the International Monetary System* (Princeton: Princeton University Press, 1996), chap. 2; Ian M. Drummond, *The Gold Standard and the International Monetary System, 1900–1939* (London: Macmillan, 1987); Robert J. Barro, "Money and the Price Level Under the Gold Standard," *The Economic Journal* 89, no. 353 (March 1979): 13–33; and Frieden, *Global Capitalism*, chap. 12.

203 See Eichengreen, chap. 4; and Mica Panic, "The Bretton Woods System: Concept and Practice" in *Managing the Global Economy*, ed. Jonathan Michie and John Grieve Smith (Oxford: Oxford University Press, 1995).

204 For a helpful discussion of the Eurodollar market by a former banker see S. C. Gwynne, *Selling Money: A Young Banker's First Hand Account of the Rise and Extraordinary Fall of the Great International Lending Boom* (New York: Weidenfeld and Nicolson, 1986), 77–88.

205 The preceding paragraphs draw on Eatwell and Taylor, *Global Finance at Risk*, 36–37, 87–89, and Eichengreen, *Globalizing Capital*, 116.

206 On this point see Lukin Robinson, "The Downfall of the Dollar," *Socialist Register 1973*, ed. Ralph Miliband and John Saville (London: Merlin Press, 1974), 407, and consult the whole article for an important analysis.

207 Frieden, *Global Capitalism*, 339, 342.

208 In a critique of my analysis of financialization and the crisis (as I advanced it in "From Financial Crisis to World Slump," *Historical Materialism* 17.2 (2009)), Joseph Choonara has considerably confused my account, accusing me of shifting the date of "financialization and credit-driven growth from the early 1980s to 1997." But I do not consider financialization and the period of credit-driven growth to be the same thing. As my explanation makes clear, I locate the structural basis of financialization in the legal de-commodification of world money in 1971-73 (not the early 1980s). I then also argue that credit becomes increasingly crucial to sustaining the neoliberal expansion after 1997—which is quite a different point, one having nothing to do with the *origins* of financialization. See Choonara, "Marxist Accounts of the Current Crisis," *International Socialism* 123 (June 2009).

209 Eatwell and Taylor, *Global Finance at Risk*, 112.

210 West German Chancellor Helmut Schmidt, as quoted by Joel Kurtzman, *The Death of Money* (Boston: Little Brown and Co., 1993), 51.

211 Eatwell and Taylor, *Global Finance at Risk*, 3–4.

212 Bank for International Settlements, *Triennial Survey 2007* (Basel, 2007)

213 Kavaljit Singh, *Taming Global Financial Flows* (London: Zed Books, 2000), 16.

214 Aaron Luchetti, "'Innovation, Imagination' Drive Derivatives-Investment Contracts," *Wall Street Journal*, March 20, 2007.

215 Gwynne, *Selling Money*, 19.

216 For an interesting treatment of transformations in banking during the neoliberal period see Paulo L. Dos Santos, "On the Content of Banking in Contemporary Capitalism," *Historical Materialism* 17, no. 2 (2009): 180–213.

217 Kurtzman, *Death of Money*, 26.

218 Scott Patterson, *The Quants: How a New Breed of Math Whizzes Conquered Wall Street and Nearly Destroyed It* (New York: Crown Business, 2010), 138.

219 Lawrence G. McDonald with Patrick Robinson, *A Colossal Failure of Common Sense: The Inside Story of the Collapse of Lehman Brothers* (New York: Crown Business, 2009), 66; and Gillian Tett, *Fool's Gold* (New York: Free Press, 2009), 86.

220 McDonald and Robinson, *Colossal Failure*, 160.

221 Michael Lewis, *The Big Short: Inside the Doomsday Machine* (New York: W. W. Norton, 2010), 23.

222 The right for anyone to buy a credit-default swap was a result of the Commodities Futures Modernization Act of 2000.

223 Lewis's *The Big Short* (see n.221) vividly tells the story of a number of contrarians who bet massively against the U.S. housing market.

224 On synthetic CDOs see Lewis, *Big Short*, 72–74; Tett, *Fool's Gold*, 93-97; and Patterson, *Quants*, 190–92.

225 Tett, *Fool's Gold*, 126.

226 Ibid., 147; and McDonald and Robinson, *Colossal Failure*, 278.

227 McKinsey Global Institute, *Debt and Deleveraging: The Global Credit Bubble and Its Economic Consequences* (Washington: McKinsey and Company, 2010), 10, 18–19.

228 Kevin Phillips, "The Destructive Rise of Big Finance," *Huffington Post*, April 4, 2008; and "The Gods Strike Back: A Special Report on Financial Risk," *The Economist*, February 13, 2010, 4.

229 As quoted in McDonald and Robinson, *Colossal Failure*, 278.

230 Lewis, *Big Short*, 129, 158.

231 For the examples in this paragraph see Tett, *Fool's Gold* .93, 134–36, 203–10; McDonald and Robinson, *Colossal Failure*, 298; and Lewis, *Big Short*, 206–15.

232 For a helpful summary see Patterson, *Quants*, chap. 3.

233 Patterson, *Quants*, 53.

234 The concept of abstract risk is advanced by Edward Li Puma and Benjamin Lee, *Financial Derivatives and the Globalization of Risk* (Durham: Duke University Press, 2004), though they do not make the link to the value abstraction that I am proposing here.

235 Lewis, *Big Short*, 170.

236 Alan Greenspan, "Testimony to the House Committee on Oversight and Government Reform," October 23, 2008, available at http://oversight.house.gov/documents/20081023100438.pdf.

237 McDonald and Robinson, *Colossal Failure*, 339.

238 Joseph E. Stiglitz, *Globalization and Its Discontents* (New York: W. W. Norton, 2003), 24. Stiglitz's book is a most useful insider's debunking of the market fundamentalism that has dominated Washington and the

International Monetary Fund. But its critical power is severely limited by its liberal Keynesian commitments and its abject apologies for the World Bank and the Clinton administration. For a proper corrective with respect to the World Bank, see Eric Toussaint, *Your Money or Your Life: The Tyranny of Global Finance*, updated edition (Chicago: Haymarket Books, 2005), especially chap. 10.

239 On capitalism as a system of alienation see especially the young Marx's manuscript, "Estranged Labor" in his *Economic and Philosophic Manuscripts of 1844*, published in Marx, *Early Writings* (Harmondsworth: Penguin Books, 1975). On the idea of capitalism as a system of social relations see Bertell Ollman, *Alienation: Marx's Concept of Man in Capitalist Society* (Oxford: Oxford University Press, 1970), chap. 2.

240 See Richard Sennett and Jonathan Cobb, *The Hidden Injuries of Class* (New York: Vintage, 1973).

241 As quoted by Richard Brooks, "Maggie's Man: We Were Wrong," *Observer*, June 21, 1992.

242 Karl Marx, *Capital*, vol. 1, trans. Ben Fowkes (Harmondsworth: Penguin Books, 1976), 899.

243 Ruth Wilson Gilmore, *Golden Gulag: Prisons, Surplus, Crisis, and Opposition in Globalizing California* (Berkeley: University of California Press, 2007), 96, 107.

244 Jordan Flaherty, *Floodlines: Community and Resistance from Katrina to the Jena Six* (Chicago: Haymarket Books, 2010), 83.

245 Todd Gordon, *Cops, Crime and Capitalism: The Law and Order Agenda in Canada* (Halifax: Fernwood Publishing, 2006) provides a highly perceptive discussion of Ontario's "Safe Streets Act," alongside a powerful analysis of the racial and class dynamics of policing in the neoliberal era. For an overview of the "law and order" agenda in the U.S. see Christian Parenti, *Lockdown America: Police and Prisons in the Age of Crisis* (London: Verso, 1999), and Ruth Wilson Gilmore, *Golden Gulag: Prisons, Surplus, Crisis and Opposition in Globalizing California* (Berkeley: University of California Press, 2007).

246 Cary J. Rudman and John Berthelsen, *An Analysis of the California State of Corrections Planning Process* (Sacramento: California State Assembly Department of Research, 1991), i, as quoted in Gilmore, *Golden Gulag*, 88.

247 Gilmore, *Golden Gulag*, 110–13.

248 Rick Salutin, "The Fear Factor in Economics," *Globe and Mail*, July 23, 2010.

249 Diana Zlomislic, "Ottawa's Prison Plan Won't Work, Critics Say," *Toronto Star*, August 7, 2010; and Campbell Clark, "Day Cites 'Alarming' Rise in Unreported Crime to Justify New Prisons," *Globe and Mail*, August 4, 2010.

250 Marx, *Capital*, vol. 1, 915

251 As Kevin Anderson has pointed out, Marx's anti-colonialism became sharper and more determined over the course of his life, just as he broke from much of his early Eurocentrism. See his *Marx at the Margins: On Nationalism, Ethnicity and Non-Western Societies* (Chicago: University of Chicago Press, 2010). Building on some of the finest historical materialist work in this area, I have attempted to outline the inner connections of racism and capitalism in my *Another World Is Possible*, 2nd ed., chap. 4.

252 For a significant theoretical statement of this point see Massimo De Angelis, "Separating the Doing and the Deed: Capital and the Continuous Character of Enclosures," *Historical Materialism* 12, no. 2 (2004): 57–87. David Harvey has made a similar argument, under the rubric of his notion of "accumulation by dispossession" in *The New Imperialism* (Oxford: Oxford University Press, 2003), chap. 4. While there are some unclarities in Harvey's formulation (see n. 273 below), the concept of accumulation by dispossession powerfully captures central features of neoliberal globalization.

253 McNally, *Another World Is Possible*, 2nd ed., 70–72.

254 See G. E. M. de Ste. Croix, *The Class Struggle in the Ancient Greek World* (London: Duckworth, 1981), 162–70.

255 See Makoto Itoh and Costas Lapavitsas, *Political Economy of Money and Finance* (London: Macmillan, 1999), chap. 3.

256 Ben Woolsey and Matt Schulz, "Credit Card Statistics, Industry Facts, Debt Statistics." Available at http://www.creditcards.com/credit-card-news/credit-card-industry-facts-personal-debt-statistics-1276.php.

257 Paulo L. Dos Santos, "On the Content of Banking in Contemporary Capitalism," *Historical Materialism* 17.2 (2009), 190–94.

258 See for instance R. Aitken, *Performing Capital: Toward a Cultural Political Economy of Popular and Global Finance* (Basingstoke: Palgrave Macmillan, 2007).

259 Paul Langley, "Financialization and the Consumer Credit Boom," *Competition and Change* 12, no. 2 (June 2008): 144; and Dos Santos, "On the Content of Banking," 191.

260 For the concept of "financial expropriation" see Costas Lapavitsas, "Financialised Capitalism: Crisis and Financial Expropriation," *Historical Materialism* 17, no. 2 (2009): 126–32. While I think this concept needs further theoretical clarification and refinement, it does capture important dimensions of neoliberal capitalism.

261 For the case of California, see Gilmore, *Golden Gulag*, 36.

262 Gary A. Dymski, "Racial Exclusion and the Political Economy of the Subprime Crisis," *Historical Materialism* 17, no. 2 (2009): 152–54.

263 Ibid., 162–63.

264 Ibid., 164.

265 Janis Bowdler, "Survival Spending: The Role of Credit Cards in Hispanic Households," National Council of La Raza, January 19, 2010.

266 Ajamu Dillahunt, Brian Miller, Mike Prokosch, Jeanette Huezo and Dedrick Muhammad, *State of the Dream 2010 DRAINED: Jobless and Foreclosed in Communities of Color* (Boston: United for a Fair Economy, 2010), sec. 2.

267 Dymski, "Racial Exclusion," 164; and Phillip Anthony O'Hara, "The Global Securitized Subprime Market Crisis," *Review of Radical Political Economics* 41, no. 3 (Summer 2009): 328; and Allen J. Fishbein and Patrick Woodall, "Women are Prime Targets for Subprime Lending (Washington, D.C.: Consumer Federation of America, December 2006). See also: National Council of Negro Women, *Income is No Shield, Part II: Assessing the Double Burden: Examining the Racial and Gender Disparities in Mortgage*

Lending (Washington, D.C.: National Council of Negro Women, June 2009).

268 Mariko Chang, *Lifting as We Climb: Women of Color, Wealth and America's Future* (Insight Center for Community Economic Development, 2010), 21.

269 Barbara Ehrenreich and Dedrick Muhammad, "The Recession's Racial Divide," *New York Times*, September 13, 2009; and Mike Davis, *Magical Urbanism: Latinos Reinvent the U.S. City* (New York: Verso, 2000), 116.

270 David Rosenberg, "Optimism Slowly Erodes as Debt Gets Piled On," *Globe and Mail*, June 16, 2010.

271 Data in this paragraph come from Andrea Orr, "One in Four Black, Hispanic Workers is Underemployed," Economic Policy Institute, January 8, 2010; Dillahunt et al. *State of the Dream 2010*; Keeanga-Yamahtta Taylor, "Black America's Economic Freefall," *Socialist Worker*, January 8, 2010; and Chang, *Lifting as We Climb*, 5.

272 Gwynne, *Selling Money*, 19, 27–28, 53.

273 The concept of "accumulation by dispossession" was coined by David Harvey in *The New Imperialism*. In some respects, its meaning corresponds with that of Marx's "primitive accumulation," which pivots on the dispossession of people from the means of life, particularly land. But Harvey subsumes under his concept a variety of "parasitic" practices through which capital profits by seizing assets at little or no cost, including virtual theft. This has produced a tendency in some quarters to see neoliberalism and accumulation by dispossession as fundamentally characterized by theft and extortion, not the expansion of wage-labor. As should be clear from chap. 2, I believe the practices described by Harvey have frequently been means of proletarianizing people, turning them into wage laborers or members of the global reserve army of labor. Accumulation by dispossession is in my analysis thus joined to exploitation of wage-labor, not an alternative to it, as Harvey and others sometimes seem to suggest.

274 Toussaint, *Your Money or Your Life*, 148–49.

275 McNally, *Another World*, 55–56.

276 See Toussaint, *Your Money or Your Life*, 225–44, and McNally, *Another World*, 227–31.

277 Toussaint, *Your Money or Your Life*, 277.

278 McNally, *Another Life*, 62–63, and *El Financiero*, May 31, 2007.

279 James Petras and Henry Veltmeyer, *Globalization Unmasked* (Halifax: Fernwood Publishing, 2001), 85.

280 This paragraph draws on the excellent analysis in Toussaint, *Your Money or Your Life*, 313–26, and James Petras and Henry Veltmeyer, *System in Crisis: The Dynamics of Free Market Capitalism* (Halifax: Fernwood Publishing, 2003), 68–86.

281 Martin Wolf, "The World Wakes from the Wish-Dream of Decoupling," *Financial Times*, October 21, 2008.

282 "Cash-Strapped Greece to Unload State Assets," *Globe and Mail*, June 3, 2010.

283 Toussaint, *Your Money or Your Life*, 153.

284 Robert Wade and Frank Veneroso, "The Asian Crisis: The High Debt Model Versus the Wall Street-Treasury-IMF Complex," *New Left Review* 228 (2002): 20.

285 See Nancy Holmstrom and Richard Smith, "The Necessity of Gangster Capitalism: Primitive Accumulation in Russia and China," *Monthly Review* 51, no. 9 (2000).

286 Stiglitz, *Globalization and Its Discontents*, 152.

287 Ibid., 146–48.

288 Holmstrom and Smith, "Necessity of Gangster Capitalism."

289 See Russel Smyth, "Asset Stripping in Chinese State-Owned Enterprises," *Journal of Contemporary Asia* 30: no. 1 (2000): 3.

290 However, because of their ties to and domination by the state bureaucracy, these were not true self-governing communes. Nonetheless, ownership was communal not private.

291 Martin Hart-Landsberg and Paul Burkett, *China and Socialism: Market Reforms and Class Struggle* (New York: Monthly Review Press, 2005), 39–40, 43.

292 For a useful overview of the commodification of land in China in recent years, see Jiang Xu, Anthony Yeh, and Fulong Wu, "Land Commodification: New Land Development and Politics in China since the Late 1990s," *International Journal of Urban and Regional Research* 33, no. 4 (December 2009): 890–913.

293 Jim Yardley, "In a Tidal Wave, China's Masses Pour from Farm to City, *New York Times*, September 12, 2004.

294 For Marx's fascinating discussion of "primitive accumulation" (more accurately translated as original or primary accumulation), see *Capital*, vol. 1, pt. 8.

295 Liu Shi, "Current Conditions of China's Working Class," *China Study Group*, 3 (November 2003), as cited by David Harvey, *A Brief History of Neoliberalism* (Oxford: Oxford University Press, 2005), 144.

296 Michael Meyer, *The Last Days of Old Beijing* (New York: Walker and Company, 2008).

297 Patti Waldmeir, "Determined to Be the Biggest and Best, *Financial Times*, April 30, 2010.

298 Ananya Mukherjee-Reed, "The South Asia Blog," November 14, 2008; and United Nations, *Human Development Index 2010*.

299 See Pablo S. Bose, "Dams, Development and Displacement: The Narmada Valley Development Projects," in *Development's Displacements: Ecologies, Economies, and Cultures at Risk*, ed. Peter Vandergeest, Pablo Idahosa, and Pablo S. Bose (Vancouver: University of British Columbia Press, 2007), 187–205; and McNally, *Another World*, 281–82.

300 See Aditya Sarkar, "Nandigram and the Deformations of the Indian Left," *International Socialism* 115 (2007) 23–34.

301 Andrew Martin, "So Much Food. So Much Hunger," *New York Times*, September 20, 2009; Susan Sachs, "More Food Being Produced, but One Billion Still Hungry, Scientists Find," *Globe and Mail*, March 29, 2010.

302 Geoffrey York, "Land: Africa's Last Great Treasure," *Globe and Mail*, May 6, 2009; and Eric Reguly, "Foreign Investors Rush to Lock up Food Supply," *Globe and Mail*, November 17, 2009; and "Buying Farmland Abroad: Outsourcing's Third Wave," *The Economist*, May 21, 2009.

303 Nestlé chairman Peter Brabeck-Letmathe, as quoted in "Buying Farmland Abroad," *The Economist*, May 21, 2009

304 "Land Grabbing in Latin America," *Against the Grain*, March 2010. Available at http://www.grain.org/atg/.

305 Frank Bajak, "Indian Political Awakening Stirs Latin America," *Associated Press*, November 19, 2009; John Vidal, "Indigenous People: 'We Are Fighting for Our Lives and Our Dignity,'" *Guardian*, June 13, 2009; and Todd Gordon, "Acceptable Versus Unacceptable Repression: A Lesson in Canadian Imperial Hypocrisy," *rabble.ca*, July 13, 2009.

306 Joel Kovel, *The Enemy of Nature: The End of Capitalism or the End of the World?* (London: Zed Books, 2007).

307 On the role of private contractors such as Blackwater and Halliburton in New Orleans see Naomi Klein, *The Shock Doctrine: The Rise of Disaster Capitalism* (Toronto: Alfred A. Knopf, 2007), 488–500. On displacement in the city see Flaherty, *Floodlines*, 67, 71, and chap. 8 generally.

308 As quoted by Flaherty, *Floodlines*, 48.

309 Alex Stonehill, "World Water Crisis," *Z Magazine*, June 2008, 13–14.

310 See Jasmin Hristov's powerful study, *Blood and Capital: The Paramilitarization of Colombia* (Athens: Ohio University Press, 2009); and Sheila Gruner, "Contested Territories: Development, Displacement and Social Movements in Colombia" in *Development's Displacements*, ed. Vandergeest, Idahosa, and Bose, 155–86.

311 As quoted by Gruner, "Contested Territories," 166.

312 Nina Bernstein, "Officials Obscured Truth of Migrant Deaths in Jail," *New York Times*, January 10, 2010.

313 See the evidence on Canadian (and other) mining companies in Africa presented by Madeleine Drohan, *Making a Killing: How and Why Corporations Use Armed Force to Do Business* (Toronto: Random House, 2003).

314 Tom Barry, "The New Political Economy of Immigration," *Dollars and Sense*, January/February 2009, 29.

315 William Fisher, "Immigration: Emma Lazarus Redux," *The Huffington Post*, January 7, 2010. Available at http://www.truthout.org/105091.

316 Eric Schmitt, "Americans (a) Love (b) Hate Immigrants," *New York Times*, May 27, 2001.

317 For examples of immigration enforcement breaking union organizing see David Bacon, *Illegal People: How Globalization Creates Migration and Criminalizes Immigrants* (Boston: Beacon Press, 2008), 12–21, 96.

318 Rachel Donadio, "Thousands Jailed After Italy's Migrant Riots," *Globe and Mail*, January 11, 2010.

319 Sandro Contenta, "How We're Creating an Illegal Workforce," *Toronto Star*, November 1, 2009. See also "What's Wrong with the Immigration System—A Statement by No One Is Illegal–Toronto," October 17, 2009. Available at http://toronto.nooneisillegal.org/node/336.

320 Susan Sachs, "Illegal Workers in Paris out of Hiding and up in Arms," *Globe and Mail*, December 8, 2009.

321 David Bacon, "Mississippi's SB 2988," *Z Magazine*, June 2008, 15–17.

322 Kari Lyderson and James Tracy, "The *Real* Audacity of Hope: Republic Windows Workers Stand their Ground," *Dollars and Sense*, January/February 2009; and David Bacon, "Chicago Workers to the Rest of the Country: Don't Let It Die!" *New American Media*, December 11, 2008.

Available at http://news.newamericanmedia.org/news/view_article.html?_id=a3d3cc49a93f6bfac1b3f2211.

323 Occasionally, workers did keep a factory open, as at Prisme packaging in Dundee, Scotland, where a fifty-one-day occupation led to reopening the plant as a workers' cooperative. For background on these struggles see Immanuel Ness and Stacy Warner Madder, "Worker Direct Action Grows in Wake of Financial Meltdown," *Dollars and Sense*, November/December 2009; and Alan Sheldon, "Tools of the Trade: Resistance to the Crisis around the World," *New Socialist* 66 (2009): 24.

324 Jessica Leeder, "Economic Uncertainty Boils Over in Workplace," *Globe and Mail*, March 26, 2009; and David Gauthier-Villars and Leila Abboud, "Kidnapping the Boss Becoming a Peculiarly French Tactic," *Globe and Mail*, April 3, 2009.

325 In Bolivia, of course, the tin miners' union was made up predominantly of workers of indigenous descent. However, they tended to articulate their grievances in exclusively class terms, sometimes underplaying the wider importance of indigenous issues.

326 Alan Sears, "The end of 20th-Century Socialism?" *New Socialist* 61 (Summer 2007).

327 Dan La Botz, "What Happened to the American Working Class?" *New Politics* 12, no. 4 (Winter 2010): 80.

328 Harvey, *Brief History of Neoliberalism*, 47.

329 See the fascinating study by Jesook Song, *South Koreans in the Debt Crisis: The Creation of a Neoliberal Welfare Society* (Durham: Duke University Press, 2009).

330 For interesting reflections on this process, see Atilio A. Boron, "Promises and Challenges: The Latin American Left at the Start of the Twenty-First Century" in *The New Latin American Left: Utopia Reborn*, ed. Patrick Barrett, Daniel Chavez and César Rodriguez-Garavito (London: Pluto Press, 2008), 236–38. While finding many of Boron's observations compelling, I have differences with a number of his political conclusions.

331 My own book, *Another World Is Possible: Globalization and Anti-Capitalism*, first published in early 2002, was in part a product of that political moment. The second edition, (Winnipeg and London: Arbeiter Ring Publishing and Merlin Press, 2006), registers the political shift that took place after 2001.

332 The term "cycle of revolt" has been coined by Jeffery R. Webber in his outstanding study, *Red October: Left Indigenous Struggle in Bolivia, 2000–2005* (Leiden: Brill, 2010).

333 Oscar Olivera with Tom Lewis, *Cochabamba! Water War in Bolivia* (Cambridge: South End Press, 2004), 13.

334 On the economic and social struggles of this period see June Nash, "Interpreting Social Movements: Bolivian Resistance to Economic Conditions Imposed by the International Monetary Fund, *American Ethnologist* 19, no. 2:275–93.

335 *Ibid.*, 111, 113.

336 *Ibid.*, 107.

337 *Ibid.*, 105.

338 Raquel Gutierrez and Alvaro Garcia Linera, "The Rebirth of the

Multitude," *International Viewpoint* 323 (July–August 2000). While this is a most informative article, Garcia Linera, now Bolivia's vice-president has played a consistently demobilizing role *vis-à-vis* the popular movement.

339 For more detail see Olivera, *Cochabamba!*, 41–49, and McNally, *Another World Is Possible*, 2nd ed., 292–95.

340 In addition to Jeffery Webber's indispensable *Red October*, see his analysis of the de-mobilization of the movement after the electoral victory of Evo Morales in 2005 in his three-part series of articles, "Rebellion to Reform in Bolivia," *Historical Materialism* 16(2): 23–58, 16(3): 1–22, and 16(4): 67–109. See also Mike Gonzalez, "Bolivia: the Rising of the People," *International Socialism* 108 (October 2005), 73–101.

341 This is a central theme of Jeffery Webber's article "The Bolivian Left and Indigenous People Join in Struggle," *Monthly Review* 57, no. 4 (September 2005): 34–48.

342 Gonzalez, "Bolivia," 92.

343 Olivera, *Cochabamba!*, 47, 125.

344 Ibid., 47, 128.

345 Author of "The *Coordinadora*: One Year After the Water War," in Ibid., 53–64.

346 Wes Enzinna, "All We Want is the Earth: Agrarian Reform in Bolivia," *Socialist Register 2008: Global Flashpoints*, ed. Leo Panitch and Colin Leys (London: Merlin Press, 2007), 223.

347 Ana Esther Cecena, "On the Forms of Resistance in Latin America: Its 'Native' Moment," *Socialist Register 2008: Global Flashpoints*, ed. Leo Panitch and Colin Leys (London: Merlin Press, 2007), 245.

348 For just one case in point, consider the decision of the Bolivian MST to abandon land occupations in 2006 at the request of Morales.

349 In what follows, my account draws from Rudolphe Lamy, "Price Protests Paralyze Martinique, Guadeloupe," *Associated Press*, February 11, 2009; Angelique Chrisafis, "France Faces Revolt over Poverty on its Caribbean Islands," *The Guardian*, February 12, 2009; United Press International, "Protests Disrupt Life on French Islands," February 13, 2009; Richard Fidler, "Guadeloupe: General Strike Scores Victory, Spreads to Other Colonies," *Green Left Weekly*, March 3, 2009; and Richard Fidler, "Martinique General Strike Ends in Victory," *Green Left Weekly*, March 21, 2009.

350 In what follows, I rely on a series of first-rate studies, including Diana Denham and CASA Collective, ed., *Teaching Rebellion: Stories from the Grassroots Resistance in Oaxaca* (Oakland: PM Press, 2008); Richard Roman and Edur Velasco Arregui, "Mexico's Oaxaca Commune," *Socialist Register 2008: Global Flashpoints* (London: Merlin Press, 2007), 248–64; B. Gloria Martinez, González and Alejandro Valle Baeza, "Oaxaca: Rebellion against Marginalization, Extreme Poverty, and Abuse of Power," *Monthly Review* 59, no. 3 (July–August 2007): 26–37; Nancy Davies, *The People Decide: Oaxaca's Popular Assembly* (Natick, MA: Narco News Books, 2007); Louis E. V. Nevaer, *Protest Graffiti Mexico: Oaxaca* (New York: Mark Batty Publisher, 2009); and Rubén Leyva, *Memorial de Agravios: Oaxaca Mexico, 2006* (Oaxaca: Primera Edición, 2008).

351 Roman and Velasco Arregui, "Mexico's Oaxaca Commune," 257.

352 See Colin Barker, ed., *Revolutionary Rehearsals* (London: Bookmarks, 1987).

It is important to emphasize here that just setting up a small organization that tries to operate outside the market, like a co-op, does not represented dual power, contrary to some recent interpretations. Dual power in its classic meeting refers to the creation of broad-based oppositional popular institutions through which hundreds of thousands, even millions, of working class people begin to manage their lives.

353 Karl Marx, "The Civil War in France" in Karl Marx and Friedrich Engels, *Writings on the Paris Commune*, ed. Hal Draper (New York: Monthly Review Press, 1971), 76.

354 However, workplace-based forms of dual power have sometimes been weak in these settings.

355 See the wonderful account of this action and other actions by a young woman activist in Denham and CASA Collective, ed., *Teaching Rebellion*, 85–96.

356 Roman and Velasco Arregui offer an instructive analysis of this dilemma.

357 Roman and Velasco Arregui, "Mexico's Oaxaca Commune," 255.

358 For an important discussion of this new multiracial urban working class, see Robin D. G. Kelley, *Yo' Mama's Disfunktional!: Fighting the culture wars in urban America* (Boston: Beacon Press, 1997), chap. 5.

359 In 1995, in fact, the LA local of SEIU (Local 339) was placed in trusteeship by its national "leadership." This was followed by forty similar acts of trusteeship in SEIU, a trend that provoked the creation of the National Union of Healthcare Workers, now under legal Assault from the SEIU. See Steve Early, "The NUWH 16: SEIU's Courtroom Payday is a Pyrrhic Victory for New Corporate Unionism," *MRZine*, April 12, 2010. Available at http://mrzine.monthlyreview.org/2010/early120410.html.

360 Davis, *Magical Urbanism*, 172–73.

361 This is the subtitle of Kelley, *Yo' Mama's Disfunktional!*, chap. 5.

362 David Bacon, *Illegal People: How Globalization Creates Migrants and Criminalizes Immigrants* (Boston: Beacon Press, 2008), chap. 6.

363 I should acknowledge here that my argument about fighting for working class power (and supporting revolutionary change via the victory of workers' dual power) goes significantly beyond the perspective Bacon proposes.

364 Kelley, Davis, and Bacon discuss some of these organizations. See also Miriam Ching Yoon Louie, *Sweatshop Warriors: Immigrant Women Workers Take on the Global Factory* (Boston: South End Pres, 2001). For a slightly dated but still interesting collection that discusses some of these groups see John Anner, ed., *Beyond Identity Politics: Emerging Social Justice Movements in Communities of Color* (Boston: South End Press, 1996).

365 Bacon, *Illegal People*, 192.

366 It is impossible to do justice to this theme here, but for interesting and important examples see Eric Arnesen, *Waterfront Workers of New Orleans: Race, Class, and Politics, 1863–1923* (New York: Oxford University Press, 1994); Neil Foley, *The White Scourge: Mexicans, Blacks, and Poor Whites in Texas Cotton Culture* (Berkeley: University of California Press, 1997); and Rick Halpern and Roger Horowitz, *Meatpackers: An Oral History of Black Packinghouse Workers and the Struggle for Racial and Economic Equality* (New York: Monthly Review Press, 1999).

367 Mike Davis, "Why We Need Rebels," Talk presented to the Socialism 2009 conference, San Francisco, September 5, 2009 and available at http://www.zcommunications.org/why-we-need-rebels-by-mike-davis.

368 Dimitris Fasfalis, "Class Struggles Heat Up in Greece," *The Bullet*, no. 366, June 8, 2010. Available at http://www.socialistproject.ca/bullet/366.php#continue.

369 "Separating Greek Myths from Truth," *Globe and Mail*, May 18, 2010; and "The Myth of the 'Lazy Greek Workers,'" *Marxisti Foni*, May 4, 2010.

370 For a summary of key events see McNally, *Another World*, 8–11, 22–24. On the revolt in the immigrant suburbs see Le Monde diplomatique, "Banlieues: Trente ans d'histoire et de revoltes," *Manière de voir* 89 (Octobre-Novembre 2006). The quotation about these events comes from p. 5 of that document, my translation.

371 Léon Crémieux, "French Workers Face the Crisis," trans. Michael Seitz, *New Politics* 12, no. 3 (Summer 2009): 35, 36. I should add that most French workers are covered by collective agreements despite not belonging to unions, and this favorably shapes the context in which unions operate.

372 SYRIZA has done so in parliamentary elections; the NPA's predecessor group managed this level in recent presidential elections.

373 "Fifty Who Will Frame a Way Forward," *Financial Times*, March 11, 2009. It is worth pointing out that the NPA does not espouse Trotskyism, though Besancenot's was an activist with a far-left group, the Ligue communiste révolutionnaire (LCR), which developed out of one wing of that tradition.

374 Olivier Besancenot, "France: New Anti-capitalist Party Defends Democratic Right to Wear Hijab," translated by Yoshie Furuhashi, February 3, 2010. Available at http://links.org.au/node/1498. It must be acknowledged, however, that there are, regrettably, significant internal divisions in the NPA over the *hijab*.

375 Roman and Velasco Arregui, "Mexico's Oaxaca Commune," 259.

376 Rosa Luxemburg, "Reform or Revolution" in *Rosa Luxemburg Speaks*, ed. Mary-Alice Waters (New York: Pathfinder Press, 1970), 36.

377 Colin Barker, "Perspectives" in *Revolutionary Rehearsals*, ed. Colin Barker (London: Bookmarks, 1987), 225–26.

378 The classic participant's account of the Minneapolis Teamsters' strike is Farrell Dobbs, *Teamster Rebellion* (New York: Monad Press, 1972).

379 Sidney Fine, *Sit-Down: The General Motors Strike of 1936–1937* (Ann Arbor: University of Michigan Press, 1969), 201.

380 While there are many excellent sources for the strikes of 1934 and the labor upsurge of 1937, for a single text it is hard to beat Jeremy Brecher, *Strike!* (San Francisco: Straight Arrow Books, 1972). The quote in the preceding sentence comes from p. 197 of that work. Another valuable work is Art Preis, *Labor's Giant Step* (New York: Pioneer Publishers, 1964).

381 In the U.S., the work of Labor Notes looms especially large in this regard. See http://labornotes.org/. The writings of Kim Moody are hugely important in articulating a rank-and-file, class-struggle unionism. See especially his *Workers in a Lean World* and, more recently, *US Labor in Trouble and Transition: The Failure of Reform from Above, the Promise of Revival from Below* (London: Verso, 2007).

382 For highly informative coverage see the articles by Adam Dylan Hefty, Zachary Levenson, Tanya Smith, Kathryn Lybarger, Claudette Begin, and Gretchen Lipow in *Against the Current*, no. 145 (March–April 2010), and the follow-up piece by Hefty, "What Next after March 4?" as well as the interview with Joshua Pechthalt, "An UTLA Leader on the California Crisis," *Against the Current*, no. 146 (May–June 2010).

383 Quotes from Tom Mitchell, "Strike Force," *Financial Times*, June 11, 2010. For further background see also Keith Bradsher, "Demand for Higher Paychecks Stirs Unrest in China," *New York Times*, May 30, 2010; and Norihiko Shirouzu, "Chinese Workers Challenge Beijing's Authority," *Wall Street Journal*, June 13, 2010.

384 Evidence of the police actions is widely available on YouTube. For information on legal and political defense campaigns, see http://g20.toronto-mobilize.org/node/391, and https://www.g20defence.ca/.

385 "The G-20 Toronto Summit Declaration," June 26–27, 2010, 11–12. Available at http://g20.gc.ca/toronto-summit/summit-documents/the-g-2-0-to-ronto-summit-declaration/. In light of the slump it has endured since the mid-1990s, the declaration excludes Japan from this commitment to radically reduce government deficits.

386 See Naomi Klein, *The Shock Doctrine: The Rise of Disaster Capitalism* (Toronto: Alfred A. Knopf, 2007).

387 Stathis Kouvelakis, "Shock and Awe on Greece," edited version of a talk given at Birkbeck College, London, May 5, 2010. Available at http://scur-vytunes.blogspot.com/.

388 Paddy Moore, "Battlefield Classroom," *Ontario Votes 2003*, CBC Ontario. Available at http://www.cbc.ca/ontariovotes2003/features/educa-tion_052803.html.

389 Doug Saunders, "The Pain in Spain," *Globe and Mail*, July 17, 2010.

390 By *depoliticized politics* I mean a public realm characterized by the trivial and mundane, by public relations, commercialized spectacle and superficial messaging, rather than one in which the mass of the population deliberates over the substantive issues of the age.

391 Kouvelakis, "Shock and Awe on Greece."

392 Michael Steen, "Anti-Islamic Party Eyes Role in Ditch Coalition After Strong Election Gains," *Financial Times*, June 11, 2010.

393 As I write these words, the Canadian government is engineering a racist backlash against hundreds of ship-borne Tamil refugees from Sri Lanka. For a superb antiracist response see Harsha Walia, "Why We Should Welcome Boatful of Tamil Refugees into Canada," *Vancouver Sun*, August 14, 2010. Available at http://www.vancouversun.com/news/sho uld+welcome+boatful+Tamil+refugees+into+Canada/3398770/story.html.

394 See Eric Reguly, "Europe's Winter of Discontent," *Globe and Mail*, February 3, 2009. On the Left and the strikes see "Ten Days that Shook the British Left: The Oil Refinery Wildcats," http://www.thehobgoblin.co.uk, February 6, 2009.

395 Antonio Gramsci, *Selections from the Prison Notebooks*, trans. Quintin Hoare (New York: International Publishers, 1971), 276.

396 Atilio A. Boron, "Promises and Challenges: The Latin American Left at the Start of the Twenty-First Century," in *The New Latin American left: Utopia Reborn*, ed. Patrick Barnett, Daniel Chavez and César Rodriguez-Garavito (London: Pluto Press, 2008), 236–37.

397 Rosa Luxemburg, "Our Program and Our Political Situation" and "What Does the Spartacus League Want?" in Luxemburg, *Selected Political Writings*, ed. Dick Howard (New York: Monthly Review Press, 1971), 396–97, 368.

398 The expression comes from the Bolivarian Revolution in Venezuela and has been used by Hugo Chávez, among others. I was fortunate to have some direct exposure to debates and discussions on this theme during the World Social Forum in Caracas in 2006.

399 On this point see McNally, *Another World Is Possible*, 2nd ed. 268–71.

400 Neil Reynolds, "The Disintegration of the European Welfare State," *Globe and Mail*, July 12, 2010.

401 See Alan Sears, "G20 Protests: Fighting Back Against the Police State," available at http://www.newsocialist.org/attachments/220_G20%20leaflet.pdf.

402 Victor Serge, *Birth of Our Power*, trans. Richard Greeman (London: Victor Gollanz, 1968), 118.

403 Nothing compares to Serge's autobiography, *Memoirs of a Revolutionary 1901–1941*, trans. Peter Sedgwick (London: Oxford University Press, 1963) for providing a sense of his remarkable life and his ethical-political stature. See also Susan Weissman, ed., *The Ideas of Victor Serge: A Life as a Work of Art* (Glasgow: Critique Books, 1997); and Weissman, *Victor Serge: This Course is Set on Hope* (London: Verso Books, 2001).

404 Serge, *Birth of Our Power*, 74.

405 Oscar Olivera with Tom Lewis, *Cochabamba! Water War in Bolivia* (Cambridge, MA: South End Press, 2004), 159, 189.

Index

abstract labor, 71, 110, 205n89
accumulation by dispossession, 10,
    42, 52, 56, 127, 139, 195, 218n273
    See also enclosure, primitive
    accumulation
age of austerity, 10, 189
alienation, 87–88, 114
American Insurance Group (AIG),
    13, 20, 21, 104, 108
APPO
    See Popular Assembly of the
    People of Oaxaca
Argentina, 130–31
Asian Crisis, 41, 54, 58–59, 131
asset bubbles, 56; 88, 101

bank bailouts, 2–10, 21, 197n4
Barker, Colin, 177
Baudrillard, Jean, 87, 88
Bear Stearns, ix, 18, 106
Beitel, Karl, 206n96
Besancenot, Olivier, 175
Bernanke, Ben, 16, 17, 200n40
Bolivia, 152–60; Gas Wars, 156;
    Water War, 152–56
Brazil, 47, 53, 59, 98, 131
Brenner, Robert, 202n61, 205n87,
    206n95, 206n96, 207n105
Bretton Woods System, 31–32, 89, 92
Britain, 6, 22, 106
business cycle, 39, 40

Callinicos, Alex, 202n61, 206n95
Canada, 13, 23–24, 43, 45, 47, 56, 118,
    136, 184–85, 197n4, 201n58, 202n63,
    225n393; migrant workers, 143,
    186; neoliberalism, 118, 120;
    racism, 225n393
capitalism, 199n31, 211–212n175;
    alienation, 87–88, 114; "disaster
    capitalism," 139; economic
    cycles, 61–67; global system,
    37; market compulsion, 114;
    neoliberal capitalism, 26, 39, 125,

136; rise in Britain, 116–17; value
    abstraction, 71
    See also Late capitalism
Central America, 138
Chile, 34, 44
China, 7–8, 9, 26, 39; "China Price,"
    57–58; growing inequality in,
    56–57; land grabs, 137–38; new
    center of accumulation, 54–56;
    Special Economic Zones, 54;
    strike wave of 2010, 181–82;
    transition to market economy,
    133–35
Chomsky, Noam, 151
Choonara, Joseph, 214n208
collateralized debt obligations
    (CDOs), 18, 19, 80, 86, 99, 105,
    108, 109, 111, 124–25
Colombia, 139–40
credit, 79–81, 86
credit-default swap (CDS), 19, 103–
    105, 108, 124, 215n222
currency trading
    See foreign exchange

Davis, Mike, 172
debt, 86–87, 97; consumers, 106–
    107; and dispossession, 121–22,
    126, 131–32; and financial sector
    106–107; and modern banking,
    121–22; of nation states, 106; and
    Third World, 98
decade of austerity, 4, 22, 45, 145,
    175, 188
deleveraging, 6, 195
deregulation, 87, 91
derivatives, 10, 19, 94–97, 108, 110,
    111; definition of, 96
displacement, 134–35
    See also Migrant workers, 140–45
dispossession
    and debt, 121–126, 131–32; and
    privatization, 130–31

227

ABOUT PM PRESS

PM Press was founded at the end of 2007 by a small collection of folks with decades of publishing, media, and organizing experience. PM Press co-conspirators have published and distributed hundreds of books, pamphlets, CDs, and DVDs. Members of PM have founded enduring book fairs, spearheaded victorious tenant organizing campaigns, and worked closely with bookstores, academic conferences, and even rock bands to deliver political and challenging ideas to all walks of life. We're old enough to know what we're doing and young enough to know what's at stake.

We seek to create radical and stimulating fiction and non-fiction books, pamphlets, t-shirts, visual and audio materials to entertain, educate and inspire you. We aim to distribute these through every available channel with every available technology — whether that means you are seeing anarchist classics at our bookfair stalls; reading our latest vegan cookbook at the café; downloading geeky fiction e-books; or digging new music and timely videos from our website.

PM Press is always on the lookout for talented and skilled volunteers, artists, activists and writers to work with. If you have a great idea for a project or can contribute in some way, please get in touch.

PM Press
PO Box 23912
Oakland, CA 94623
www.pmpress.org

FRIENDS OF PM PRESS

These are indisputably momentous times—the financial system is melting down globally and the Empire is stumbling. Now more than ever there is a vital need for radical ideas.

In the four years since its founding—and on a mere shoestring—PM Press has risen to the formidable challenge of publishing and distributing knowledge and entertainment for the struggles ahead. With over 175 releases to date, we have published an impressive and stimulating array of literature, art, music, politics, and culture. Using every available medium, we've succeeded in connecting those hungry for ideas and information to those putting them into practice.

Friends of PM allows you to directly help impact, amplify, and revitalize the discourse and actions of radical writers, filmmakers, and artists. It provides us with a stable foundation from which we can build upon our early successes and provides a much-needed subsidy for the materials that can't necessarily pay their own way. You can help make that happen—and receive every new title automatically delivered to your door once a month—by joining as a Friend of PM Press. And, we'll throw in a free T-shirt when you sign up.

Here are your options:

- **$25 a month** Get all books and pamphlets plus 50% discount on all webstore purchases
- **$40 a month** Get all PM Press releases (including CDs and DVDs) plus 50% discount on all webstore purchases
- **$100 a month** Superstar—Everything plus PM merchandise, free downloads, and 50% discount on all webstore purchases

For those who can't afford $25 or more a month, we're introducing **Sustainer Rates** at $15, $10 and $5. Sustainers get a free PM Press T-shirt and a 50% discount on all purchases from our website.

Your Visa or Mastercard will be billed once a month, until you tell us to stop. Or until our efforts succeed in bringing the revolution around. Or the financial meltdown of Capital makes plastic redundant. Whichever comes first.

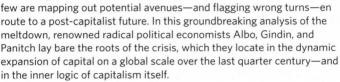
In and Out of Crisis: The Global Financial Meltdown and Left Alternatives

Greg Albo, Sam Gindin, Leo Panitch

ISBN: 978-1-60486-212-6
$13.95 144 pages

While many around the globe are increasingly
wondering if another world is indeed possible,
few are mapping out potential avenues—and flagging wrong turns—en
route to a post-capitalist future. In this groundbreaking analysis of the
meltdown, renowned radical political economists Albo, Gindin, and
Panitch lay bare the roots of the crisis, which they locate in the dynamic
expansion of capital on a global scale over the last quarter century—and
in the inner logic of capitalism itself.

With an unparalleled understanding of the inner workings of capitalism,
the authors of *In and Out of Crisis* provocatively challenge the call
by much of the Left for a return to a largely mythical Golden Age of
economic regulation as a check on finance capital unbound. They deftly
illuminate how the era of neoliberal free markets has been, in practice,
undergirded by state intervention on a massive scale. In conclusion,
the authors argue that it's time to start thinking about genuinely
transformative alternatives to capitalism—and how to build the collective
capacity to get us there. *In and Out of Crisis* stands to be the enduring
critique of the crisis and an indispensable springboard for a renewed Left.

*"Once again, Panitch, Gindin, and Albo show that they have few rivals and no
betters in analyzing the relations between politics and economics, between
globalization and American power, between theory and quotidian reality,
and between crisis and political possibility. At once sobering and inspiring,
this is one of the few pieces of writing that I've seen that's essential to
understanding—to paraphrase a term from accounting—the sources and
uses of crisis. Splendid and essential."*
—Doug Henwood, *Left Business Observer*, author of *After the New Economy*
and *Wall Street*

*"Mired in political despair? Planning your escape to a more humane
continent? Baffled by the economy? Convinced that the Left is out of ideas?
Pull yourself together and read this book, in which Albo, Gindin, and Panitch,
some of the world's sharpest living political economists, explain the current
financial crisis—and how we might begin to make a better world."*
—Liza Featherstone, author of *Students Against Sweatshops* and *Selling
Women Short: The Landmark Battle for Worker's Rights at Wal-Mart*

Also from SPECTRE from PM Press

Capital and Its Discontents: Conversations with Radical Thinkers in a Time of Tumult

Sasha Lilley

ISBN: 978-1-60486-334-5
$20.00   320 pages

Capitalism is stumbling, empire is faltering, and
the planet is thawing. Yet many people are still
grasping to understand these multiple crises and to find a way forward
to a just future. Into the breach come the essential insights of *Capital
and Its Discontents*, which cut through the gristle to get to the heart of
the matter about the nature of capitalism and imperialism, capitalism's
vulnerabilities at this conjuncture—and what can we do to hasten its
demise. Through a series of incisive conversations with some of the
most eminent thinkers and political economists on the Left—including
David Harvey, Ellen Meiksins Wood, Mike Davis, Leo Panitch, Tariq
Ali, and Noam Chomsky—*Capital and Its Discontents* illuminates the
dynamic contradictions undergirding capitalism and the potential for its
dethroning. At a moment when capitalism as a system is more reviled
than ever, here is an indispensable toolbox of ideas for action by some of
the most brilliant thinkers of our times.

"*These conversations illuminate the current world situation in ways that are
very useful for those hoping to orient themselves and find a way forward to
effective individual and collective action. Highly recommended.*"
—Kim Stanley Robinson, *New York Times* bestselling author of the *Mars
Trilogy* and *The Years of Rice and Salt*

"*In this fine set of interviews, an A-list of radical political economists
demonstrate why their skills are indispensable to understanding today's
multiple economic and ecological crises.*"
—Raj Patel, author of *Stuffed and Starved* and *The Value of Nothing*

"*This is an extremely important book. It is the most detailed, comprehensive,
and best study yet published on the most recent capitalist crisis and its
discontents. Sasha Lilley sets each interview in its context, writing with style,
scholarship, and wit about ideas and philosophies.*"
—Andrej Grubačić, radical sociologist and social critic, co-author of
Wobblies and Zapatistas

Also from SPECTRE CLASSICS **from PM Press**

William Morris: Romantic to Revolutionary

E. P. Thompson

ISBN: 978-1-60486-243-0
$32.95 848 pages

William Morris—the great 19th-century
craftsman, architect, designer, poet and writer—
remains a monumental figure whose influence
resonates powerfully today. As an intellectual (and author of the seminal
utopian *News From Nowhere*), his concern with artistic and human
values led him to cross what he called the "river of fire" and become
a committed socialist—committed not to some theoretical formula
but to the day-by-day struggle of working women and men in Britain
and to the evolution of his ideas about art, about work and about how
life should be lived. Many of his ideas accorded none too well with the
reforming tendencies dominant in the Labour movement, nor with those
of "orthodox" Marxism, which has looked elsewhere for inspiration. Both
sides have been inclined to venerate Morris rather than to pay attention
to what he said. Originally written less than a decade before his
groundbreaking *The Making of the English Working Class*, E. P. Thompson
brought to this biography his now trademark historical mastery, passion,
wit, and essential sympathy. It remains unsurpassed as the definitive
work on this remarkable figure, by the major British historian of the 20th
century.

"*Two impressive figures, William Morris as subject and E. P. Thompson
as author, are conjoined in this immense biographical-historical-critical
study, and both of them have gained in stature since the first edition of the
book was published... The book that was ignored in 1955 has meanwhile
become something of an underground classic—almost impossible to locate
in second-hand bookstores, pored over in libraries, required reading for
anyone interested in Morris and, increasingly, for anyone interested in one
of the most important of contemporary British historians... Thompson has
the distinguishing characteristic of a great historian: he has transformed
the nature of the past, it will never look the same again; and whoever works
in the area of his concerns in the future must come to terms with what
Thompson has written. So too with his study of William Morris.*"
—Peter Stansky, *The New York Times Book Review*

"*An absorbing biographical study... A glittering quarry of marvelous quotes
from Morris and others, many taken from heretofore inaccessible or
unpublished sources.*"
—Walter Arnold, *Saturday Review*

The Nature of Human Brain Work: An Introduction to Dialectics

Joseph Dietzgen
With an afterword, notes and
bibliography by Larry Gambone

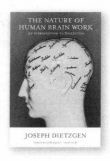

ISBN: 978-1-60486-036-8
$20.00   144 pages

Called by Marx "The Philosopher of Socialism," Joseph Dietzgen was
a pioneer of dialectical materialism and a fundamental influence on
anarchist and socialist thought, who we would do well not to forget.

Dietzgen examines what we do when we think. He discovered that
thinking is a process involving two opposing processes: generalization,
and specialization. All thought is therefore a dialectical process. Our
knowledge is inherently limited however, which makes truth relative and
the seeking of truth ongoing. The only absolute is existence itself, or the
universe; everything else is limited or relative. Although a philosophical
materialist, he extended these concepts to include all that was real,
existing or had an impact upon the world. Thought and matter were no
longer radically separated as in older forms of materialism. *The Nature of
Human Brain Work* is vital for theorists today in that it lays the basis for a
non-dogmatic, flexible, non-sectarian, yet principled socialist politics.

"Here is our philosopher!"
—Karl Marx

"...brilliant contributions to the theory of knowledge."
—Anton Pannekoek

"left...a fine legacy of wisdom in his writings"
—Friedrich A. Sorge